BEYOND ANDROCENTRISM
NEW ESSAYS ON
WOMEN AND RELIGION

AMERICAN ACADEMY OF RELIGION
AIDS FOR THE STUDY OF RELIGION

edited by
Gerald Larson

Number 6
BEYOND ANDROCENTRISM
NEW ESSAYS ON
WOMEN AND RELIGION

Edited by
Rita M. Gross

SCHOLARS PRESS
Missoula, Montana

BEYOND ANDROCENTRISM
NEW ESSAYS ON
WOMEN AND RELIGION
Edited by
Rita M. Gross

Published by
SCHOLARS PRESS
for
The American Academy of Religion

Distributed by

SCHOLARS PRESS
Missoula, Montana 59806

BEYOND ANDROCENTRISM
NEW ESSAYS ON
WOMEN AND RELIGION

Edited by
Rita M. Gross

Library of Congress Cataloging in Publication Data

Main entry under title:

Beyond androcentrism.

(Aids for the study of religion ; no. 6)
Includes bibliographical references.
1. Women and religion—Addresses, essays,
lectures. I. Gross, Rita M. II. Series.
BL458.B49   291.1'7834'12   77-13312
ISBN 0-89130-196-8 pbk.

Printed in the United States of America
1 2 3 4 5

TABLE OF CONTENTS

INTRODUCTION

This volume, which grows out of the 1975 meeting of the Women and Religion section of the American Academy of Religion, reflects the continuing paradigm shift that is occurring in the discipline of the Academic Study of Religion, as well as in all other disciplines in the humanities and the social sciences. This paradigm shift is the scholarly and philosophic dimension of the feminist transformation of culture. In simplest terms, the paradigm shift involves a transition from an androcentric model of humanity, which views males as carriers and embodiers of the human norm, and women as alien or "other" to that central normative version of humanity to a new model of humanity. In the new model of humanity, female and male modes of being, whether they are similar or different, are co-equally modes of the human, and, therefore, co-equally subjects of speculation and research.

Since these articles are part of a significant paradigm shift, it is important that they be viewed and received in the proper context—not only as of concern and interest to feminists and women in the Academic Study of Religion, but also as significant to the entire Academy of Religion and to all members of the discipline of religious studies. One of the continuing frustrations of the feminist scholar engaged in effecting this paradigm shift is the widespread assumption that her or his work is of limited, specialized interest, relevant only to other feminists, but irrelevant to the Academy as a whole. However, the work we are doing *should not* be confined to the feminist scholars in the discipline. It needs a wider audience, not so much for our sakes, as for the sake of the whole discipline of religious studies. The issues we are raising concern not only our understanding of women and religion; they concern our understanding of *religion* per se. If the discipline's methods of dealing

1

with women and religion are inadequate, the discipline
cannot have an adequate understanding, model, or methodology of religion. In other words, given what we are
doing, the entire discipline of religious studies should
never be the same again. There should be a transformation
of religious studies from a limited model of humanity and
methodologies to more whole and adequate models and methodologies. Therefore, this book is addressed to the entire
discipline of religious studies since it is of concern to
the entire discipline. It is explicitly directed towards
explicating and facilitating the basic paradigm shift
that feminist scholarship entails. Though elements of
some essays are critical of prevailing current androcentric modes of scholarship, in the main these articles
attempt a new construction beyond the inadequacies of
androcentrism.

The articles in the first section deal explicitly
with the methodologies of some sub-disciplines within the
academic study of religion. These essays provide succinct
and lucid theoretical definitions of the paradigm shift
from androcentrism to full humanism in the perspective and
research program of several disciplines in religious
studies. These statements are followed by specific
instances of the application of the paradigm shift in
several disciplines within religious studies, both in
historical and cross-cultural studies. The concluding
set of essays is both general and specific. The utilization of feminine language and imagery in concepts of the
ultimate is of utmost significance for understanding and
transcending androcentrism. On the one hand, it is
crucial to explore such language and imagery in existing
religious language and imagery, since existing feminine
language and imagery is usually underreported and down-
played in most scholarship. On the other hand, it is
crucial to discuss the problems and potential of feminine
imagery in constructing new images and language. Several

attempts to assess the scope and significance of feminine
imagery in constructs of ultimacy, whether in existing
examples or in theology-in-the-making, are presented together, in the hope of cross-fertilization and mutual
stimulation. Culture-bound assumptions of a lack of feminine imagery in constructs of ultimacy skew and impair
scholarship on cross-cultural and historical materials,
and ignorance of such cross-cultural and historical precedents limits the theologian's imagination.

The entire collection of essays is offered in the
conviction that it represents only the firstfruits of
feminist scholarship, the beginnings of the paradigm
shift, which will continue to challenge the foundations
of the discipline.

Rita M. Gross

University of Wisconsin, Eau Claire
November 15, 1976

I. THE FEMINIST TRANSFORMATION OF RELIGIOUS STUDIES:
Statements from Several Disciplinary Perspectives

ANDROCENTRISM AND ANDROGYNY IN THE
METHODOLOGY OF HISTORY OF RELIGIONS

Rita M. Gross
University of Wisconsin, Eau Claire

The questions that a feminist scholar asks of her
discipline when she is a historian of religions must be
understood within the context of the paradigm shift that
feminist thought requires of all disciplines in the humanities and social sciences. That basic paradigm shift
is the transition from an androcentric methodology to an
androgynous methodology. The resulting transformation of
the history of religions would be quite subtle and overwhelming, though not total. The unconscious androcentric
presuppositions undergirding almost all work done to date
in the history of religions cause serious deficiencies,
especially at the primary level of data-perception and
gathering, and this deficiency in turn generates serious
deficiencies at the level of model-building and theorizing
whenever any hint of sexuality or sexual imagery is present
in the data being analyzed. However the most abstract
level of history of religions theory—regarding questions
such as the nature and scope of religion itself—is not so
vulnerable and inadequate.

The scope and the limitations of the feminist critique
and reformulation of history of religions methodology will
be dealt with as answers to two frequent, somewhat defensive, questions asked by those who want history of religions methodology to be adequate, but also wish to assert
that the feminist critiques that can be leveled at other
disciplines in religious studies do not apply to history
of religions. The first question is, "Yes, but we investigate religious situations in which women are scarcely
involved and work with texts that reflect that androcentrism, so what can we possibly do?" Those who ask this
question believe that if there is any androcentrism in the

history of religions, it resides in the data itself and
that the discipline is free of any distortion or bias
towards androcentrism. The second question is, "Yes, but
even if the feminist critique has some validity, aren't
these concerns peripheral and trivial compared to questions like discerning an adequate model of religion or
comprehending myth or understanding Buddhist philosophy?"
Those who ask this question do not wish to be bothered
themselves with the feminist critique and often wish to
dismiss or denigrate those who are. They wish to assert
that they already are dealing with the central questions
in history of religions, without ever having thought about
androcentrism and androgyny.

Do most of the books written about history of religions and non-Western religions talk only about men and
their religious lives simply because that accurately
represents the religions being studied? If there is male-
centered perspective in the history of religions, is it
the unavoidable result of the materials being studied and
not part of the outlook of the scholars? The feminist
critique could not be so easily dismissed even if the
religions studied by a historian of religions were indeed
androcentric. The question of whether or not the religious ideas and practices investigated by the historian of
religions are part of an androcentric world view is irrelevant from a methodological point of view because even a
highly male-dominant and male-centered set of rituals and
images could not be adequately or fully understood if only
the data about the males is reported and analyzed. The
real question is whether the investigator is androcentric
in outlook and thus more interested in or liable to study
the males and their involvement in the religious symbol
system, while overlooking the data about the female half
of the religious community. Furthermore, though the
investigated religions may well be at least somewhat
androcentric, I suspect most of them would appear less

androcentric if we stopped projecting our own androcentrism onto them. Every religious system and set of data that I have investigated thoroughly has turned out to have been seriously misunderstood by historians of religion because of an unconscious androcentric bias and not to be nearly so male-dominated and male-centered as it is generally portrayed in the scholarly literature. I cannot over-emphasize that statement: the real issue is whether or not the historian of religions has an androcentric set of presuppositions, not whether the systems s/he investigates are male-centered.

Thus far, I have made explicit my conviction that the conventional program and methodology of history of religions, rather than, or perhaps, in addition to, the data discussed, reflects an intensely androcentric world view and that the average historian of religions is intensely and unconsciously androcentric in outlook. What precisely do I mean by this statement? The literature defining and demonstrating androcentrism is already large, so all that is needed is a brief summary of the three central characteristics of an androcentric outlook, followed by an equally brief demonstration of their scope in basic dimensions of history of religions methodology.

First of all, in androcentric thinking, the male norm and the human norm are collapsed and become identical. That is to say, it is assumed that one standard and one norm really are applied to all humans, both male and female. Therefore, secondly, because the male norm and the human norm are collapsed, it is assumed that the generic masculine habit of thought, language, and research, is adequate. To study males is to study humanity. No special attention to women is required since they are assumed to be fully covered by the generic masculine. Third, and most important, when women, per se, are considered, after it becomes obvious that there is sex role differentiation in every religion and that, therefore women are not adequately discussed in research, language and thought couched in the generic masculine, they are discussed as an *object* exterior to mankind, needing to be explained and fitted into one's worldview, having the same ontological and epistomological status as trees, unicorns, deities or any other object that must be discussed to make experience intelligible. They are there in the world, but they are discussed as an "other"[1] to the human Subject attempting to understand his world (generic masculine deliberate), as the problem to be solved, not as a Co-Subject in a mutual attempt to understand human sexual differentiation and all its manifestations.

If all the above statements are the case, then it should be no surprise that one of the primary constructs in the history of religions, *homo religiosus*, really turns out to be *vir religiosus, relating to woman as a symbol*, constructing a religious universe in which she functions as something exterior to mankind (generic masculine used deliberately), as a symbol of good or of evil, as a deity or a demon, as an object to be excluded or included in ritual, as a being whose ontological status can be debated. But *homo religiosus* as constructed by the history of religions does not include women as religious subjects, as constructors of religious symbol systems and as participants in a religious universe of discourse. History of religions really only deals with women and feminine imagery *as they are thought about by* the males being investigated, whether specific males in a specific religious situation or the abstract model *homo religiosus* are the subject of inquiry. Since the discipline of history of religions is basically concerned with discovering and understanding humans as religious beings, the androcentric limitations of the construct *homo religiosus*, religious humankind, constitute a very severe liability indeed.

Once one has become fully aware of androcentrism, the habits of thought compacted into the previous paragraphs are glaringly, frustratingly omnipresent, in every book, almost in every line. They account for the fact that the usual method of discussing women is either total silence about women and sex role differentiation or a special chapter or footnote. They also account for the fact that we *never* find discussions in which *full* information about women and the feminine in a religious context is presented as naturally and completely, with the matter-of-factness that information about men is presented; nor do we find discussions in which that *full* information is interwoven with the other data and integrated into the entire presentation. These habits of thought also explain why even the most sympathetic outsiders expect discussions of women and religion either to be about men's views of women, the restrictions imposed on them, what they are allowed to do, etc., or else to be about female symbolism, deities, mythic characters, etc. They do not think of the possibility that the discussions might be about women's religious lives and roles, their appropriations of the culture's symbol system, their deviations and independence from it. Even less likely is the expectation that the study of topics like "men's views of women" or "the female deity" might yield different results if the student began with less androcentric presuppositions.

Actually the three central propositions that characterize the general ideology of androcentrism contain an interior contradiction that makes androcentrism glaringly inappropriate as a mind-set for cross-cultural or historical research. The first two elements of androcentrism, when combined, proclaim that the generic masculine is adequate to illumine the human--that *homo religiosus* is genuinely *homo religiosus*, not just *vir religiosus*. But those two propositions hide what the third covertly recognizes--that this is not the case, that woman-the-object is essentially not encompassed by *homo religiosus*. She is different and is instead an object of contemplation and symbolization by *vir religiosus*. So we are left with a situation in which sex role differentiation is assumed to be a part of the human condition, and women are assumed to be different from men, but because of the authority of the generic masculine, we have no conceptual tools for rigorously dealing with the sex role differentiation that is so pervasive in all religious symbol and ritual systems, and, therefore, no knowledge about women.

Thus, we paint ourselves into a corner with the androcentric habit of thought. The generic masculine would work only for a religion in which there is no sex role differentiation, but there is no such religion, not even our own, to say nothing of the religious situations usually investigated by historians of religion. However, the authority of the generic masculine is great. In that conflict between the authority of the generic masculine and the reality of sex role differentiation, our knowledge about and understanding of women is crushed out. Nor can the problem be solved by expanding our knowledge about woman-the-object. Making sure that a footnote or a chapter about women and religion is tacked onto the rest of the book or curriculum simply is not intellectually satisfying, rigorous or adequate, given the pervasiveness of sex role differentiation. That would only perpetuate the woman-as-object syndrome, the attempt to define woman's place in man's world, in a slightly less inadequate fashion. Instead, we must find other methods, other models of humanity, that require us to have *full knowledge about women thoroughly integrated into* our discussions of the human, if we want to contend that we are doing adequate scholarship. Nor is this paradigm shift of relevance only to a few female scholars. It affects everyone trying to think about

the human phenomenon. I might add in passing that the
failure of conventional methodologies even to raise these
issues, let alone to deal with them, is at the same time
most condemning and most confirming of our own androcentrism.

Therefore, instead of patching up the androcentric
habit of thought, I would argue that we should abandon
forthwith all three components of androcentrism and substitute an alternative outlook. I must emphasize once more
that I am discussing an internal change in our own outlook,
which is prerequisite ever to understanding religion fully
and which has nothing to do with whether or not the religions being studied are androcentric. Even an androcentric
religion cannot be understood if the scholar is androcentric in outlook and therefore does not or cannot provide
clear and complete knowledge and understanding of women's
involvement in the religious situation.

I choose the word "androgyny" for the alternative
method and model of humanity because even the simplest
meaning of the term--"both male and female"--involves the
negation of all three components of androcentrism. We no
longer collapse the male norm and the human norm. Because
that is no longer done, the generic masculine habit of
language, thought, and research is no longer adequate.
Then the whole woman-as-object syndrome also collapses.
Simply put, there is a fundamental reorientation of consciousness to the deeply internalized realization that,
however similar or different men and women may be in any
religious situation, however dominant one sex or the other
may be, they both represent modes of the human. Therefore,
information about and understanding of both must be a part
of the data that goes into creating a human perspective on
a human world, a model of religion, or an analysis of any
specific religious situation. All this represents a
profound and subtle shift in basic thought-patterns,

for the thought-patterns of woman-as-object and men as sole
representatives of the human are deeply ingrained in our
intellectual heritage. We are advocating a basic paradigm
shift from models of humanity and modes of research and
thought that perceive males at the center and females on
the edges to modes that perceive both females and males at
the center and reflect the essential "femaleness-maleness"
of androgynous humanity.

Thus far, androgyny has been discussed very abstract-
ly. This abstract level of definition is also most basic.
It is more difficult to suggest more concrete and specific
guidelines for an androgynous methodology because as each
historian of religions internalizes the basic paradigm
shift from androcentrism to androgyny, s/he will see new
ways in which the model of religion as well as the theories
and monographs dominant in her specialization are skewed
by androcentrism and will have numerous concrete suggestions for deriving an androgynous understanding and ordering of the data. So the specific suggestions with which
I conclude this section of my paper should be taken, not
as foolproof guidelines, but as the formulations I have
derived thus far in my attempts to do more adequate scholarship in several areas within history of religions. I
might also say in passing that the amount of data not perceived by androcentric scholarship is astounding and that
the hypotheses used to understand and order the perceived
data simply are manifestly inadequate after one leaves
behind the androcentric model of humanity. I cannot over-
emphasize how subtly different the entire discipline of
history of religions looks after an androgynous perspective
is internalized.

I would like to suggest that both the ritual dimension
of religion, i.e., the religious life of humankind, and the
symbolic dimension of religion, i.e., the mythic prototypes
and constructs of the Ultimate by means of which religious

humankind understands itself, need to be reinvestigated
from an androgynous perspective. First, I would like to
suggest two guidelines for research into the ritual dimension of religion that yield a more adequate and whole
portrait of and theories about that dimension of religion.
These two suggestions are the result of my attempt to find
androgynous descriptive and theoretical handles on the role
of women in aboriginal Australian religions, and I am convinced that they would illumine most other religious situations as well.

The first suggestion is exceedingly simple and I
think exceedingly basic, since so much of the passage from
androcentrism to androgyny simply involves new ways of
organizing material and of relating data and ideas to one
another. I suggest that women's religious lives and roles
should be investigated and understood as a *pattern* of
exclusion and *participation*. This methodological-organizational formula meets several very important criteria.
It is reversable, i.e., we could also investigate men and
religion as a pattern of exclusion and participation, and
therefore, it is non-heirarchic, treating males and females
as co-equally modes of the human, whichever sex is dominant. In addition, instead of ignoring or suppressing sex
role differentiation, it deals head-on with this important
facet of all religious situations. It allows us to discuss
all aspects of women's religious roles and lives in a sexually differentiated religious situation and *requires* consideration of significant data that is glossed over in
androcentric, heirarchic considerations of women and religion. Implicit in this methodological-organizational
framework is the demand to study not just the *exclusion of*
women (which turns out to be much more complex than androcentric scholars imagine), but also *exclusion by* women--
that whole dimension of any religious situation exhibiting
significant sexual differentiation that will be known *only*

to women. It also is conducive to a more sensitive and subtle understanding of *co-participation* than hierarchic, androcentric presuppositions generally provide.

The data and interpretations that arise when sexual differentiation is acknowledged and studied as a pattern of exclusion and participation rather than ignored give rise to the second important guideline for androgynous study of the ritual dimension of religion. When the patterns of exclusion and participation are analyzed, they reveal that male and female modes of being in a situation of sexual differentiation *hide* a *pattern* of *overarching* and *parallel experiences* and *expressions* of *sacrality*. To understand the total pattern of exclusion and participation, both modifiers of "sacrality" must be understood and recognized and their relationship with one another carefully delineated. On the one hand, both men and women participate in the sacred cosmos and are sacred; in that sense there is overarching sacrality. However, at the same time the *expression* of that sacredness usually occurs by means of parallel, separate rituals for males and females because it is felt that to have one set of rituals for both men and women or to allow men to observe or participate in the women's spiritual universe or vice versa is dangerous and inappropriate. This dual recognition is fundamental, for without it one cannot understand the complexity and ambiguity of women's role in most religious situations. At the most generalized and abstract level, both males and females have access to the same experiences and expressions of sacrality. However, in the concrete, most everyday and visible dimensions of the religious situation, that overarching sacrality is reached and expressed by differing, parallel and mutually exclusive modes of religious experience and expression. This facet of women and religion in sexually differentiated religious situations has been almost totally overlooked. Instead, scholars have

noticed *only* the mutual antagonism of male and female approaches to the sacred and have misinterpreted these different avenues to the sacred as a male monopoly of religion and the sacred.

Finally, I would like to suggest that, although
throughout this paper I have stressed the religious life
and criticized the history of religions for insufficient
and androcentric attention to the role of women in religion, the studies of the symbols and constructs of ultimacy
used by religious humankind are almost as inadequate, for
precisely the same reasons, as are the studies of the religious life of humankind. This suggestion grows out of
an incomplete, continuing study of Hindu concepts of deity
which makes me ever more dissatisfied with standard presentations of Indian concepts of deity because androcentric
presuppositions obscure what is clearly present in the
iconography and even the texts relating to Indian concepts
of deity. Basically, androcentric presuppositions have
led most scholars unconsciously to view feminine symbols
and constructs of ultimacy as secondary, unusual and aber-
rant. As a result, feminine symbols, like women, receive
a chapter, usually short and at the end of the book, in
which consideration of them is *tacked on* rather than *integrated into* the full presentation of the symbols and constructs of ultimacy. That, I am convinced, is a subtly,
but fundamentally, wrong model of deity for most religious
situations. Instead I suggest that we should not be surprised by a fundamental bisexuality or androgyny in theistic imagery but rather should be surprised when it is lacking. As humanity is male and female, whatever hierarchic
relations between men and women may be, so in most cases
will anthropomorphic symbolisms be fundamentally female-
and-male, whichever is dominant. Furthermore, I suggest
that the female dimensions of deity-images are too fundamental to be appended, androcentric-wise, to the central

and normal subject matter--male images of deity. A more
integrated, androgynous model of deity is much more in
order. Such is certainly the case with Indian images of
deity and probably also with many other theistic systems.
Only an androcentric model of humanity could have made us
so insensitive to this fundamentally bi-sexual imagery and
then led us to present the miniscule portion of female
imagery that was perceived as an appendage to discussions
of the male images of deity.

Answering the first of the skeptical, defensive, "Yes,
but..." questions with which historians of religion often
respond to the feminist critique of the discipline and its
methodology has taken us deep into a discussion of the nature of androcentric thinking, its scope within the discipline, the inherent unfeasibility of androcentrism as a
mind-set conducive to good cross-cultural research and
theorizing, as well as into a discussion of corrective mea-
sures for history of religions methodology. It seems completely clear that we cannot weasel out of feminist criticisms of history of religions methodology by appealing to
the supposed androcentrism of the religious systems studied
by historians of religion.

Now, in conclusion, what of my second, "Yes, but..."
question? "Yes, but isn't all of this peripheral compared
to other issues in the history of religions?" I understand
the question, but the wrong word is chosen. These issues
are not peripheral. They are terribly central. But they
are also *preliminary*. They are not the only program that
I, or any historian of religions, would want to investigate
for my entire scholarly career. However, despite their
preliminary nature, they are also absolutely central.
Therefore, I can't get out of this corner, called "women
and religion," that I've been backed into, until the discipline reforms itself so that we always deal with women and
religion whenever we discuss religion. We should not

really need to spend time and scholarly energy discussing
something so completely preliminary as the inadequacy of
androcentrism for a cross-cultural and historical discipline like the history of religions, nor should we have to
discuss whether we need to know and understand women and
religion as well as men and religion ever to understand
religion or *homo religiosus*. It would be advantageous to
the discipline simply to accept the feminist critique and
make the requisite corrections in methodology and research
programs. Then we could get on with doing history of religions instead of arguing about preliminaries. For "women
and religion" is by no means the only or even the central
issue for history of religions. But until an adequate
solution of that problem is integrated into the discipline,
no other subject matter can be dealt with adequately, because all our theories and models are based on the data of
religion and so far we have been blind to much of the data
and have looked at the rest of it with very skewed percep-
tions and presuppositions.

NOTE

[1] The best discussion of women as "the other" in androcentric culture is Simone de Beauvoir's classic, *The Second Sex*.

THE FEMINIST TRANSFORMATION OF THEOLOGY

Judith Plaskow
Wichita State University

Feminist theology has reached a rather important point
in its history. It has set out its dissatisfactions with
the western religious traditions in both general and specific terms. It has suggested some of the ways in which it
would view things differently both substantively and methodologically. It has begun to delineate the basis of its
own authority. And yet, having done all this, feminist
theology still remains curiously bound to what it rejects.
It can claim few works within its growing corpus which do
not define themselves in contrast to the traditions they
oppose and thus in some sense depend upon them. For perhaps obvious reasons, feminist theology has begun to feel
its way toward a truly independent voice, but has yet to
find one. At such a juncture, an effort to read the future
of feminist thought would be inappropriate and probably
fruitless. Who could possibly pin down the many paths
which feminist exploration might follow? Rather than attempting this, and rather than simply focusing on some
routes which feminist theology has already taken, I would
like to say something about the issues I see myself facing
as I approach my own work, for I think my situation may
shed some light on the problems and possibilities of feminist theology in general.

It is important to begin with some history, for the
future of feminist theology as a constructive discipline
is necessarily linked with its critical past. Its critique
of tradition both sets it certain boundaries and points it
in certain directions. The present wave of feminist theology can be traced to Valerie Goldstein's article, written
in 1960, "The Human Situation: A Feminine View."[1] Arguing
that the theologies of Reinhold Niebuhr and Anders Nygren

speak to the life situation of men but not women, Goldstein
set out--at least implicitly--what were to become the two
basic tenets of all feminist theology: first, theology,
whether it recognizes it or not, is rooted in the particularities of human experience, including the theologian's
experience as male or female. Second, theology has in fact
been rooted in *male* experience in such a way as, on the one
hand, to ignore women's experience, and on the other hand,
to reinforce a very traditional conception of women's nature and role.[2]

While Goldstein has long since been joined in her
theological criticisms by a host of other writers, as long
as feminist theology has stuck to its critical task, these
two basic tenets have not been superseded. Instead they
have been applied in an increasingly farreaching way.
Thus Goldstein argued that Niebuhr and Nygren fail to
speak to women's experience because they equate sin with
pride and self-centeredness, while the sins fostered by
women's situation are more likely characterized by lack of
centeredness, underdevelopment and negation of the self.
She was concerned with theological anthropology, in other
words. Since 1960 when she wrote, other women have
brought her line of argument to bear on the doctrine of
God, pointing out that traditional notions of God are not
free from male bias either. All attempts to purge theological language of anthropomorphism notwithstanding--and
all protestations that these attempts have been successful
notwithstanding--God has continually and consistently been
depicted in terms of qualities and activities which in our
society are associated with men. This argument, it is important to point out, while it focuses on different theological material from Goldstein's, is not unrelated to
hers. If God is Lord, Father, King, sole creator, sole
initiator, it is not surprising that he resents invasions
of his territory, that he finds pride more damnable than

self-abnegation when either appears in his subjects and children. Nor is it surprising that he expects these subjects and children to be "feminine" before him, "femininity" being defined in entirely traditional terms. Tracing the connections between theology and social roles, feminist theologians have discovered that individual obnoxious theological statements about women are not aberrations. They are expressions of a total understanding of the nature of humanity and God, and to attack any one part of this understanding is to attack the others.

Now it seems to me that it is in the launching of this attack--in the formulation of the destructive interconnections between anthropology, God-language, and a specific understanding of women--that feminist theology has been most successful. Indeed, one could say that today, fifteen years after Goldstein's article first appeared, no self-respecting theologian should be able to look at his or her work without asking whose experience it reflects, who is addressed by the doctrine of "man," and in whose image God is created. It is these questions which mark the beginning of the theological transformation to which feminist theology points us.

Feminist theology does not stop with criticism, however. It also turns its two central insights--theology's rootedness in experience and its male bias--on itself. It acknowledges the particularity of its own starting point, and it glories in it. As Sheila Collins says in her book *A Different Heaven and Earth*, feminist theology is like a good novel or play: it clarifies the universal in human experience through attention to the details of human life.[3] Feminist theology believes that the neglected experience of half the human race can and must become a source of theological insight, and so it uses women's experience, in all its particularity, as a theological norm. I think this generalization is applicable to all feminist theology.

That is, whether it uses feminist experience as a sole
norm, as in the case of Mary Daly's *Beyond God the Father*,
or coordinates it with other norms, as in Letty Russell's
Human Liberation in a Feminist Perspective, feminist theology is feminist precisely insofar as it bases itself on
women's--feminist--experience.

Construction is always far more difficult than criticism, however. And it seems to me that as feminist theology has turned to construction, it has become subject to
certain tensions or contradictions. I would like to focus
on two of these contradictions now, for I believe they indicate two different directions in which feminist theology
might go, and while implicit in each direction is an imperative to which this theology must be faithful, these
imperatives may not be easily reconcilable.

First, there appears to be a certain amount of tension
between feminist theology's critical principles and its actual practice. In other words, feminist theology has not
applied its theological critique to itself in a radical
enough manner. It has been proud to speak from women's
experience, but it has too often equated particular dimensions of women's experience with women's experience as a
whole. It has forgotten that women's experience is as
diverse and complex as the experience of the human race.
Naomi Goldenberg, in the first draft of her thesis, shows
very nicely how in Daly's *Beyond God the Father*, the experience of nothingness opens into an experience of sisterhood which is in many respects quite coercive.[4] Women's
experience of our failures and evasions, our collusion with
a patriarchal system, our own capacity for evil is relegated to the past, swept aside in a great "hoorah" for the
transforming power of sisterhood. The reader is made to
feel that she must share certain affirmations to qualify
as a feminist--or perhaps even as a woman, for that matter.
This is just one instance of a particular image of women's
experience coming to claim ultimacy for itself.

Of course, in absolutizing particular experiences, feminist theology fails to say and mean what it is asking male theologians to say and mean, namely: "This is *some* people's experience"; "this is *an* image"; "this is *one* way of looking at things." It thus falls into self-contradic- tion. This in itself is a problem, naturally, but there is also a greater danger with elevating some individual aspect of women's experience. To do so may be to create the impression that women's experience has been understood and thus to short-circuit continued exploration of women's experience--precisely when we should be seeking to uncover and understand women's experience in all its variety. I would argue, that is, that the real impact of our criticism of the universalizing tendency of much theology should be to send us delving more and more deeply into the experiences of all kinds of women--black women and white women, middle class women and working class women, Jewish women and Christian women, and so on. This is the only way to avoid the pitfalls of a "universal" analysis of women's experi- ence which is really an analysis from the perspective of the dominant (white middle class) group. It is also the way to educate ourselves to the genuine diversity of wom- en's experiences, experiences which are necessarily dimin- ished and falsified when reduced to a single theme.

As to the form this exploration must take, it must begin by taking seriously everything which is an authentic reflection of women's experience. By everything, I mean letters, diaries, artwork, dreams, literature by and about women, and so on--all of our hidden history, anything which expresses women's experience of ourselves as opposed to male definitions of women's experience. It may be that for some people, such researches will entirely absorb the im- pulse to theologize or lead to its suspension, at least for a time. But such explorations may also have a theological

point--the recovery of images, metaphors, and stories
which resonate with and express our own experiences and
which contribute to a widened and enriched vocabulary of
religious experience upon which theology can reflect and
draw. This is one direction, then, in which feminist theology can, and I think should, move.

The second tension I want to deal with is more difficult to define; its implications are less clear to me. It
is a tension not between feminist principles and practice
but between feminist principles and what I hesitate to call
"the nature of theology itself." If in one sense, feminist
theology has not applied its criticisms to itself in a
thorough enough manner, in another sense, it has applied
them all too thoroughly. While it has deliberately limited itself to speaking out of and to women's experience--is
unabashedly partisan, as Sheila Collins puts it[5]--there may
be something in the nature of theology which lures us, perhaps even compels us, to move beyond the exploration of our
particular experiences. I take it that this "something" is
the fact that theology talks about God. As long as feminist theology is monotheist, its content will have to come
to reflect the fact that the God of women's experience is
also the God of androgynous experiences of women and also
the God of men. I suppose feminist theology need not remain monotheist, but I do not think it is a coincidence
that it has up until now. Insofar as feminist experience
involves an "intuition of Being" as Mary Daly says,[6] it
makes us want to speak in terms which point beyond our own
experience; it makes us want to say: "This is the way the
world is. Despite all appearances to the contrary, the
ultimate power of the universe is on the side of the free
self-actualization of human life."

And if speaking about God leads us in a universalizing
direction, so do certain aspects of feminism. The theological dynamic is reinforced by the political dimension of

feminist theology. Because this theology is rooted in experiences of oppression, it must make ethical statements
which apply beyond the boundaries of the feminist community. The very term "oppression" implies an absolute moral
claim. Moreover, while exploration of women's experience
undoubtedly has its intrinsic importance, feminist theology
uses such exploration as a vehicle for social change. It
cannot be content to say, "these are some aspects of wom-
en's experience," and then live and let live. To reconstruct the hidden history of women is to imagine a different social order--and to judge those persons and forces
which stand in the way of its implementation. I do not
mean to separate political and theological insight too
sharply here; any feminist theological insight which points
beyond itself emerges in a political context and has political implications.

Obviously, where these theological and political considerations are taken seriously, feminist theology is led
in a very different direction from the examination of particular women's experiences. It is led, rather, toward
the envisaging of a new world order, an order which presup-
poses the transformation of inter-human relationships and
the transformation of the human relationship to the world
and God. It may well be that at this point, only soundings in this direction are possible. A more concrete
theology may require a deeper understanding of women's experience than we now have. Perhaps we have not yet ex-
plored women's experiences fully enough to say where they
lead us. Yet it seems to me we are beckoned in this direction as surely as in the other.

Feminist theology has two tasks, then: first, the inquiry into the nature of women's experience; second, the
statement of the implications of women's experience in
wider and wider terms. As I suggested earlier, however,
these tasks are not all that easily held together. If we

deal with *aspects* of women's experience, we somehow fail
to be faithful to the total dynamic of that experience
which points beyond itself. If we seek to apply the insights of women's experience to an ever wider community,
we run the risk of absolutizing our particular perspectives. This is not a conflict peculiar to feminist theology. It has been discussed by others under a variety of
different names--the tension between particularism and
universalism, finitude and freedom, and so on. And yet in
a feminist context, this problem has a certain poignancy,
and perhaps even a certain irony. It is ironic that a
theology which begins with a critique of theological absolutism cannot reject the premise on which theological ab-
solutism--and with it the dismissal of the feminist theological enterprise--rest. I mean by this that the claim
that "true" theology transcends sex, culture, etc. is, I
think, based at least partly on the idea that theology
deals with a transcendent and unifying God.

Feminist theology has never been without a response
to this claim, though, and a response which suggests how
the tension between the two tensions I mention can--if not
be resolved--at least become a fruitful one. I mean that
feminist theology has shown us, through its criticism of
male God-language, that while *God* may transcend and unify
human experience, the theologian does not. The theologian
can witness to God's unity, but only as s/he experiences
it from her or his particular perspective. S/he has no
way to get inside transcendence and speak for it. Concerning the unity of human experience, too, feminist theology
has shown us--this is the point of Goldstein's article--
that while there may be structures of human experience
which are universal, they are actualized differently and
have different meaning in different cultures and in different groups within cultures. These differences, moreover,
are as significant and interesting as the universal

structures they modify, and theology ignores them only at the cost of cutting itself off from its roots in experience, which is to say from what keeps it honest and alive.

These last two points should not be taken to resolve the contradictions I described on the side of particularity. Rather, they should suggest once again the nature of the contributions which feminist theology has to make to theology as a whole. First, of course, it raises to consciousness a whole range of human experiences which theology has largely neglected. But second, it reminds theology that in expanding on the ramifications of particular experiences--as it inevitably will--it must neither lose touch with these experiences nor cease to hear the balancing voices of the experiences of others. What feminist theology has to teach theology, in other words, is how to be bold with its ears open. And it will best teach this by finding such a delicate balance itself.

NOTES

[1] *The Journal of Religion* (April, 1960) 100-12.

[2] This point is developed at greater length in my dissertation, "Sex, Sin, and Grace: Women's Experience and the Theologies of Reinhold Niebuhr and Paul Tillich" (Yale University, 1975).

[3] (Valley Forge, PA: Judson, 1974) 44.

[4] "Gods and Genders in a New Mythology: The Place of Depth Psychology in a Feminist Critique of Religion," p. 50 (privately circulated).

[5] Collins, p. 43.

[6] *Beyond God the Father* (Boston: Beacon, 1973) 36.

FEMINIST STUDIES IN RELIGION AND LITERATURE:
A Methodological Reflection*

Carol P. Christ
San José State University

The recent feminist criticism of the androcentric bias of the major traditions of Western religion, reflected in such books as *Beyond God the Father*,[1] *Religion and Sexism*,[2] and *A Different Heaven and Earth*,[3] has sent feminist scholars searching for alternative texts and traditions which may reflect an authentically female religious outlook.[4] Sources for such study include the diaries, journals, letters, and other writings of women from all periods of history. The feminist historian of Christianity, for example, might study the writings of Julian of Norwich, Teresa of Avila, or Christine de Pisan with particular attention to the female perspective reflected in them.

In twentieth century religious studies, which is my field, the novels and poetry of women writers are a particularly fruitful source for the study of women's religious outlook. Inasmuch as such study must draw on and integrate the work of scholars in the areas of religion and literature, theory of religion, and feminist literary criticism, methodological reflection is clearly called for. Since the area of religion and literature, as has been noted elsewhere,[5] is in a state of methodological chaos, simple reflection on the feminist transformation of this area of study is impossible. Therefore, I will proceed in this essay from the concrete case of my own feminist studies in religion and literature, in the hope that my reflections here will clarify and chart the way for other feminist scholars. My reflections here will also reveal the implicit androcentric bias in traditional religion and literature studies which make the texts discussed and the theories developed less than immediately relevant to women.

Before proceeding to the body of the essay, a clarification is in order. When I refer to female religious outlook or sensibility, I mean a viewpoint rooted in and reflecting the experiences of women in a particular time and place. I do not refer to an "eternal feminine" principle, nor do I imply that the female outlook necessarily excludes men. I simply refer to a religious outlook which is both *as conditioned and as potentially appropriable* by others, as are the religious writings of men which we call the Western religious tradition. I use "appropriation" in a technical sense to mean "to take possession of" an experience not immediately one's own. This act of appropriation, I would argue, is made by all women who call the Western tradition "their own." It is also made by every female reader who "identifies" with a male character in a novel. There is no reason why men cannot do the same with characters and outlooks rooted in female experience. I would insist, however, that psychic damage is done to the sexual identity of those who never find the experience of their own sex reflected in text or tradition, and who must always appropriate texts and traditions mediated through the experiences of those of the opposite sex.[6] The same is true, *mutatis mutandem*, of persons of racial, ethnic, or class groups which lack their own literary texts and traditions.

To return to the subject, religion and literature studies spring equally from the exigencies of the literary texts themselves,[7] and from the increasing distance of twentieth century theological studies from cultural and personal experience. My current research on the religious outlook reflected in the writing of twentieth century women writers is dually motivated. Both my desire to understand and find an interpretative scheme adequate to a powerful and moving literature, and my desire to discover sources for the discussion of the spiritual consciousness of modern women, have pushed my interests in twentieth century religious studies beyond the boundaries of traditional texts and methodologies.

The problematic methodological issues in my work arise at the junction of women's experience, religion, and literature in the works I study. Each of these three terms is problematic, if not in essence, at least as a subject for critical inquiry. My work is based on four methodological decisions about their relation, which at least require explication, and at most will provoke controversy. Let me first note the areas of my work which require methodological clarification or justification, and then proceed to discuss each in greater detail.

(1) Like feminist critics of literature; I assume a relation between literature and life--a view which is not necessarily popular in the literary establishment.

(2) Like religion and literature critics, I assume and interpret the religious dimension of modern literature--thus entering a territory largely unrecognized and uncharted by feminist, or other, literary critics.

(3) Unlike most religion and literature critics, I make little use of three of the most common approaches to the relation of religion and literature--and instead use a representational theory of literature together with the story and religion theory.

(4) Unlike androcentric critics, I use a sex-differentiated model of humanity in discussing modern literature--a model which would be disputed even by some feminist critics.

(1) The first methodologically problematic assumption I make is that there is a relation between literature and life. An obvious assumption to anyone not trained in literary studies or theory, the connection between literature and experience is explicitly acknowledged in feminist studies in literature. Feminist critics take their cue from

Doris Lessing's Martha Quest, who searched to find in literature or in life, that woman, who, she vaguely put it,
is "a person."[8]   In an article in a recent volume of feminist literary criticism, Florence Howe, past president of
the Modern Languages Association, boldly admitted that the
ultimate purpose of feminist literary studies is to learn
to "love being a woman."[9]   Feminist critics are clearly
interested in the function literature plays in shaping
lives.

The typology of Eliseo Vivas places feminist critics
in relation to other critics. According to Vivas, theories of literature and literary criticism may be divided
according to whether they focus on (1) the *artist* in the
act of creation, (2) the *work* in its autonomy, or (3) the
function which literature plays in life.[10]   Modifying Vivas
only slightly, we may call the first theory a *Romantic* one
in which the critic treats the artist as a species of religious genius and the work of art as a quasi-divine creation. In the second theory, the autonomist view, recently
canonized as the New Criticism, the work of art is treated
as an isolated aesthetic creation, its connections to the
life of the author or reader relentlessly ignored. The
third theory is the *representational* or mimetic theory in
which the work of art is considered as in some sense a
representation of actual or possible life, its connections
with the social world it reflects or engenders a matter of
critical inquiry.

Using this scheme, feminist criticism clearly falls
into the third category. Feminist criticism views the
work of literature as a representation of actual or possible ways of organizing perception and action. In its
negative phase, feminist criticism exorcises negative images of women presented in "great works" of literature by
showing how they reflect and perpetuate androcentric
stereotypes of women. In its positive phase, feminist criticism aids women's quest for self by discussing the shape,

value, and direction given to women's experience in certain works of literature, especially those written by women. The feminist critic seeks to discover a literature in which her own experience is given form through representation. Her first criterion of judgment is realistic--she judges literature according to the adequacy of its representation of women's experience. Second, she searches to discover paths to her own future in those works of women's literature which assist transformation by beginning with the common experiences of women and moving beyond them into a vison of a fuller, richer way of being a woman person. Her second criterion of judgment is realistic-imaginative--she judges literature according to whether it succeeds in imagining a world in which women can move beyond androcentric stereotypes.

Since feminist criticism is based on the representational view of literature, the Romantic and autonomist theories of literature and criticism are not particularly useful to it. Romantic and autonomist theories are, it seems, the prerogatives of those whose selfhood has been so adequately defined by literature over the years as to render representational concerns and criticism boring. Since the Romantic theory is not currently popular in the literature field, it has not been explicitly rejected by feminist critics. The autonomist theories of New Criticism have, however, been explicitly attacked by feminist critics. Two articles in the recent volume of feminist criticism mentioned above, state the case against New Criticism very clearly.[11] One critic, Fraya Katz-Stoker put the feminist objection this way, "Feminist criticism can never be merely formal because women recognize out of their own oppression (that)...literature is a major component of the educational process...(that) shapes our destiny."[12] The feminist rejection of autonomist theories of the work of art challenges the exclusive claim of literature departments to

works of literature. If literature stands in relation to
life, then its interpretation must become open to inter-
disciplinary criticism from sociology, psychology, political science, and *religion*.

(2) The second problematic assumption I make is that
literature, in this case, twentieth century women's literature, has a religious dimension. This is particularly
true of the literature of female quest which has thus far
been the focus of much feminist literary criticism. Quest
literature has a long history in the West. The quest for
self has always had two aspects, the social and the spiritual. In the social quest, the heroine searches for self
in alienation from and reintegration into human community.
In the spiritual quest, the self's journey is in relation
to ultimate or cosmic powers, and it generally reflects a
greater interiority. The social quest has received far
more attention to date in feminist literary studies.
Novels such as *The Golden Notebook*,[13] *Memoirs of an Ex-
Prom Queen*,[14] *Fear of Flying*,[15] and *Small Changes*[16] which
focus on the social aspect of the female quest have inspired many critical studies. Novels which focus on the
spiritual dimension of the female quest like Lessing's *The
Summer before the Dark*,[17] or Atwood's *Surfacing*[18] have remained opaque or have been misinterpreted by critics[19] who
expect them to display the conventions of the social quest
novel.[20] Religious studies can aid feminist studies in
literature by calling attention to the spiritual dimension
of the female quest.

It is unlikely, however, that religious studies can
provide more than a formal definition of women's spiritual
quest. Preliminary research indicates that the stages of
the female quest differ from the stages of the male
quest.[21] A great deal of research needs to be done with
the literature of female quest--fiction, poetry, biography,
and autobiography--in order to bring to light the

characteristic stages of the female quest. My studies indicate that awakening from the androcentric world to a
world of greater terror, risk, and potential healing, and
the movement from victimhood to power are two structures
of the female quest which have immense spiritual significance.[22]

(3) In developing an approach to the spiritual quest
in modern women's writing, I have found three of the most
common approaches to the relation of religion and literature to be of little use. One of these approaches relies
too heavily on theological categories which are simply not
appropriate for the literature in question. The other two
use the Romantic and the autonomist views of literature,
which, as I have said above, are not central to feminist
literary criticism. A fourth approach, which combines the
representational theory of literature with the story and
religion theory, seems to be the most useful for feminist
criticism in religion and literature.

The oldest approach to religion and literature is the
theology and literature approach, represented in the work
of Nathan Scott and the Chicago School.[23] In this approach
theological categories are correlated with themes and images
in the literary work, or the literary work is found lacking
from an antecedent theological standpoint. The categories
of Christian theology are not adequate for defining the
spiritual quest in modern men's writing, and they are even
less adequate to modern women's writing. While this approach might be useful for introducing certain themes or
images from women's writing into the Christian vocabulary,
it does not provide an adequate scheme for understanding
this literature on its own terms.

The more recent direction of studies in religion and
literature, reflected in the American Academy of Religion
section name, "Arts, Literature, and Religion," is more
promising for feminist studies. There is a religious

dimension in female quest literature, even if there is not often a theological one. It remains to specify that dimension.

Theories of the relation of religion and literature may be divided according to the typology of literary theories suggested above. The work of Stanley Romaine Hopper and the Drew-Syracuse school reflects the first type. Hopper's view of literature is a Romantic one in which the poet is viewed as the religious genius of the modern world and the art work is viewed as a revelation of Being, a kind of divine revelation.[24] While the feminist literary critic might agree with Hopper that new possibilities of being are revealed in the new women's literature, this formal observation is not the focus of her critical work. She is far more concerned to discern and interpret the shape of this new being in women's writing. To do this she must go beyond the Romantic theory of the relation of religion and literature.

A second theory of the relation of religion and literature makes great use of the autonomist theories of literature. Formal similarities. such as metaphor, symbol, paradox, and ambiguity, are used to create a theory of the relation between religious and literary language.[25] Sallie TeSelle's recent book, *Speaking in Parables* makes this point quite effectively.[26] Again, the feminist critic would not deny the insights gained through this approach. However, her interest in the shape of the self and world represented in women's writing in relation to possible selves and worlds, requires a theory and model of criticism which can take her beyond the primarily formal observations available through autonomist theory.

The third theory views the work of art at the reflection of a world which is, and is not, our own. A version of the representational theory, it holds more promise for the feminist critic. Giles Gunn has recently defended this

view, seeing literature's function as "always that of mediating a form of otherness, a sense of things not quite our
own."[27] His words might be used to describe the feminist
critic's search to find a new way of being a woman through
the reading and interpretation of literature. My only
quarrel with Gunn is a minor one. Speaking of literature
as a "hypothetical world," as he does, might possibly obscure the connections between literature's world and our
own. It seems to me that the best literature, and certainly the best women's literature, elicits the sympathy of the
reader with an accurate representation of the known world
of experience, and moves from there into the "hypothetical
world."[28] This objection to Gunn's language notwithstand-
ing, the representational theory seems most useful for feminist criticism in religion and literature because it focuses on the world presented in literature in relation to
our own world. It remains to specify more clearly just
what the religious dimension of these worlds is.

The story and religion theory articulated by Stephen
Crites,[29] Michael Novak,[30] and others,[31] provides a way
of talking about the religious dimension of the world projected in literature. According to Crites, religion is the
fundamental story which creates a sense of self and world
for a group. Feminist critics are dealing with just such
fundamental stories--stories which have created woman's
place in man's world, and stories which may have the power
to create a new self for women in new world. According to
Crites, fundamental stories orient people to "the great
powers that establish the reality of their world."[32] The
notion of "great powers" which provide orientation is a
definition of the religious dimension of stories which is
extremely useful for feminist criticism in religion and
literature. It provides a tool for discussing the religious
dimension of the world projected in the novel of female
quest. A novel in which such great powers appeared only

implicitly could be classified as a novel primarily concerned with the social aspect of the female quest. A nov-
in which such great powers appear and directly influence
action and perception, as for example the powers of the
lake in *Surfacing* or the currents and forces of energy in
The Four-Gated City, would be classified as a novel of
spiritual quest. Crites' theory is particularly useful for
religion and literature criticism for three reasons which
set it apart from other theories of religion: (1) it reflects the narrative element in literary genres; (2) it is
a functional definition which can be adjusted to different
content (i.e., different great powers) in different stories; and (3) it is a definition which is not necessarily
monotheistic.

Crites, like most theorists of religion, is not concerned with the differences between women's and men's stories. The theory, as he projects it, treats culture and
cultural stories as monolithic. And, in fact, a number of
those identified with the story and religion school are
using the theory to reassert an old style confessional
theology.[33] Feminist critics will be wary of this potential of the theory, while using it for their purposes. In
order to use Crites' theory, the feminist critic must pos-
it a difference between the fundamental stories and great
powers of androcentric religious traditions and the new
fundamental stories and great powers reflected in women's
literature. This implies that one of the structures of
the new fundamental story may be a conversion from the old
world of woman's place into a new world of women's potential and power. My studies of women novelists and poets
suggest that at least one of the great powers that assists
women's transition from one world to the other is the life
energy revealed in nature mysticism, sexual mysticism, and
social mysticism (identification with the currents of power and energy of an age or time).[34]

(4) The fourth and possibly most controversial methodological assumption I make is the decision to use a sex-
differentiated model in my work.[35] The model of humanity
shapes the selection of texts and the questions asked of
them. Traditional research in religion and literature,
like traditional research in all fields, uses the androcentric model couched in the "male generic." Texts written by men are interpreted as reflections of the "human"
spirit. Feminist studies rejects the androcentric model
because it distorts or ignores the experience of one-half
of humanity. A disputed question in feminist studies is
whether to use a sex-neutral model of humanity which
points beyond the polarities of androcentric culture, or
to use a sex-differentiated model which reinterprets the
polarities.

Those who propose a sex-neutral or androgynous model
of humanity, like Mary Daly in *Beyond God the Father*[36]
and Carolyn Heilbrun in *Toward a Recognition of Androgyny*[37]
seek to overcome the negative effects of androcentric sex-
role stereotyping. They believe that genuinely human po-
tentialities and characteristics are equally available to
both sexes. They seek to describe and interpret those human qualities without reference to sexual differentiation.
In Heilbrun's work, literature written by women and men is
considered equally capable of revealing the "androgynous"
qualities of all human beings. Heilbrun's goal is a form
of literature and literary criticism which is indifferent
to sex.

Like Sheila Collins in *A Different Heaven and Earth*[38]
or Patricia Meyer Spacks in *The Female Imagination*,[39] I
find the move to a sex-neutral model of humanity premature,
if not wrong-headed. Even Mary Daly has recently expressed
second thoughts about the use of the term "androgyny" in
her work.[40] I use a sex-differentiated model of humanity
in recognition of the *fact* that cultural conditioning, and

perhaps biology, have encouraged *propensities* in perception
and action which are different for women and men. These
propensities are reflected in differences in plot, character, theme, orientation to powers, and possibly language
in works of literature written by women and men. I believe it is the task of feminist studies to define and
interpret these differences. I recognize that a sex-differentiated model of humanity has been used in androcentric
culture to denigrate women's experience. But I nonetheless
find a sex-differentiated model important and healing for
women. Finally, the sex-differentiated model is useful
for bringing to light modes of perception and action which
can provide alternatives to the destructive aspects of androcentric culture.

The mention of a sex-differentiated model of humanity
usually triggers a fear which is expressed as a question,
"but if you talk about women's experience, what possible
relevance can your work have to a male scholar?" The
short-sightedness of this question is revealed by putting
it into words. I have deliberately used the word "propensities" to talk about differences in female and male experience. A propensity is a tendency, not a necessary course.
Study of women's experience can open up possibilities for
men to enlarge the range of their experience through sympathy and appropriation, as stated at the beginning of
this essay. Even if women's experience were completely
closed to men's sympathy or appropriation, male scholars
would still need to know about women's experience to have
complete knowledge of the world. The sex-differentiated
model does not close women's studies to men, or vice versa.

In conclusion, then, feminist studies in religion and
literature is a vast and exciting area of study, which suggests a potentially enormous transformation of the area of
religion and literature. First, it would mean the introduction of a whole new set of texts written by women, and

the creation of theories and methods for their interpretation. Second, it suggests the need for a fuller articula-
tion of a theory of the relation of religion and literature
in which, on the one hand, religion is discussed in broad,
non-Christian terms, and on the other, literature is discussed in terms of its representational function in human
life. Finally, if a sex-differentiated model of humanity
were broadly accepted, not just for feminist studies, but
for all studies in religion and literature, two conclusions
would follow. The androcentric bias of most of the work in
the area would need to be examined; and the specifically
male character of the religious outlook reflected in literary works written by men would require exploration.

NOTES

*This article has appeared in the *Journal of the American Academy of Religion* 44/2, pp. 317-25.

[1] Mary Daly (Boston: Beacon, 1973).

[2] *Images of Women in the Jewish and Christian Traditions*, ed. Rosemary Ruether (New York: Simon and Schuster, 1974).

[3] Sheila Collins (Valley Forge, PA: Judson, 1974).

[4] The meaning of "female religious outlook" is discussed below. This essay is concerned with a feminist criticism in religion and literature which uses a sex-differentiated model of humanity. I recognize that not all feminist scholars share this premise.

[5] Giles Gunn, "Threading the Eye of the Needle: The Place of the Literary Critic in Religious Studies," *Journal of the American Academy of Religion* (June, 1975) 164.

[6] Strictly speaking, every text is mediated except to its author, and then only if it is an autobiography. Here, however, I use "mediation" to refer to the process of making one's own or finding relevant to one's own experience, literature written by persons of the other sex. This use of terms is justified by sex-role differentiation which renders the experiences of persons of one sex alien to persons of the other.

[7] It was painful for one trained in religious studies to listen to literary critics use the terms "Jungian," "unconscious," "irrational," and "unrealistic" to interpret the spiritual dimension of Doris Lessing's recent novels at the 1975 meeting of the Doris Lessing Seminar of the Modern Languages Association.

[8] *A Proper Marriage* (New York: New American Library, 1970) 206.

[9] "Feminism and Literature," in Susan Koppelman Cornillon, ed., *Images of Women in Fiction*: Feminist Perspectives (Bowling Green, OH: Bowling Green University Popular Press, 1973) 259.

[10] *Creation and Discovery*: Essays in Criticism and Aesthetics (New York: Noonday, 1955) 90-91, quoted in Sallie McFague TeSelle, *Literature and the Christian Life* (New Haven: Yale University, 1966) 71.

[11] "Modernism and History, "*Images of Women in Fiction*, 278-307; and "The Other Criticism: Feminism vs. Formalism," 315-27.

[12] "The Other Criticism," 326.

[13] Doris Lessing (New York: Ballantine, 1968).

[14] Alix Kates Shulman (New York: Bantam, 1973).

[15] Erica Jong (New York: New American Library, 1974).

[16] Marge Piercy (New York: Doubleday, 1973).

[17] New York: Alfred A. Knopf, 1973.

[18] New York: Simon and Schuster, 1972.

[19] See Alison Lurie's review of *The Summer before the Dark*, "Wise Women," *The New York Review of Books* (June 14, 1973) 18-19.

[20] See my article, "Margaret Atwood: The Surfacing of Female Spirituality," in *Signs*: Journal of Women in Culture and Society, (Winter, 1976) 316-30, for a fuller discussion of the spiritual quest-social quest distinction.

[21] See Annis Pratt, "The New Feminist Criticism," *College English* (May, 1971) 872-78, and "Women and Nature in Modern Fiction," *Contemporary Literature* (Fall, 1972) 476-90; also see my article on Atwood, and my article, "Explorations with Doris Lessing in Quest of the Four-Gated City," in Judith Plaskow and Joan Arnold Romero, eds., *Women and Religion*, Rev. Ed. (Missoula, MT: Scholars Press and The American Academy of Religion, 1974) 31-61, and "Spiritual Quest and Women's Experience," *Anima*: An Experimental Journal (Spring, 1975) 4-15.

[22] See my articles on Lessing and Atwood.

[23] See, for example, *The Broken Center*: Studies in the Theological Horizon of Modern Literature (New Haven: Yale University, 1966).

[24] See "The Poetry of Meaning," in *Literature and Religion*, Giles B. Gunn, ed. (New York: Harper and Row, 1971) 220-35. Hopper defers to Heidegger as the one who brought forward "the poem and the art work as the model for that kind of unconcealing of Being that is central to his notion of *a-lethia*" (229).

[25] See, for example, Philip Wheelwright, *Metaphor and Reality* (Bloomington: University of Indiana, 1962).

[26] A Study in Metaphor and Theology (Philadelphia: Fortress, 1975).

[27] "Threading the Eye of the Needle," 181.

[28] Ibid.

[29] "The Narrative Quality of Experience," *Journal of the American Academy of Religion* (September, 1971) 291-311.

[30] *Ascent of the Mountain*: Flight of the Dove (New York: Harper and Row, 1971).

[31] See, for example, James B. Wiggins, ed., *Religion as Story* (New York: Harper and Row, 1975). Also see my dissertation, "Elie Wiesel's Stories: Still the Dialogue," Yale University, 1974, unpublished.

[32] "The Narrative Quality of Experience," 295.

[33] See, for example, James W. McClendon, Jr., *Biography as Theology* (Nashville: Abingdon, 1974).

[34] This is borne out in my studies of Atwood and Lessing referred to above, and in my unpublished studies of Denise Levertov and Adrienne Rich.

[35] Because the use of a sex-differentiated model is so controversial, I have already spoken briefly about it at the beginning of this essay.

[36] Op. cit.

[37] New York: Alfred A. Knopf, 1973.

[38] Op. cit.

[39] New York: Alfred A. Knopf, 1975.

[40] "The Qualitative Leap beyond Patriarchal Religion," *Quest*: A Feminist Quarterly, pp. 20-40.

JUNG AFTER FEMINISM

Naomi R. Goldenberg
University of Ottawa

I decided to call my paper to you this morning "Jung After Feminism" since what I want most to present is the story of my own thinking about Jung—the reasons I was attracted to his works and what I had to come to terms with in them. Because I became interested in Jung and Jungian thought after two years of work and study in the feminist movement, the glass through which I view this branch of depth psychology is heavily influenced by feminism. My fans will say that this results in giving my analysis a unique clarity. My critics will find it reason to dismiss my views—seeing them as greatly distorted. Whatever your opinion, let my statement this morning stand as an example of a feminist revision of Jung—of the theoretical moves one feminist had to make in order to use Jungian psychology constructively.

The reasons I was attracted to Jungian thinking initially had a lot to do with the way I was beginning to view the world through feminism. The feelings of estrangement and alienation which I had sensed in the Jewish and Christian religious systems were beginning to be articulated for me in feminist theory. No wonder the hierarchies of rabbis and priests had so little to say to me about religion! Feminist analysis taught me that because I never fit traditional views of what my proper place in this world should be, I could never be comfortable with theological formulations which both reflected and justified that place. The early feminism of the sixties, however, did little more to address religious matters than to point out how traditional religions reinforced the subjugation of women. It is only very recently that feminists have begun to experiment with constructing alternative religions for spiritual

development.[1] Before the appearance of these movements,
Carl Jung was the thinker to whom I turned for methods of
understanding religious growth outside of traditional institutions.

Jung's attitude to the established religious systems
proved very helpful. He hypothesized that there is a religious process in every human being. Dreams, images, symbols and myths are the manifestations of this process. He
saw religions like Christianity, Judaism and Buddhism as
elaborate communal ways of organizing the basic progression.
Jung thought a person quite lucky if she or he could be a
devout follower of the religion she or he inherited. Then
the road would be easy, well-planned and secure. In the
Collected Works he often states that his first effort in
therapy is to try to connect the patient to his or her native
religion since many of his patients did not suffer from a
sense of the impossibility of coping--but rather from a
sense of the meaningless, barren quality of life. Contact
with "religion" could help in the cure of these souls. If
connection with the native religion could not work, the
patient had to become expert in listening and being guided
by his or her own religious authority and adept at seeing
the basic process within. The people who saw too much
hypocrisy and too little relevance in their native religion
were both cursed and blessed. Cursed because they could
not refer to any established text or doctrine to make the
way easier. Blessed because their religious creations had
the chance of being much more creative.[2]

I see Jung's importance for feminism as residing in
his theories and methods concerning estrangement from traditional religious forms. Many feminists are in the same
position as Jung himself and those he saw as "patients."
Many of us are irrevocably estranged from traditional religious thought. We can not go home again--and, because of
this, must seek religion elsewhere--if religion is

something we want. Thus, we too are both blessed and
cursed. Cursed by the difficulty of feeling so estranged,
and blessed with the opportunity to locate the inadequacy
in some of the old forms and to build new ones. Jung can
help feminists in understanding both the nature of their
curse--the estrangement, and the essence of their bles-
sing--the chance to construct new forms. But before feminists use him for any task--a thorough critique is necessary, for Jungian psychology has largely become a form of
patriarchal religion itself.

I am going to concentrate primarily on the demolition
work this morning. I think that once a feminist is alert-
ed to what may be "wrong" in Jungian thought--she can accept and reinterpret what feels right about it for herself.
The first portion of my demolition job has to be questioning the veneration of Jung himself. This is something I
can not find in the works of "Jungians." The vast majority
of those who get into print never dare question the master.
Instead, they see him as the great man--the word "prophet"
is not too strong. (I am restraining myself from saying
they see him as a god which probably is too strong.) They
see themselves as teachers of the word who can, at most,
"clarify" Jung. Thus, in bookstores, one will see rows of
books summarizing Jungian thought.[3] The closest most works
come to being original are those that extend Jung's assumptions without questioning any premises. Erich Neumann and
Marie Louise von-Franz have engaged in this sort of thing.
Neumann first assumed that archetypes were already proven
and then arranged "the" archetypes in succession.[4] Von-
Franz shared the assumption of archetype by looking at the
"archetypal" truth of various fairytales.[5] Many "Jung
books" pick on one aspect of the man's theories and try to
"explain." Ann Belford Ulanov's book on *The Feminine in
Jungian Thought and Christian Theology* is an example of
this. It is a work which tries to clarify what Jung said
about the feminine without disagreeing with anything at all.[6]

There are two major flaws which all these writers share because they see Jung as the great one and themselves as clarifiers or disciples. First of all, with such an attitude, they are not likely to prune any theories which need pruning or even discarding. Second, the clarifying does not work well. Jung, like most of us, thought different things at different points in his life. He often reworked theories, added to them or changed his interests and, with them, his emphases. On top of this, he was a very uneven sort of thinker and writer who would often make several contradictory statements within a single work.[7] The summary books gloss over all of these complexities and failures in an effort to make everything simple, cohesive and inoffensive. As a rule, Jungians are eager never to harm the image of Jung the-great-one by letting on that he often made statements which were misinformed, ignorant and just plain prejudiced. In one unpublished seminar, for example, Jung is noted as saying that when you are talking of Negroes, you are quite close to the gorilla.[8] Feminists can not ignore such statements from a man who claims so much of his theory is based on anthropological "fact."

One of the great services feminists can render in academics in general and in religion and depth psychology in particular is to bring a useful critical perspective on the works of the great men. It takes a group as disenchanted as we are with cultural givens to have the motivation to uncover what is wrong with those givens and the thinkers who gave them.

After feminists have put Jung the man in some perspective, we have to confront the sexism of his theories and the ways in which this has been glossed over by his followers. Here I would like to try to put my finger on the way I found sexism present in the theory and then discuss what implications the erasing of it might have for depth psychology.

The first sexist issue--the tip of the iceberg--lies
in the way Jung values woman. This might seem strange to
some, since it is often held that because Jung valued the
"feminine," he valued women. Jung is often cast as the
"good guy" in relation to Freud who supposedly only saw
woman as a deficient version of the masculine norm.

Let me quote from Jung to illustrate just how he
valued "woman." This is a characteristic statement:

> Woman is compensated by a masculine element and
> therefore her unconscious has, so to speak, a
> masculine imprint. This results in a consider-
> able difference between men and women, and ac-
> cordingly, I have called the projection-making
> factor in women the animus, which means mind or
> spirit. The animus corresponds to the paternal
> Logos just as the anima corresponds to the ma-
> ternal Eros. But I do not wish or intend to
> give these two intuitive concepts too specific
> a definition. I use Eros and Logos merely as
> conceptual aids to describe the fact that wom-
> an's consciousness is characterized more by
> the connective quality of Eros than by the dis-
> crimination and cognition associated with Logos.
> In men, Eros, the function of relationship, is
> usually less developed than Logos. In women,
> on the other hand, Eros is an expression of
> their true nature, while their Logos is often
> only a regrettable accident.[9]

From this quotation one can see that Jung had a clear idea
of what a "woman" was despite his caveats that his "in-
tuitive concepts" should not be taken too literally. Wom-
en were characterized by Eros, an ability to make connections, while men were oriented toward Logos, the function
of analytic thought. Though Jung never made the definitions of these two terms "too specific" as he said, he and
his followers continually used them to specify and define
male and female roles. The terms became much more than
useful descriptions of psychological events in individuals.
Instead they evolved into universal prescriptions of how
everyone should live. It is true that Jung valued woman
for her remarkable and all too often overlooked "Eros."

But, it is equally true that he wanted her to stay in the sphere of that "Eros." Once she moved into a "Logos" arena, she was not only at a great disadvantage, but extremely annoying as well.

In essence Jung and Jungians have a definitive concept of "The Eternal Feminine." Mary Daly has made an acute remark about this sort of thinker in *The Church and the Second Sex*. She says that people like Jung never stay on a symbolic or harmlessly vague level with their ideas of "feminine" and "masculine," but quickly get around to making "dogmatic assertions" about what should or should not be the role of "existing individuals."[10] Jung fits this description very nicely. In his essay "Woman in Europe" he says:

> No one can get around the fact that by taking up a masculine profession, studying and working like a man, woman is doing something not wholly in accord with, if not directly injurious to, her feminine nature. She is doing something that would scarcely be possible for a man to do, unless he were a Chinese. [Note the racism.] Could he, for instance, be a nurse-maid or run a kindergarten? When I speak of injury, I do not mean merely physiological injury, but above all psychic injury. It is a woman's outstanding characteristic that she can do anything for the love of a man. But those women who can achieve something important for the love of a thing are most exceptional, because this does not agree with their nature. Love for a thing is a man's prerogative.[11]

Such is the way in which Jung valued woman--in the same place she always had--using her "Eros."

Once I had observed this overt sexism in Jung's work vis-à-vis the ineradicably "Eros" nature of "the feminine," I had to dig deeper. This led me to examine the anima-animus model of the psyche. I felt that there was something wrong with the theory even though many people have praised it as a liberating concept because it supports that marvelous unseen creature--"the androgyne." (I believe

that if there is a modern day unicorn--it has to be the
androgyne. It's out there somewhere, running around--but
nearly impossible to catch.) The anima-animus theory pos-
tulates a contrasexual personality in each sex. In men
this personality would be female--in women, male. The
word "personality," however, is too light. In Jungian
thought, "anima" and "animus" are weighty words conjuring
up associations to "the unconscious" and "the soul." The
terms "Eros" and "Logos" are analogous to "anima" and
"animus" in that both sets of words are never clearly defined and often used with different connotations. As with
most Jungian concepts, this slippery quality serves to in-
sulate the ideas from much questioning. In the use of
anima and animus, the only element one can be sure of is
that an "anima" is man's picture of his female "other"
side, while an "animus" is woman's picture of her "other."
The model also sets a psychological task of somehow getting in contact with this "other."

Despite the obvious flaw of imprecise definition of
terms, I accepted the vagueness of the Jungian usage and
set about trying to pinpoint the inequity which I sensed
in the model itself. Research has helped me document this
imbalance more specifically.

The crux of my objection to "anima" and "animus" lies
in statements of Jung like the following:

> Since the anima is an archetype that is found in
> men, it is reasonable to suppose that an equiva-
> lent archetype must be present in women; for just
> as the man is compensated by a feminine element,
> so woman is compensated by a masculine one. I
> do not, however, wish this argument to give the
> impression that these compensatory relationships
> were arrived at by deduction. On the contrary,
> long and varied experience was needed in order
> to grasp the nature of anima and animus empiri-
> cally. Whatever we have to say about these
> archetypes, therefore, is either directly veri-
> fiable or at least rendered probable by the
> facts. At the same time, I am fully aware that
> we are discussing pioneer work which by its very
> nature can only be provisional.[12]

The hesitation, the assertion of probability, and the mention of "pioneer work" at the end of the paragraph reveal Jung's uncertainty about the idea. The key statement is the first sentence: *Since the anima is an archetype that is found in men, it is reasonable to suppose that an equivalent archetype must be present in women.* Jung certainly seems to have deduced the presence of the animus in women from his hypothesis of an anima in men.

Whether one agrees with me on this point or not, it is a fact that Jung never developed the animus idea to the extent of his anima theory. I suggest further development was impossible because he was forcing a mirror image where there was none. He hypothesized the animus in woman to balance the anima in men. The reasoning went that if the unconscious (or, perhaps, "soul") in men were a feminine anima; in women, it must be a masculine animus. According to the Jungian stereotypes of masculine and feminine, this gives women and men qualitatively different kinds of unconsciouses (or souls); and this is a big assertion based on so little "evidence."

On a practical level the anima/animus model and its goal of unification works better for men than for women. The model supports stereotyped notions of what "masculine" and "feminine" are by adding mystification to guard against change on the social sphere where women are at a huge disadvantage. In practice, men can keep control of all "logos" activities and appropriate just whatever "eros" they need from their women as a kind of psychological hobby. Women, on the other hand, are by no means as encouraged to develop "logos," since they are thought of as handicapped by nature in all "logos" arenas such as those found at the top of any important profession. Belief in the anima/animus theory, which rests on shaky grounds, does not lead to integration of the sexes, but rather to more separatism. Intrapsychically, it might do some good in permitting people who have been afraid of experiencing certain things because these things have been seen as appropriate for just one sex or the other. To people with this outlook, the anima/animus theory says "Go ahead, develop your contrasexual element." However, the model is decidedly inadequate if a person is questioning the masculine and feminine stereotypes themselves.

All the work I have seen about anima and animus indicates a tremendously forced quality about the model. It makes far more sense to postulate a similar psychic task for both sexes. Freud did this in a negative sense by speaking of "repudiation of femininity" as the task of successful psychoanalysis for men and women.[13] In the current theology of women's religions the goal is understood in a positive sense by posing contact with female energy as the end for which both sexes should strive.[14] What is relevant here is not so much the labeling of a basic human drive as male or female, but the notion that it is the *same* force which is a prime impetus in human libido. Perhaps in future work this model might be developed more profitably than the petty anima/animus division of the psyche.

Along with every other facet of Jung's theory, the imbalance of the anima/animus model was never challenged by any of his immediate circle of followers. In fact, they were and are prone to emphasize it to an even greater degree. Dr. Jolande Jacobi, one of the most successful female members of the second generation of Jungians insisted that "Just as the male by his very nature is uncertain in the realm of Eros, so the woman will always be unsure in the realm of Logos..."[15] The fact that Dr. Jacobi's very successful career as author and lecturer in the realm of "Logos" seemed to contradict this statement never bothered her at all.

To Jungians the anima, the animus and their verbal handmaidens Eros and Logos are "archetypes"--and if a something is an archetype, it is unchanging and unchangeable. It is the concept of archetype that allows Jungians

like Erich Neumann[16] and Esther Harding[17] to write studies
on the "archetypal" nature of the feminine psyche. All of
these studies rest on selecting mythological material to
document conclusions. There seem to be only two rules in
the selection process--one, never contradict a prevailing
notion of Jung and two, call whatever you come up with
"archetypal."

Thus, it became very important for me to examine the
entire idea of archetype in Jungian thought if I were ever
to confront sexism at its base, for it was this idea of
archetype which created the absolutes of Logos and Eros,
Masculine and Feminine, and Anima and Animus.[18]

I believe that changing the assumption of "archetype"
is the major implication of any feminist critique of Jung.
It will be my last effort at demolition today. If feminists do not make the move to redefine the archetype, we
are left with two options:

> One is to accept the patriarchal ideas of the
> "feminine" as ultimate and unchanging and work
> within those.
>
> Or, the second is to indulge in a rival search
> to find our own archetypes...this time the "true"
> ones to support our conclusions.

I pause over this second option a bit, since quite a
few feminists are taking it. An example is the trend to
use *The First Sex* by Elizabeth Gould Davis,[19] which is an
essentially imaginative work, and claim it to be true because it is "science." The result is the proclamation of
"matriarchy" as an *empirical* absolute. This assertion of
factual absolutes is the very same means which men have
employed to justify the subjugation of women. I think
feminists can arrive at a more honest methodology.

My wariness of the trend to set up rival archetypes
or absolutes is complicated, since I do see the great use
in recovering our lost herstory and finding buried images
of women. However, if we set up these images as "archetypes," we are in danger of setting bounds to experience,

defining what the "proper" experience of women is. I see
this as a new version of the Eternal Feminine enterprise
which could become just as restrictive as the old Eternal
Feminine ever was.

It is on a possible redefining of the concept of absolutes that I would like to close this morning--hopefully
on a constructive note. Perhaps the thinking I've done
about Jungian archetypes can help in developing a useful
attitude toward setting up a new mythology or iconography.
I suggest that feminists abandon the hierarchical idea
of archetype prevalent in most of Jung's work--that we
renounce the idea of separating "archetype" from its
expression in "images" and action. In most Jungian
thought "images" are the contents of experience which
usually appear in visual form in the mind and are expressed
in active form in the world.[20] "Archetypes," on the other
hand, are asserted to be transcendent ideals of which our
"images," i.e., our experiences, are only inferior copies.
This separation leads to making a distinction between the
ideal "form" out there in archetype land and the expressed
"content" in here, in individuals--in their activities,
dreams and meditations. It is this separation of absolute
from experience which lies at the base of all patriarchal
religion. We are told that we women are the way we are
because we are conforming to something out there which can
never change. It is such a concept of "archetype" which
allowed much of Jungian thought to become racist, sexist
and closed to experience.

Instead of setting up rival absolutes, ultimates or
"archetypes," we could use a line of thought in both depth
psychology and religion which begins to equate "image"
(and, its correlate, "action") with archetype. Toward the
end of his life, Jung toyed with the idea of a psychoid
continuum on which our action in the world, our images of
that action, and the ideal spiritual "archetype" were
linked. Although he continued to insist on the transcendence of archetypes, he was beginning to join them to the

material world of experience in images.[21] Such a theoretical movement could lead us to put a much greater value
on what is happening in the individual psyche. Each fantasy, dream or life story becomes archetypal to the degree
that it has psychic effects--to the degree that it moves
things and partakes of what we might want to call "numin-
osity." "Archetype" then can be understood as referring
to the psychic or religious process itself rather than to
past documents of that process.

   With this sort of notion we can stay open to all data
of experience. We might cease looking for authority words
outside the experience itself to label that experience
archetypal, mythological or religious. I see this as
nothing less than breaking down the hierarchy of mind--to
which all other hierarchies and authority structures are
linked--whether political, economic or religious. Since
feminists have suffered more than most from these hierarchies, I see it as a task which those of us working in
psychology of religion are obliged to do.

NOTES

[1] Z. Budapest and the Feminist Book of Lights and Shadows Collective, *The Feminist Book of Lights and Shadows* (The Feminist Wicca, 442 Lincoln Boulevard, Venice, CA 90291, 1975). Also see *Quest*: A Feminist Quarterly, "Women and Spirituality" 1/4 (Spring, 1975) and *Womanspirit* (Womanspirit Publications, Box 263, Wolf Creek, OR 97497) all issues.

[2] See especially: C. G. Jung, *Psychology and Religion, The Collected Works of C. G. Jung*, trans. R. F. C. Hull, Vol. 11 (Princeton, NJ: Princeton University, 1973) and idem, "The Meaning of Psychology for Modern Man," pp. 134-56 in *Civilization in Transition, The Collected Works of C. G. Jung*, Vol. 10 (Princeton, NJ: Princeton University, 1970).

[3] See for example: Frieda Fordham, *An Introduction to Jung's Psychology* (London: Penguin Books, 1954) and Jolande Jacobi, *The Psychology of C. G. Jung* (New Haven: Yale University, 1971).

[4] Erich Neumann, *The Origins and History of Consciousness*, trans. R. F. C. Hull (Princeton, NJ: Princeton University, 1954).

[5] Marie Louise von-Franz, *Creation Myths* (New York and Zurich: Spring Publications, 1972); idem, *Interpretation of Fairytales* (New York and Zurich: Spring Publications, 1970); idem, *The Problem of the Puer Aeternus* (New York and Zurich: Spring Publications, 1970); and idem, *The Feminine in Fairytales* (New York and Zurich: Spring Publications, 1972).

[6] Ann Belford Ulanov, *The Feminine in Jungian Psychology and Christian Theology* (Evanston, IL: Northwestern University, 1972).

[7] Philip Rieff has pointed out some of the worst features of Jung's style in *The Triumph of the Therapeutic* (New York: Harper Torchbooks, 1968) 44-45.

[8] All of the seminars consist of notes transcribed by some of Jung's students. These notes can not yet be directly quoted in print. One can only report their contents.

[9] Jung, *The Collected Works*, Vol. 9, Part II, p. 14.

[10] Mary Daly, *The Church and the Second Sex*, With a Feminist Postchristian Introduction by the Author, Harper Colophon Books, New York, 1975, pp. 148-49.

[11] Jung, *The Collected Works*, Vol. 10, pp. 117-18.

[12] Ibid., Vol. 9, Part II, p. 14.

[13] Sigmund Freud, *The Standard Edition of the Complete Psychological Works*, trans. James Strachey, Vol. 23 (London: Hogarth Press, 1964) 252.

[14] From class given on the Wicca taught by Star Hawk, High Priestess of the Compost coven in San Francisco, December, 1975.

[15] Jacobi, op. cit., pp. 117-18.

[16] Erich Neumann, *The Great Mother*: *An Analysis of the Archetype*, trans. Ralph Mannheim (Princeton, NJ: Princeton University, 1972) and idem, "The Psychological Stages of Feminine Development," trans. Rebecca Jacobson, *Spring* 1959).

[17] Esther Harding, *Women's Mysteries* (New York: Bantam Books, 1971).

[18] See my article, "Archetypal Theory After Jung," *Spring--A Journal of Archetypal Psychology and Jungian Thought* (1975).

[19] Elizabeth Gould Davis, *The First Sex* (Baltimore, MD: Penguin Books, 1973).

[20] James Hillman pointed this out in relation to instinct in his *Essay on Pan* in *Pan and the Nightmare* (Zurich: Spring Publications, 1972) 23-26.

[21] Jung, "On the Nature of the Psyche," *The Collected Works*, Vol. 8, pp. 159-237.

BIBLICAL PROPHECY AND MODERN FEMINISM
For George E. Mendenhall

Mary K. Wakeman
University of North Carolina

There is an analogy between the prophetic movement in
biblical times and the women's movement in our own time
that I would like to describe and explore. The similarities that I see between them are that 1) the movement begins in a personal experience of inner convulsion 2) under
pressure of historical circumstances which results in 3) a
radical break with prevailing values; that inner convulsion
depends on 4) the resurrection of suppressed values (that
have in fact underpinned the dominant ethos), and the radical break then results in 5) subversion of the dominating
institutional forms 6) including language.

My object in describing the prophetic movement in
such a way as to emphasize these characteristics is to
raise questions for and invite realization of the impulse
underlying the women's movement, which, as I see it, is not
only analogous to, but also continuous with the prophetic
movement.[1] In exploring this analogy and continuity, I
have four points to make.

1) The Bible can be read as a prescriptive description of
"the way things are," or as a paradigm of cultural transformation. We are in the midst of a transvaluation of
values which, I would like to suggest, is analogous to the
transvaluation of values in the ancient Near East, of
which we have a record in the Bible, particularly as it is
reflected in the prophetic movement.

2) Hosea's image of a marriage between Yahweh and Israel
was effective as a projection of a new and viable reality.
It was the fruit of his willingness to suffer through the
contradictions in his own thoughts and experience, just as
we must now bear new visions out of our struggle to accomo-
date conflicting realities.

3) Hosea was torn between the archaic view of the world as
an eternal hierarchy in which human society reflected the
divine order and the historical view of states in conflict,
necessitating that humans take initiative in devising forms
of order among peers. Brotherhood was affirmed as a value.
4) We are pressed further to envision a world in which persons, each her/his own source and norm of order, have scope
to develop and express our full humanness. Respect for the
uniqueness of persons is expressed in the notion of "the
sisterhood of man."[2]

Already in Elizabeth Cady Stanton's time it was recognized that the Bible is a man's book. The women in it are
presented as men see them. Women play a largely symbolic
role. The laws protect a man's interests.[3] The poetic
language itself is permeated with imagery that plays on
sex-role differences. It is important to realize that our
noticing the uses to which references to gender were put,
depends on our having moved out (thanks in part to the work
of people like E. C. Stanton) of a world shaped by biblical
images, where it is taken for granted that God is a He, and
that the Church is a She. Such interest in the symbolic
significance of gender as it appears in ways of speaking
about the people, the city, God, chaos, etc., is relatively
new.[4] It testifies to a sense of alienation (experienced
by many of us) from the norms of Western civilization more
radical than that expressed by our nineteenth century forerunners. Out of our awareness of being disconnected from
it, we call into question the whole imaginative frame of
reference within which biblical language signifies. Every
aspect of the biblical tradition is then opened up as a
potentially rich field for a new kind of exploration. I
deliberately use the word "rich" referring to the mining of
gold as a geological image, rather than "fruitful," as an
agricultural one, to remind us that the development of
international empires was related to the invention of
bronze, and later of iron. Such technological innovations

entailed radical changes in the ordering of human community, and eventually, in the experience of self. They involved practices which inevitably conflicted with practices rooted in agricultural values. At the risk of raising more questions than I can deal with at the moment I want to suggest that along with this shift of interest from gardening to *metallurgy occurred* a changed conception of human possibilities and that we are still working to realize those possibilities.

I start with the assumption that feminism is one expression of the attempt to adjust ideologically to changes in our material circumstances brought about by the industrial revolution. What is involved is a radical leap into a new reality, and then an attempt to communicate across the cultural gulf, or, to secure the rope on which one had swung so that others may use it to cross by. When "a whole symbolic universe is being confronted by another whole symbolic universe"[5] the problems of communication are profound. My stance is that the Bible provides evidence of cultural transformation in its own time that may be peculiarly relevant, because it belongs to us, to our present task of transformation.

The prophets of Israel took language and imagery that was familiar to their people and used it in unorthodox ways to tell them something unheard of. "Is not the day of the Lord darkness, and not light?" (Amos 5:20). They did so at the risk of their lives, in passionate love, for the sake of diverting their people from a suicidal course. The analogy I am suggesting between the prophetic and the women's movements may become clearer if we can see how the practices the prophets condemned made sense to their practitioners. Our success in changing practices that are evidently lethal depends on our achieving equal understanding of the prevailing idiom/idiocy. The fact that those practices are often justified with reference to scripture (you shall "have dominion...over...the earth" Gen 1:28) should

not deter us. We will confront the exploitative mentality
which finds support in the Bible more effectively, the
more we come to appreciate the symbolic world in confron-
tation with which the biblical view took shape. To understand what is being said it is necessary to reconstruct
the other side of the conversation. Let me provide one
example.

There is a difference between scholars who unself-
consciously refer to Israel as "she," and the feminist
awareness of the significance of so doing, given the history of symbolizing the relation between divinity and humanity in terms of a marriage. It is Hosea who first referred to Israel as the Bride of Yahweh. This image had
a power that depended on his hearer's familiarity with the
ancient Near Eastern understanding of the relation between
the divine and the human community (the city-state) as
fruitfully consecrated in the sacred marriage of goddess
and priest/king. That marriage expressed the "cosmological
conviction"[6] of consanguinity and continuity in the orders
of nature and society. Man was made from the blood of the
rebel god, to serve the gods.[7] Divorce was out of the
question: man served the gods in a hierarchical order which
was immutable. Hosea, though, was calling the convenant
community of Israel to recognize its relation to the divine
sovereign. The husband here was God rather than man.

To understand the very possibility of imaging the
relationship between God and the human community in these
terms and to appreciate the significance of so imagining
it in Hosea's own time, we must recall Israel's origin in
"a peasant's revolt against the network of interlocking
Canaanite city states....From its very beginnings, the
Yahwistic faith...functioned in a way to create a community
above the tribal level....Land tenure, military leadership,
'glory,' the right to command, power, are all denied to
human beings and attributed to God alone."[8] In this simple
shift of orders from man being king to God being King,

there is implied the profoundly disturbing social and political upheaval in the ancient world toward the end of
the second millennium B. C. "The 100 years between 1250
and 1150 B. C. saw the complete destruction, or reduction
to virtual impotence, of every major political state in
the eastern Mediterranean region."[9] As reflected in the
Song of Deborah, Israel in its beginnings was a community
of semi-autonomous groups, regionally associated with the
ancient Canaanite city-state boundaries. That is, Israel
consisted for the most part of ex-Canaanites, bound in
covenant relationship through common loyalty to a God who
defended their independence from any other king. The definition of the covenant changed with time, and was understood differently by different elements of the population.[10] But the notion of a supra-city-state God whose
will was manifest in historical events was fundamental
from the start. It thrived along-side the notion of the
gods of the land, with which it was in basic contradiction.

It was recognition of this contradiction that historical circumstances finally forced, so that the prophets
were radical in both senses of the term: Going back to the
root, and extreme in their conviction of discontinuity.
In what sense this is also true of the women's movement
will be made clear later in the paper. Here, I am saying
that it was only in the prophet's time that the implications of the principle underlying Israel's existence were
realized: There could be no going back to the sacred state
as it was embodied in Egypt under the Pharaohs, in Babylon,
or in ancient Sumer or Canaan. There was no hope of continuing as a state defined by land, king and temple. It
was only as the People of the Book that Israel could retain a sense of identity. I am not saying that all of
this was realized overnight, or by any one person such as
Hosea. But that the prophetic movement successfully
weaned Israel from its dependency on archaic institutions

is evident in the very survival of the tradition, of the
Bible. Its existence testifies to the survival of a community to whom it was of critical importance.

To understand how Hosea's image of Israel as the Bride
of Yahweh served his purpose, I must explore the idea that
developments in international diplomacy affected the conception of a God who transcends nature.[11] Comparison with
the international treaty forms dating from the mid-second
millennium B. C. up until Hosea's time is illuminating of
the implications of relating to such a God, if we see Him
as the suzerain, the author of the covenant. These forms,
in review, might include the title and attributes of the
great king or suzerain, a historical prologue reviewing his
benevolent acts toward the vassal states whose loyal response was guided by the stipulations of the covenant.
Among them were prohibitions against foreign relations,
and against hostility between vassals; requirements to
answer the call to arms, to trust the suzerain, to pay tribute, to submit controversies for his judgment, to accept
whomever the suzerain appointed as sovereign. Provision
was made for deposit in the temple and public reading of
the treaty, which was witnessed by the gods. The covenant
was ratified by an oath in the names of the gods of the
parties involved, and sanctioned by blessings and cursings
formulae in lieu of other non-military enforcement proce-
dures, or, to justify the use of force.[12]

The question before us now is how, as the initial experience of God as a liberating and unifying force took
imaginative shape in accord with the international treaty
form, it transformed and reflected a transformation in the
understanding of human community. I will limit my remarks
to comparisons that clarify what it might mean for the ordering of a nation to be conceived after the pattern of the
international treaty. Whereas the city-state hierarchy had
been authorized by an assumed natural, given relationship
between the community of men and of the gods, with the

international treaty there was provision for and divine
sanction recognizing a relationship that was not "natural,"
that was admittedly rational, man-made. A distinction was
made within the treaty form between 1) autonomy at the
local level (the divinely sanctioned authority of the king
was still recognized within the vassal state), and 2) the
responsibility of kings to the suzerain (including obedience to laws that regulated the relations between vassal
states). This international community constituted a qualitatively different kind of order in the sense that it was
willed, chosen, legal. The vassal states obligated themselves to the suzerain in return for services rendered and
for the sake of continuing to enjoy the commercial and
other security benefits the relationship provided.

What happened to the conception of self when the relationship between the community and God was conceived
after this pattern? Some brief statements may be sugges-
tive. In choosing Yahweh, the people with Joshua at
Shechem rejected enslavement to the sacred state, and took
on the responsibility for being witnesses against themselves (Josh 24:22). They had no king, but divine guidance was provided, in the law, and by the spontaneous appearance of inspired leaders who interpreted the law and
bore witness to God against themselves. They were prohibited from making images, but perhaps because they recognized in their very autonomy the image of God.[13] They
forfeited whatever security there was in the notion of
their consubstantiality with the divine, as that notion
would now seem to implicate the suzerain-god in mortality.
But this immortal suzerain, as (mytho-)logical successor
to the king-servant of the Goddess, was most naturally
imaged as male. As a vestige from the archaic sexualizing
of the relationship between divine and human worlds, the
new consciousness was associated with masculinity. Significant differences between the archaic and biblical consciousness may be summarized in the following table:

Under Goddess	Under God
Kingship descended from heaven	The law descended from heaven (Sinai)
The gods bear witness	You are witnesses against yourselves
Man is made from the blood of the rebel god	Man is made in the image of God

Hosea's tour-de-force depends on a figure-ground play of mutually exclusive possibilities of understanding contained in the image of Yahweh as husband. *Either*, as a god like those of the other nations, he is jealous of the Baalim of international commerce, *or*, it is as the ultimate Lord of history that his husbandry of Israel concerns him. ("The baalization of YHWH appears to be overcome where Israel is thought of as His wife, and so His husbandship pictured as something not of nature but of history.")[14] Hosea's prophecy challenged the Israelite leaders' willingness to enslave his people for the sake of military security and commercial advantages. Thus those who truly heard Hosea were seduced/converted from commitment to international politics, in which there was no hope for Israel, to a living federation under Yahweh of those for whom significance attached to historical rather than to mythical events. These survived the vicissitudes of historical fate through faith that it was meaningful ("I will betroth you to me in faithfulness; and you shall know the Lord" 2:20), through acceptance of their terrifying independence from land, king and temple ("For the children of Israel shall dwell many days without king or prince, without sacrifice or pillar, without ephod or teraphim." 3:4). Hosea's image, then, marked a major shift of values in the direction of increasing human autonomy. It testified to the recognition that it was within the God-given possibility of human imagination to accept as meaningful events that threatened the structures of meaning on which life had seemed to depend. The word remained, the concept of regulation, the possibility of a self-defining community.

The next step in the same direction leads toward self-regulation: If there can be an authoritative word, then there can be many words, each embodied in a life that speaks to another life in a revelatory way. The very notion of "a people" becomes devoid of meaning as the significance of persons is recognized. The prophetic movement set the direction that led through Jeremiah's vision, "I will put my law within them and I will write it upon their hearts....No longer shall each man teach his neighbor and each his brother, saying 'know the Lord,' for they shall all know me" (31:33-34), through Joel's "I will pour out my spirit on all flesh" (2:28) to the current necessity to trust ourselves and one another, to find in our differences more cause for celebration than for fear. Thus the prophetic movement is not only analogous to, but continuous with the women's movement, as it provides, in its outcome (Judaism, Christianity and Islam) the view with which we find ourselves in vital conflict now. The notions of progress, of development, of defense, the value of which has up until recently been taken for granted, are all dependent on a linear view of history. They are dependent on the idea of a normative word that defines reality for a group, which has a destiny, that is threatened by the existence of dissenting groups. Suppose each person is a "group," with its own peculiar destiny, for which there are no precedents, for whom the urge to self-transcendence is the only guide? "The tradition" takes on a quite different meaning, as one among a number of expressions of this urge, as it has manifested itself in various times and places.

At this point I would like to provide a conceptual model of how I see the process of cultural change as I am describing it here. The next step will be to demonstrate that we are on a similar cultural brink, called to reconcile, in a new vision, a contradiction that has been basic to western/christian civilization, as well as that women as a

group are peculiarly equipped to do so by the nature of
our participation in it. (Our "acculturation"). I have
recently realized why the fact that a snake sheds its
skin makes it an appropriate symbol of immortality. We
live within a skin (which we might call "conceptual structures")[15] that allows us to grow, to expand within it. At
a certain point that skin, which had provided the organi-
zation and the space to grow in, becomes constricting. It
is no longer liberating: it must be burst. The possibility
of bursting a skin that has grown too small, however, depends on there already being a skin on us capable of holding the new growth in order. And of course the shape of
that new skin is in some way determined by the old one.
Part of what characterizes the new one, I imagine, is what
enables it to tear off the old, which means that once the
old skin *is* torn off, aspects of the new one atrophe, and
fester. Nelle Morton said recently, "It's not that the
church has become too much like the world, but that the
world has become too much like the church."[16] Christianity burst the old hierarchy by democratizing sacred marriage (e. g. "wives be subject to your husbands, as to the
Lord" Eph 5:22) but now sexism has permeated every aspect
of culture. It has become big business rather than a
vehicle for spiritual growth. Or, as Rosemary Ruether observes, "The irony...is that Christian culture took over
and absorbed the classical view of man and its myth of
salvation, and so molded its social institutions accordingly that it now finds itself the foe to the new culture-
bearers of its own original tradition."[17] The "original
tradition" can be realized only by throwing off the skin
that protected its growth.

In bringing together ancient international treaty
forms, the prophet Hosea, and modern feminism, I am suggesting a relation between political order, religious
ideal, and subjective experience, as a spiral of expanding
possibilities. At any one point in time there may be a

relation between subjective experience and political order,
but they are not a direct reflection of one another. The
religious ideal is pivotal. It is the snakeskin in its
double aspect of retaining wall and blueprint for the
future. (In Hosea's case, the image of the covenant as a
marriage refers back to the sacred state, and forward to
the understanding that everyone is a king.)[18]

What does it mean, to be a king? Kingship is a
mediating role, between the unknowns within and without,
whether we are talking about selves, or states, or the
cosmos. It depends on the support of subjects, and the
election of the gods. Consider as a paradigm: There is a
story about Inanna the Goddess of Life who is released
from the grip of death on condition that her husband, the
king, take her place. His sacrifice, accepted as necessary
to continuing life, is celebrated in the yearly festival
of renewal in which the king suffers a ritual death and
rebirth. The shift of emphasis within the tradition concerning this figure from triumphant warrior against mythical chaos (Marduk in *Enuma Elish*) to suffering servant of
unfathomable historical forces (Isa 42:1-4, etc.) reflects
Israel's experience, until the motif is taken up and transformed by the figure of the suffering Christ, in whose
death and birth into eternal life anyone may participate
through baptism (Rom 6:3).

The Christian ideal of universal kingship coincides
chronologically with the political order of the Roman Empire, and the subjective experience of enslavement. "The
kingdom of God is within you/Render unto Caesar what is
Caesar's." But the relationship is clear, in chronological
sequence, between the ancient political order of sacral
kingship, the religious ideal of participation in the suffering and resurrection of Christ (for which Hosea's suffering is a prefiguration), and the subjective reality of
the individuation process which requires each one of us to
take responsibility for mediating the divine/human relation
within ourselves.

Hosea's experience as symbolized by his unhappy marriage was that of a responsible leader (i.e., a king) who knew that Israel was doomed as an autonomous state. The conflict between this knowledge and his commitment to Israel was resolved by encompassing both in one order that for the moment could exist only in idea. Israel was saved as a community of *knowers*. The basis of community was acceptance of historical process as real and meaningful. The form in which this community could be envisioned so that it would survive the destruction of the state was the international treaty form which, in granting greater autonomy to its separate parts, was better able to withstand disruption. The new direction, then and now, came from those with strength to encompass the ideological contradictions within their own souls (for Hosea, between reverence for the state, and reverence for himself as a knower) where they could be suffered through to the point of issue in a new word that provided order also for other persons. "The order of society in history is reconstituted in fact through the people who challenge the disorder of the surrounding society with the order they experience as living in themselves."[19] The authority to validate that living order is sought and found in the tradition (for Hosea, of the pre-state federation). The prophet's responsibility is to deal adequately with his own present moment, in faith that the embodiment of his vision in social form will follow as a matter of course if he does so. "The attitude of the prophets is tantalizing in that it seems to violate common sense"[28] only if common sense assumes that we wish to limit the future to what we already know.

Follow the track laid down by the previous paragraph exactly, just to see how it will come out. In the next turn of the spiral: Our experience, symbolized by Jungian syzygy, is that of androgynous, whole, persons who know that patriarchy is doomed as a self-alienating state. The conflict between this knowledge and our commitment to humanity is resolved by accomodating both in action and

speech that is personally anchored. Humanity is saved as
a community of persons who take responsibility for ourselves. The basis of community is acceptance of imaginative process as real and meaningful. In an important
sense, if we are not to "follow the leader," we each have
to do our own learning, and need to encourage one another
to persist where we are effectively working. The form in
which this community can be envisioned so that it will survive the disintegration of "brotherhood" is something like
anarchy, but it needs a word that indicates the presence,
rather than the absence of something. The people who make
it up lead each other as we can see our way, each according to our own vision. Ideological contradictions between
reverence for the word, and for ourselves as experiencers
is suffered through to the point of issue in new being, or
what Mary Daly calls "contageous freedom"[21] that provides
validation of unique being for other persons. The authority to confirm that living order can be found in the record we have of cultural transformation.

It remains for me to show how and why this paragraph
displays the values of the women's movement. The plural-
istic value that we affirm today has its origin in the
international empires of the ancient Near East. The or-
ganization of an empire requires recognition of the
brotherhood of peoples who are not the same, who do not
share the same values, or the same institutions, but who
do share the characteristic of being "a people." This
value emerges on the personal level insofar as the process of coming to a sense of personal identity involves
awareness of one's differences from other, like persons.
This experience becomes available to women in "sisterhood."
But the possibility of women relating to each other independently from their relationship to men, depends on the
fact that brotherhood, which emerged as an *idea* only when
the ancient treaty form provided a means of recognizing
peer relationships between kings, *has been* realized on the

personal level: (We have assumed that the ideal form of
government was democracy, not autocracy). This is what I
meant when I said that the future is rooted in what patriarchy has accomplished.

Let me clarify this by referring again to the prophetic movement as exemplified in Hosea. It was possible
for Hosea to speak of the Lord of history as husband, and
so to make nought the gods of the nations, only by figur-
ing the people, rather than the Goddess, as His bride.
But Hosea's prophecy also contained within it an invitation
to join *him*: to shift from identification with apostate
people (the bride that has become a harlot), to faithful
husband (God). It was not his intention to recall the
harlot to faithfulness. The Deuternomist may have been
intent on reform, exhorting people to change their actions.[22] But the prophet knew that the only action that
could be taken was that of understanding, of accepting
disaster. No action could be effective that did not issue
out of a radically altered understanding of God's inten-
tions for Israel. And if you understood, in a saving way,
you would see things as he did. You would share his position. You would give up hope of temple, land, and king.
You would bear witness, reflect God's image, accept his
will. As a religious ideal, this was a call to full personhood. In terms of the history of these images, it was
effective for Hosea to ask that his audience cease being
female and become male: a whole nation of priest-kings
(4:6). This shift of gender correlated, then, with the
shift in the conception of human community. In the representative person of the king, the community had been the
servant to the divine power manifest in nature. Now it
shared creative initiative as the *people* were recognized
as righteous ("holy," Exod 19:6).

But there still, *now*, attaches to the notion of "person" the assumption of masculinity. The more one identifies positively with the tradition as a source of support

in the effort to become human (become a king), the more
she comes to experience herself as "other." ("The subju-
gated group...largely take on the appearance, not only in
the presence of the oppressors, but even in their own eyes,
of the character vested in them."[23]) It's not just that
you are told that because you are a woman you can't be a
priest and you answer indignantly, "why, that's nonsense,"
but that you experience within *yourself* a tendency to sabo-
tage every move toward self-realization because it conflicts with the order in which "self" is realized through
sex-roles. It is here that we can locate the contradiction
that historical circumstances, or perhaps now I should say
technological developments,[24] require us to resolve. I
observed earlier that the prophets were radical in both
senses of the term, and so are we, but the root for us is
the biblical tradition of the word incarnate. The discontinuity we experience is that we can no longer live by
the authoritative word. We have lost confidence in brotherhood, in peer relations regulated by law in which women are
regarded as property. We are beginning to realize the revolutionary potential in each one of us to make up our own
story, affirming our differences as they explode the biblical "givens" of the human situation. We seek the growing
edge. The balance-point or moment of skin-shedding is different for each of us. "Only the human speaks. God
hears."[25] In faith that we are hears, we become significant. It is in speaking our own word out of our own circumstances that we come to recognize the rightness of each
other's, different order, and so to *love* one another.
Trust in the new skin, in the coherence natural to organ-
isms allows us to risk disintegration, to risk relationship
in response to a call toward something as yet undetermined.

The battle with the sexist patriarchal order is being
fought with our lives. In the process we are discovering
that, to put it simply, there are alternatives to what once
appeared to be a choice between subordinating oneself to a

man who required the sacrifice of one's self-development, and, not subordinating oneself to a man, as was required for one's self-development. In like manner the prophets forged an alternative to the ancient Israelite choice between experiencing national disaster as abandonment to the forces of chaos, or as ungodly punishment for breach of covenant. As Job discovered, it is to those who hold fast to their integrity that God reveals him/herself.

The exploitative mentality of our culture that is now threatening to life can be changed from within through the energy of people who experience that mentality as threatening to them personally. Women who have internalized patriarchal values *at the same time* that they have accepted their position as women within the patriarchal order often experience a personal convulsion that conforms closely to the pattern of religious conversion, the experience of turning the back, of passing over from the "immemorial misdirection of human life"[26] to self-surrender to the divine. In this case the sense of alienation arises, not through blind identification with one's cultural role, but with the cultural other. The discovery that the Worm has been taken into one's own bosom marks the turning point, because in the very moment one catches herself in the act of self-betrayal, she affirms *the discovering self* that determines the new direction. The advantage of a woman over a man in the moment of disillusionment, typically, is that she is already identified with alternative values that have persisted underground, as the back-side of the "man's world." She, like the prophet, has another foot to stand on, to begin the process of self-affirmation that gives birth to a new style of human community. It is not a matter of rejecting one way for another way, but of going beneath both: of laying claim to and exercizing responsible choice in the expression of those traits that have traditionally, or unconsciously, been associated with woman. In this I think it becomes clear why it is women who take the lead in cultural change now.

What if we are each a whole empire? The vision implies radical differences between people, who trust in
each other's capacities for self-regulation, and are
mutually appreciative. "Us and them" thinking gives way
to the awareness of the radical otherness and preciousness
of all others. Pluralism means living with people at a
level that recognizes our incommensurability, means evolving institutions that are responsive to the various and
changing needs of persons, means giving voice to, recognizing the right to expression, of all parts of oneself.
The bursting of the old skin testifies to faith in the new
skin to hold, though its form be unpredictable. We emerge,
trusting the process of growth, affirming transformation,
resolutely refusing to calculate the future as we take
responsibility for our present in all its ambiguity.

NOTES

[1] The future is created by how we describe the past. There are more and less fruitful ways of reflecting on the past as a mode of moving in the present. One less fruitful way, it seems to me, is to idealize a pre-patriarchal age as a time when women had more power than they do now, relative to men. It has always been so, that freedom lies in the direction of acknowledging that it is by our own choice that we are where we are. In that move, we recover our autonomy and our freedom to exercise it. For that reason, I locate the root from which the future must flower in the "patriarchal" move to break with enslavement to natural cycles, however much I long for a future in which we realize that our humanity is natural. What possible sense does it make for me to denounce Eve for eating the apple?

[2] Mary Daly, *Beyond God the Father* (Boston: Beacon, 1973) 4.

[3] Phyllis Bird, "Images of Women in the Old Testament," in *Religion and Sexism*, ed. Rosemary Ruether (New York: Simon and Schuster, 1974).

[4] E. g., "Images of Women in the Bible (*Women's Caucus-Religious Studies Newsletter* 2/3 [Fall, 1974]) edited by myself.

[5] Kathleen Brewer at a conference on "The Feminine in Religion" organized by members of The Georgetown University Religious Studies faculty, held at The College of Preachers in Washington, DC, September 12-14, 1975.

[6] Cornelius Loew, *Myth, Sacred History and Philosophy* (New York: Harcourt, Brace & World, 1967) 13.

[7] *Enuma Elish* VI:8, 29-33 in *Ancient Near Eastern Texts* 3, ed. J. B. Pritchard (3rd ed.; Princeton, NJ: Princeton University, 1969) 68.

[8] George E. Mendenhall, "The Conquest of Canaan" in *The Biblical Archeologist Reader* 3, E. F. Campbell and David Noel Freeman, eds. (New York: Doubleday-Anchor, 1970) 107, 108, 110.

[9] George E. Mendenhall, "Covenant," *Encyclopedia Britannica* 15th ed., 5:227b.

[10] Dale Patrick, "A Study of the Conceptual Models of the Covenant," unpublished Th.D. dissertation (Berkeley: Graduate Theological Union, 1971).

[11] George E. Mendenhall, "Covenant Forms in Israelite Tradition" in *The Biblical Archeologist Reader* 3, op. cit.; Dennis J. McCarthy, *Treaty and Covenant* (Rome: Pontifical Biblical Institute, 1963); and Patrick, op. cit.

[12] McCarthy, op. cit., p. 94: "The religious sanction, the oath and the intervention of the gods was sought to justify the overlord's intervention and to assure its efficacy."

[13] G. Mendenhall, *The Tenth Generation* (Baltimore: Johns Hopkins, 1973) 211: "Prohibition against images correlates with the fact that man himself is the image of God."

[14] Martin Buber, *The Prophetic Faith* (New York: Harper-Torchbook, 1960) 120.

[15] Clifford Geertz, *Interpretation of Cultures* (New York: Basic Books, 1973) 27.

[16] Conference on "The Feminine in Religion," see n. 5.

[17] Rosemary Ruether, "Women's Liberation in Historical and Theological Perspective" *Soundings* (Winter, 1970) 372f.

[18] Or in the case of Christianity, the subjective experience of slavery (under empire) demands an ideal (everyone is a king) which is expressed in terms that are known (the obsolete sacred state) and which in turn implies a political order (democracy) in which the experience of people who take responsibility for government leads to a new demand (self-regulation) that is familiar from the (obsolete) definition of empire.

[19] Eric Voegelin, *Israel and Revelation* (Louisiana: Louisiana State University, 1956) 483.

[20] Daly, op. cit., p. 438.

[21] Voegelin, op. cit., p. 447.

[22] Patrick, op. cit., p. 438.

[23] Ruether, *Soundings* op. cit., p. 367.

[24] Above, p. 2.

[25] Nelle Morton, in a personal letter of March 23, 1976.

[26] W. E. H. Stanner, "On Aboriginal Religion II" (*Oceania* 30 [June, 1960] 278); as quoted by Robert Bellah, "Religious Evolution," *American Sociological Review* 29/3 (June, 1964) 363.

II. RECOVERING THE DATA:

Cross-Cultural and Historical Studies on Women and Religion

DRAUPADĪ AND THE DHARMA

Nancy Falk
Western Michigan University

"A wife that speaketh disagreeable words," says the massive Indian epic Mahābhārata, should be avoided "like a vessel splitting in the sea."[1] She is comparable to a preceptor that can't expound the scriptures, an illiterate priest, a king who cannot protect, a cowherd who won't go to the fields, and an outcaste with religious aspirations. Her home, it is said, is no different from a wilderness.[2] In contrast, "a beloved and sweet-speeched wife," together with wealth, health, sons, and knowledge "comprise the happiness of men."[3] Again and again, in its many descriptions of ideal womanhood, the epic praises the sweet and docile tongue.

Yet the same epic praises the princess Draupadī--perhaps the sharpest-tongued heroine of all Indian literature--as "the best of her sex"[4] and "eminently virtuous."[5] In some of the most arresting passages of the epic, Draupadī decries the seeming spinelessness of her five hero husbands. She does not mince words. They are "eunuchs" not warriors.[6] Given their behavior, she says, "husbands...have I none."[7] She reserves her most bitter castigations for Yudhiṣṭhira, the oldest of the five brothers and hence the most deserving of honor. On one occasion she cries (this time not to his face):

> What grief hath she not who hath Yudhisthira as
> her husband?[8]

He is "addicted to dice,"[9] a "desperate gambler,"[10] and as such she holds him fully responsible for the misfortunes of his brothers and herself. When he wins the war she has urged him to fight, she blames him for the loss of her five sons.[11] And when, driven by remorse, he wishes to renounce

the kingdom he has won and retreat to the forest, she calls
his plan "folly" and a "path of madness."[12] Addressed to
a king and senior husband, these are strong words indeed.
(They are even grounds for suicide: after Yudhisthira's
brother Arjuna addresses his senior in similar fashion in
a fit of anger, Arjuna offers to kill himself in expiation
for his disrespect.)[13]

Ironically, others in the epic consider Yudhisthira
to deserve the highest praise. He is called "Yudhisthira
the Just,"[14] "the best of virtuous men,"[15] "the very embodiment of virtue."[16] He is "wise in all the laws,"[17]
and "knows every rule of morality."[18] In fact, in those
passages of the epic which attribute divine fathers to
each of the five brothers, Yudhisthira is the engendered
son of Dharma, the embodied principle of morality and justice that is supposed to guide all of Hindu behavior. He
is spontaneously righteous; he cannot tell a lie; he must
treat all men (and also women) justly. These paeans persist despite an endless procession of scenes that depict
Yudhisthira as in fact the indecisive bungler of Draupadī's charges.

This great Yudhisthira, like all of his brothers,
accepts the stinging words of his wife meekly and without
response. And when he speaks of her, she is "our beloved
wife, dearer to us than our lives,[20] "ever engaged in doing
what is agreeable to us."[21] She is "devoted to her lords,
and eminently virtuous,"[22] she deserves "to be cherished
by us like a mother and regarded like an elder sister."[23]

In many ways, Draupadī *is* an ideal wife as described
in the epic itself and in so many contemporary and later
writings on the *dharma*. According to her own description,[24] she always serves her husbands with devotion and
shows no jealousy towards their other wives (her favorite
husband Arjuna has several; she is angry when the first,
Krsna's sister Subhadrā, is brought home, but quickly cools
off and comes to treat her like a sister.) She indulges in no

lies, improprieties, or flirtation and in no way is attracted to other men. She bathes, sleeps, and eats after
her husbands, and always offers them a seat when they return (this is a reference to an honorific ritual). She
keeps her house and food clean, tends her rice carefully
and serves it at the proper time. She does not imitate
wicked women. She is never idle, never giggles or dilly-
dallies. She practices penances when her husbands leave;
she renounces what her husbands renounce; she maintains
the household duties to the ancestors, gods, and guests.
She never acts against her husbands' wishes; she honors
her mother-in-law and worships the Brahmans. When acting
as queen, she knows all the activities of her thousands of
servant-girls and manages her entire household successfully, keeping track even of her husbands' horses, elephants
and total income and expenditure. When in exile, she takes
complete charge of feeding her little troop, together with
any wandering and irascible holy men who demand susten-
ance.[25] The most remarkable expression of her wifely virtue is the exile itself. Her husbands are forced to wander
in the forests for eleven difficult years and then to live
in disguise among men for another year. During this time
she follows them faithfully (though not without complaint),
leaving behind not only her ornaments and servants but also
her five precious sons, whom she will not see again until
they are young men and ready to fight in the war that takes
their lives.

It is only the lady's tongue that seems somehow out of
place. There is a common and easy explanation, based on an
internal critique of the epic. It is generally accepted
that the epic has been woven together out of many strands
of oral tradition, of which the nuclear stories about the
Pāṇḍavas and Draupadī and the great Bhārāta war form some
of the older material. [26] The passages about ideal wife-
hood are probably more recent than the memories of Draupadī herself. She is a throwback; her stories come from

a time when women were more highly respected than in the
days of the meek and submissive wifely models. Furthermore, the central story of the epic must have already been
well known before the final versions were produced. The
redactors would have been loathe to tamper with a figure
whose personality was already well set. This approach is
probably valid, as far as it goes. It can readily be
demonstrated that the status and freedom of women under-
went a sharp decline during the years in which the epic
was probably acquiring its final shape.[27] It is also true
that many of the epic's portrayals of ideal womanhood (as
well as virtually all of its misogynist passages) are contained in its Śānti and Anuśāsana Parvans--both very likely insertions of a later age.[28]

But such an explanation does not go far enough. It
fails to take into consideration the very crucial role
that Draupadī plays in the epic. The truth is that, even
if the redactors had wanted to make Draupadī over, they
could not have done so without destroying their work. Her
words are too important to the epic, too crucial to the
delineation of its central problem.

Let us briefly review the epic itself, so that we can
determine accurately the role of Draupadī. The Mahābhārata,
or Great Narrative of the Bhāratas, is the longest poem in
the literature of the world. It consists reputedly of
100,000 *ślokas*, or two-line verses. As has been previously indicated, it was constructed out of an oral tradition
that developed over a period of perhaps as long as a thousand years, reaching its final form sometime in the vicin-
ity of 400 A. D.[29] The epic as it stands contains at least
four basic types of material: 1) The nuclear story about
the five Pāṇḍavas, their early fortunes and misfortunes
with their mother Kuntī, their later fortunes and misfortunes with their wife Draupadī, their quarrel over the
"lordship of the world" with their hundred cousins, the
Kauravas, and its resolution in a horrible war which leaves

only a handful of warriors alive. 2) A group of peripheral
myths and legends used to cite precedents for various types
of actions undertaken or proposed in the epic and also to
create a semi-historical context for the Pāṇḍava-Kuru story. 3) A great deal of didactic material about the
dharma--i.e., the moral and social law. This usually
takes the form of long, dry expositions, placed in the
mouth of one of the epic's many characters who are regarded to be authorities on the *dharma* (excluding Yudhiṣṭhira,
who is more frequently in the position of inquirer in such
sessions). As we have already noted, much of the material
on ideal womanhood (though not all of it) is contained in
such expositions. 4) Equally long theological/philosophi-
cal expositions on the ultimate nature of the world, its
relationship to various gods, the "Supreme Soul" and so on;
and also presentations of the various approaches to enlightenment. These are also placed in the mouths of authorities on the *dharma*. The most famous of such passages
is the Bhagavad-Gītā; but there are far more lengthy and
complicated versions of such discourses in the Śānti-Parvan, recited by the old hero Bhīṣma as he lies on a bed
of arrows waiting to die.

J. A. B. van Buitenan has pointed out, in the introduction to the recently released first volume of his *Mahābhārata* translation, [30] (in process) that the framework of
the epic is a dispute over a royal succession whose rights
have been clouded by generations of irregularities. In
the final dispute that brings on the great war, the five
sons of Pāṇḍu (the Pāṇḍavas) challenge the 100 sons of
Dhṛtarāṣtra (the Kauravas). Dhṛtarāṣtra was the older
brother of Pāṇḍu, and under ordinary Indian norms for succession, should have automatically occupied the throne of
Hastināpura. But Dhṛtarāṣtra was born blind, and hence,
in accordance with the *dharma*, was disqualified to rule.
Unfortunately for the Pāṇḍavas, their father, the legitimate heir, refused to occupy the throne, preferring instead

to live the life of a hermit in the forest with his two
wives and his five sons. Dhṛtarāṣṭra was therefore in-
stalled as regent; because his brother's children were
still very young at the time of their father's death, he
continued to hold that position as they grew into young
adulthood. The Pāṇḍavas were therefore left in the con-
spicuously weak position of being heritors by right--but
not in fact or even by precedent. Their claim was further
weakened by the fact that the boys were not biologically
Pāṇḍu's sons. Because of a curse he did not dare beget
children himself; hence he had them "sewn in his field"[31]
(namely his two wives) by proxies (because of a boon earlier won by his first wife Kuntī, he was able to have this
done by the five gods Dharma, Vāyu, Indra, and the twin
Aśvins).[32] The difficulties inherent in the situation are
initially resolved by splitting the kingdom; the five
rightful, but weaker heirs are given an undeveloped region.
They promptly expand it and increase their own wealth and
power by conquest and alliance; they construct the magni-
ficent capitol Indraprastha and prepare to perform the
rājasūya, a great sacrifice that will bestow "universal
sovereighty" on Yudhiṣthira, the eldest. Needless to say,
this situation is highly threatening to the Kauravas.
They challenge Yudhiṣthira to a dicing match, which should
probably be understood as a requisite of the *rājasūya* ritual itself.[33] The match is rigged; the comparatively in-
ept Yudhiṣthira is forced to face a highly skilled chal-
lenger.[34] In the first eighteen throws, he loses everything, including his brothers and himself who are to become
slaves to the Kauravas. On the nineteenth throw, he stakes
Draupadī, and loses her; she is subsequently subjected to
a series of the most degrading insults that woman of her
proud descent and station could possible be made to bear.
She wins her freedom and that of her husbands when she asks
the assembly of kings a questions about the *dharma* that no
one can answer: if her husband enslaved himself on the

eighteenth throw, did he have rights over her on the nine-
teenth--and hence was he able to stake her? But their re-
lief is short-lived; Yudhiṣṭhira is called back to fin-
ish the game with the twentieth throw. This loss condemns
the Pāṇḍavas to a twelve-year exile, with the last year
spent in disguise. They complete the assignment successfully and return willing to accept even a portion of their
former kingdom. But the Kauravas will release nothing and
they are confronted with the alternatives of war or dis-
grace.

The epic, however, has long been recognized to have
a larger theme--a theme of which, I suspect, the succession dispute is itself a part. For the work is an exploration of the *dharma*.[35] It is not merely true that the
Mahābhārata incorporates a great deal of didactic material
on the *dharma*. Its stories--even the shorter, peripheral
stories--frequently turn on motifs of the *dharma's* ambi-
guities and paradoxes.

A good example is the story of the Brahman girl
Devayānī and the princess Sarmiṣṭhā.[36] As a result of the
latter's angry and disrespectful actions, Devayānī acquires
Śarmiṣṭhā as her personal slave. When the jealous Brahman
girl subsequently acquires the great prince Yayāti as her
husband, she does not wish to share her husband with her
attractive slave--who carries the additional advantage of
being of his caste.[37] She therefore has her powerful *ṛṣi*-
father[38] demand of her new husband that he will not exercise the privileges of his lordship with her slave. All
goes well until the unmarried Śarmishthā approaches Yayāti
during her *ṛtu*, the traditionally accepted period of fertility immediately following the menstrual period. According to the *dharma*, a woman had the absolute right to demand that her *ṛtu* be satisfied so that she might bear
children; if she had no husband, she might approach any
male suitable for a match with her.[39] Yayāti, thus soli-
cited, is faced with a dilemma: according to the *dharma*

he must service a woman demanding the rights of her *ṛtu*.
He resolves the impasse by following his heart and silences
his angry wife by citing the *dharma* of *ṛtu*. And later, as
Devayānī had feared, it is Śarmishthā's son who ascends to
his father's throne.[40]

"The course of morality is subtle."[41] Just as the
theme of Draupadī's insult recurs again and again through
the epic, inciting and justifying its horrible carnage, so
the supposedly all-wise Bhīṣma's shamefaced answer to her
question before the assembly about her own legal position
is illustrated again and again in its major persons and
actions. The *dharma* is ambiguous. It does not always
give the clear answers that one might hope or desire from
it. It has often been noted that Yudhiṣṭhira's character
itself constitutes a central problem or the epic. For on
the one hand, he is the son of Dharma, acting supposedly
in spontaneous righteousness. And on the other, he is a
rather second-rate warrior; the specific *dharma* of his
kṣatriya class--which is to win kingdoms and to battle
furiously in defence of the right--has little attraction
for him. The epic itself points out on numerous occasions
that he is better suited to be a *brahman* than the warrior
he was born to be. As a result the great son of Dharma
must have his own *dharma* recalled to him. This is done at
various times by a number of other characters: his second
brother Bhīma, son of the wind and a naturally furious--
and unreflective--warrior; his third brother Arjuna, son
of the gods' chief Indra and a superlative archer (whose
own single uncharacteristic moment of hesitation about the
proper interpretation of the *dharma* prompts the great revelation of the Bhagavad-Gītā); and Arjuna's brother-in-law,
ally, and inseparable friend Kṛṣna, an awesome warrior
who is revealed from time to time also to be a living manifestation of the supreme god. But it is Draupadī who most
persistently and perceptively lays bare the inconsistencies
in Yudhiṣṭhira's supposedly righteous behavior. And it is

Draupadī who so deeply feels these inconsistencies that
she is finally led to question the justice of the *dharma*
itself: There is no justice, she says. Man is like a pup-
pet on a string:

> And the Supreme Lord, according to his pleasure,
> sporteth with his creatures, creating and destroy-
> ing them, like a child with his toy....Like a
> vicious person, He seemeth to bear himself
> towards them in anger.[42]

(For this outburst of bitterly spoken doubt, the noble
Yudhishthira calls her a heretic.)

Draupadī is in fact the major counterpoise to
Yudhisthira. Her questions expose the heart of the is-
sue--Yudhisthira is not simply obeying the call to a
dharma that is difficult to accomplish but clear. He is
making a choice between *dharmas*--one that will allow him
to preserve for a period the peace he so ardently desires,
but also one that entails great cost for the innocent
people who surround him. He chooses according to the
priorities designated by his own "innate" righteousness.
But these priorities are not necessarily appropriate for
his own station and/or shared by his own associates.

Why Draupadī? Why the supposedly fragile and self-
effacing woman--the wife who reckons as the least of the
six, according to all of the many passages that reveal the
relative status of the group's members? I suggest that it
is precisely because Draupadī is a woman and a wife that
she is assigned her extraordinary role. There seem to be
at least three factors at work in the account: 1) Draupadī's vulnerability, as a woman and a wife, leaves her a
victim of Yudhisthira's choice in a way that no masculine
character could be. She is the only major character remaining with the Pāndavas throughout their wanderings who
has no way of defending herself. Hence she is the only
visible representative of the defenceless ones who are
trapped by Yudhisthira's refusal to act like a *ksatriya*.

Or to put it another way, as wife and defenceless woman,
she has rights under the *dharma* that are violated by
Yudhisthira's theoretically noble choice.   2) At the same
time Draupadī bears the responsibility, as a woman and a
wife, of seeing that her husband's proper duties are carried out.   In the religious domain (and *dharma* is an inherently religious concept), Draupadī is her husband's
equal and partner, not his subordinate.   As such she is
not in a position analogous to the younger brothers; she
must speak freely.   3) I have also come to suspect that the
male/female dichotomy itself may be an important factor at
least in the epic's later development.   For it gave the
compilers, consciously or unconsciously, a ready-made device for underscoring the paradox and opposition in the
two positions.   We may even go a bit further, given the
traditional and ancient symbolisms of maleness and femaleness in the Indian tradition, and suggest that it offered
the opportunity to create the appearance of a resolution
for the position where, in fact, no true resolution was
possible.

Defenceless Draupadī.   Let us return to the epic and
examine closely the episode most frequently cited as the
source of her indignation.   After she has lost her freedom
in Yudhisthira's gambling match, Duryodhana, the oldest
of the Kauravas and hence their leader, dispatches a servant to go and summon her before the assembly.   He says:
"Let her sweep the chambers...and let the unfortunate one
stay where our serving-women are."[43]   Draupadī is located,
living in seclusion and dressed scantily "in a single piece
of cloth with her navel exposed," because it is the time
of her monthly period.[44]   She refuses to come, and instead
sends the servant back with her question about the order
of the losses.   He returns to the assembly but is told
that the Kauravas will answer her question only in her
presence.   The servant refuses to approach her again--he

is justifiably afraid of Draupadī's anger, as well as the
ascetic power (*tapas*) that she has acquired through devoted service to her husbands. Duryodhana then sends his
brother Duḥśāsana, who is less wise. Draupadī runs before
him, trying to reach the relative security of the other
household ladies. But he seizes her by her long hair and
drags her before the assembly. She protests that she cannot stay before the assembly in her present state and asks
why she has no protectors. Her tormentor calls her
"Slave!"[45] She asks that her question be answered by the
so-called experts on *dharma*, but none can resolve it. The
torment resumes as an old suitor and major protagonist of
the epic, the half-caste Karṇa, justifies her treatment by
calling her a whore (because she has five husbands, an
irregular arrangement in Hindu practice).[46] It is not improper, he says, to bring her in public half-clothed; in
fact, she should be stripped completely. The attempt is
made; but as her cloth is pulled off, others appear miraculously, and the attempt fails. She cries bitterly and begs
that her question be answered. Karṇa, still stinging from
his early rejection, suggests that she take another husband, now that her five are slaves, while Duryodhana himself exposes his left thigh and shows it to her. Ominous
omens begin to appear and finally the situation is resolved,
not through an answer to her question, but by the old king's
offer of a number of boons. She uses these to acquire her
freedom and that of her husbands.

The scene is dramatic enough to the Western reader--
but it loses considerably in cross-cultural translation.
In fact it represents a sequence of the most intense insults to be found anywhere in the literature of the world.
These begin with Duryodhana's comment about sweeping--a
remark that prompts an instant objection from King Dhṛtarāṣṭra's wise counselor Vidura. Sweepers have been one of
the lowest occupational groups throughout Indian history.
Royal sweeping would be an act of total humiliation--so

dramatically so, in fact, that some kings deliberately
swept the temples of the gods who protected their kingdoms
to demonstrate the degree of their own submission.[47]

Draupadī is pulled into the assembly of kings. She
protests that she has been exposed to the public gaze only
once before--on the occasion of her *svayaṃvara*, the public
competition for her hand in which the five Pandavas won her.
The wives of royal heroes are not to be subjected to the
stares of others. She belongs to her husbands alone. But
she is being seen now in a time and condition where no man
should see her--during her monthly period, with her clothes
stained by the outflow. This is surely one of the most
serious offences; it is rarely left unmentioned when Draupadī's ills are recited in the epic. For a woman was truly
forbidden territory during her period.[48] During the four
days when the menses flowed, she was a source of pollution;
for with the blood flowed out any of the impurities of the
last month's sexual congress.[49] She was expected to iso-
late herself and was accustomed to doing so. Not even her
husband might talk with her, or eat food that she had prepared;[50] a gift from a menstruating woman brought to merit.[51] To be forced to enter an assembly of senior males
at this time would be not merely a source of intense personal embarrassment, but also a source of enforced religious demerit, for she would bring defilement to all who
were in her presence.

Draupadī is scantily dressed, probably as part of the
menstrual retreat that she is observing. The phrase "clad
in a single cloth" is instructive here, for it appears
many times in the epic, always in one of two contexts.
Either it is used to emphasize a woman's seductiveness--
women bent on arousing men are always "clad in a single
raiment;"[52] or it is used to signify humiliation--when the
revealing dress is taken by necessity and exposes the woman
so clothed to the public eye.[53] The term suggests that
Draupadī is willy-nilly seductive, in a place and at a time

when it is terribly inappropriate for her to be so. Hence
her objections, and hence also Karṇa's response about her
normal lack of chastity, with the consequent effort to
complete her exposure.

She is dragged into the assembly by her "long and
blue and wavy" tresses.[54] This is again an offense which
increases its awfulness when considered in the Indian context. The head is sacred; any violent touch is an act of
defilement--particularly when a man who is not a husband
thus violently touches the head of a faithful wife. To
seize a head by the hair appears to have been especially
terrible. When Draupadī's own twin brother Dhṛṣṭadyumna
grabs the hair of the preceptor Droṇa in battle (in order
to cut his head off), not only his enemies but also his
allies are horrified; his ever-proper brother-in-law Yudhiṣṭhira rebukes him sharply.[55] Furthermore Droṇa's son
Aśvatthāma cites the insult of the hair-pulling as the
chief instigation of the final grisly raid that destroys
both Dhṛstadyumna and all of Draupadī's sons.[56]

The scene culminates when Duryodhana exposes his left
thigh--an action that prompts Bhīma to promise that he will
smash it. Again we learn elsewhere in the epic that the
left thigh is a seat reserved for wives and lovers.[57]
Duryodhana has offered a contemptuous invitation--which I
suspect would be roughly equivalent to an American's giving a woman the finger. Again the impropriety of the act
is heightened by the fact of Draupadī's marriage (which
Duryodhana is of course suggesting should now be null and
void) and also be her tabood condition; to have congress
with a menstruating woman is to incur a burden of demerit
equal to 1/4 to that of a brahmanicide.[58]

Draupadī's husbands witness the entire scene. They
do not take it easily; Bhīma, in particular, is barely held
in check. But they remain properly obedient to the decision of their king and elder brother Yudhiṣṭhira. He has

lost himself and them and Draupadī and, being an upright
man, he intends to honor his losses. Yet Draupadī perceives the ambiguity of the choice. She is defenceless,
and it is a *kṣatriya's* duty to protect the defenceless.
She is a wife, and it is the husband's duty to protect the
wife. Her complaints against Yudhisthira and the Pāndavas
return again and again to this theme: they have failed
their duty of protection:

> Where are those mighty warriors today, who,..
> have always granted protection unto those who
> solicit it? Oh why do those heroes, quietly
> suffer...their dear and chaste wife to be thus
> insulted?[59]

> I blame the Pandavas..; for they saw (without
> stirring) their own wedded wife...treated with
> such cruelty....
> This eternal course of morality is ever fol-
> lowed by the virtuous viz...that the husband,
> however weak, protecteth his wedded wife! The
> Pandavas never forsake the person that solic-
> iteth their protection, and yet they abandoned
> me.[60]

She entreats her chief husband to "blaze up"--to display
his wrath, his prowess, his warrior's energy.[61] But
Yudhishthira's righteousness has all the fire of a wick
implanted in a mud puddle.

The other half. But I have also claimed that Draupadī speaks out of responsibility--a responsibility that
is uniquely given her by her role as wife. This aspect of
my argument is not as richly documented; but it is consistent, I believe, with the role of the wife both as this is
presented in the didactic sections and as it is modeled in
the Mahābhārata's many stories. It is true that women are
shown consistently in the epic to carry a status subordinate to that of men. The many passages about the sweet-
voiced and docile women who shall worship their husbands
as their gods give plentiful evidence of women's status.
But the epic also prescribes a religious role for women
that has nothing to do with superiorities and inferiorities
or matters of who shall speak and who keep silent. This

role is one of complementarity. For religious purposes--
which means both for ritual purposes and also in the observance of the *dharma*, the woman formed a unit with her
husband. "The wife is half the man,"[62] says the epic. As
such, in the performance of the duties, she bore a responsibility equal to his:

> A woman becomes, in the presence of the nuptial
> fire, the associate of her husband in the per-
> formance of all righteous deeds.[63]

In doing so, she can expect to attain to whatever status
he has attained.[64]

This is an old concept, traceable at least into the
sacrificial tradition of the Vedas, where man and wife together constituted the ritual unit. It clearly reflects
the older, freer status of Indian women that, as we have
previously noted, appears throughout the Vedic literature
and, like Draupadī herself, remains at odds with later
claims about the role and status of women. At least one
incident in the frequently misogynist Anuśāsana Parvan
shows that it was beginning already in late epic times to
become a problem. In this passage, Yudhiṣthira asks the
dying *dharma*-expert Bhīṣma the following question:

> Women in particular, the Rishis have said, are
> false in behavior....When women in particular
> have been declared in the ordinances to be
> false, how, o sire, can there be a union be-
> tween the sexes for the purposes of practising
> all duties together?[65]

Unfortunately the great expert on the *dharma* does not
choose to respond to the question asked. If he had answered, we could expect a more generous insight into the
the phrase "practising all duties together." Instead he
tells a story illustrating the wickedness and deceit of
women. But fortunately a number of the Mahābhārata's other
stories give content to the concept of shared responsibilities.

A favorite type of account, for example, portrays a

husband who is about to leave home for a time. Before
going, he admonishes his wife to make sure that the duty
of honoring guests will be fully observed in his absence.
This presents, of course, an opening for the kind of ambiguous situation that the epic so loves to explore, for
the demands of a guest on a lone and gracious woman do not
necessarily always allow her also to observe the duties of
wifely morality. The ultimate happens to Sudarśana, son
of the god Agni, when he returns to find his unhappy but
dutiful young wife in bed with a not-so-dutiful Brahman
guest who has requested her services.[66]

The scene is as often reversed as wife reminds husband of the sacred responsibilities that the two of them
share. The most striking example here is Gāndhārī, wife
of the old blind king Dhṛtarāstra. She is so faithful
to her husband that she refuses to have an advantage over
him; hence she puts on a blindfold on the day of her marriage and wears it for the remainder of her life.[67] But
she is not too reticent to let her husband know what she
thinks of his actions as war gradually becomes imminent.
She speaks to him in public with words as biting as Draupadī's:

> Indeed, O Dhritarashtra, thou so fond of thy son,
> art very much to be blamed for this, for knowing
> well his sinfulness, thou followest yet his coun-
> sel....Thou art now reaping the fruit, O Dhrit-
> arāshṭra, of having made over the kingdom to an
> ignorant fool of wicked soul, possessed by ava-
> rice and having wicked counsellors. Why is the
> king indifferent (today) to that disunion, which
> is about to take place between persons related
> so closely?[68]

Disaster, she rightly perceives, is upon them, and her
husband's indulgence is part of the problem. Her attempts
to sting her husband into firmness are unfortunately unsuccessful.

And the wise and independent tongue is by no means
restricted to the major characters. In another of the

guest-honor stories, for example, a nāga husband (i.e., a
snake-godling) has just asked, in a highly patronizing
tone, whether his wife has followed the observances.[69]
And she, acknowledging his supremacy and the supreme honor
which she owes him, replies that she has. She then informs
him of a human guest who has come and is waiting to see him
in a place where the nāga must go to see him. The mighty
snake-being senses a slight in the lowly human's behavior
and immediately flies into one of the rages for which such
beings are famous. His virtuous and submissive wife immediately tells him to cool it. The nāga as quickly does
so, ruing his regrettable temper, citing the destruction
which evil temper has brought on others, and praising his
faithful wife for her most excellent instructions.[70]

Draupadī, that is to say, has plenty of precedent for
her actions in stinging so sharply the men to whom she's
normally subordinate. And as in her case the stings come
from women whose conduct is basically irreproachable. The
wife is half the man--sometimes the half that receives instructions on the *dharma*, and sometimes the half that offers them. She is certainly allowed to criticize her hus-
bands--in a way that, it seems, a younger brother is not
allowed to criticize an older brother. She is expected to
keep them on the path of morality.

You are woman; I am man. My final point is the most
tenuous of all. At this point in my research it should
probably be taken more as a suggestion than as an argument.
To state it briefly, I have come to suspect that the male/
female opposition alone may be of considerable significance
when one considers the respective roles of Yudhiṣṭhira and
Draupadī. I am unfortunately not adept at structural
analysis, with its highly developed sensitivity to symbolic
oppositions and reconciliations. But I have noticed that
the epic frequently develops its representations of ambi-
guities in the *dharma* in the context of conflicts between
males and females.[71] The sexual polarization then serves

quite effectively to accentuate the paradoxes in the issues
under consideration. This could be a conscious literary
device. It is more likely, I suspect, given recent dis-
coveries about narrative and mythic structure, to be a
spontaneous by-product of the story-telling process.

In the peripheral stories, especially where the opposition is between husband and wife,[72] either sex can
voice the final resolution of the problem. This is quite
consistent with the old model of balanced responsibility
between husband and wife that has been described in the
preceding section.[73] There is some reason to suspect, however, that later redactors of the essay were becoming un-
comfortable with the wifely last word. Thus in the story
of the nāga's wife cited above, we find the woman's final
triumph muted by the nāga's earlier pompous and patronizing speech of leave-taking, in which all the frailties of
her sex are carefully pointed out to her.[74]

Fortunately for the epic's redactors, the respective
arguments of Draupadī and Yudhiṣṭhira came from mouths
appropriate to the sexual preferences of the later age.
In the meantime, developments were occurring, or at least
gaining in popularity and currency, in the symbolic association of the sexes that would have furnished a unique
opportunity for a subtle elaboration and coloring of the
argument at the narrative level. I am referring to the
tendency, very well documented in post-Vedic India,[75] to
associate maleness with qualities of spirituality, tran-
scendance, and intelligence, and femaleness with qualities
of materiality, immanence, and blind and whimsical passion.
These associations are most explicity expressed in the dualistic Sāṃkhya system of Indian thought, where a male, spiritual, transcendant and intelligent soul-principle, the
purusha, is opposed to a female, material, immanent and
blind creative force called prakṛtī. The Sāṃkhya system
is well-known to the didactic sections of the epic. It has
been shown, for example, that the famous Bhagavad-Gītā was

strongly influenced by Sāmkhya. But the system also appears in the Śānti-Parvan, where the *purusha*/male, *prak-
rtī*/female identifications are explicitly made.[76]

Let us consider the potential effects of such a set of
symbolic overtones upon the epic controversies of Yudhiṣthira and Draupadī. The side of the male becomes by definition the side of superior spirituality, transcendant intelligence. By contrast woman's side is blind, unreasoning,
limited in its perspective, fabricated of passion. Draupadī loses the argument before it is begun, for it is pre-
judged by the sex of its speaker. The sexual associations
allow, that is to say, a resolution at the symbolic level
of an issue that remains essentially unresolvable at the
level of reason.[77]

Ironically, in the context of this new assessment of
the sexes, Draupadī's unwifely stridency would tend to fur-
nish evidence of her inherent frailty--and hence, by implication, that of her charges against her negligent husband. For the later portions of the epic make it unequivo-
cably clear that harsh speech is an inevitable by-product
of the inferior constitution of the female sex. Not even
the goddesses are free of it, for it is reported in Anuśā-
sana-Parvan that the great goddess Uma addressed harsh
words to husband Śiva "in consequence of her being of the
opposite sex."[78] It is noteworthy, however, that Draupadī's
formidable speeches never draw so explicitly sexist a commentary. Instead they are undermined by subtle innuendo.
The speaker is delicate; she is fragile; she lacks faith
(this from the all-wise Yudhiṣthira on the occasion of her
outburst against the gods). She manipulates the devoted
and not-too-bright Bhīma.[79] And worst of all, she is partial not to the senior husband and king who has given her
so much pain, but to the junior Arjuna who won her in the
first place and should have kept her as his own.[80] This
last feminine failing seals Draupadī's fate in the epic's
final judgment on the Pāṇḍava righteousness. For as she

and the five brothers walk to meet their death in the final
ascetic fast that they have chosen to end their endeavors,
the woman who could not love according to the stipulations
of the *dharma* drops first, while the senior husband who
brought her so much suffering survives all his brothers
till the gods take him bodily into heaven.

In summary. I have argued in the preceding paper that
Draupadī's tongue is an indispensable factor in the epic's
reflection on a central issue of the *dharma*. As a woman,
Draupadī has a unique perspective on this issue which is
granted by her inherently defenceless position. She alone
is in a position to point with full dramatic power and
poignancy to the contradiciton in her first husband's
actions. Her arguments probably would not have sounded as
radical to the audiences for the initial narrative cycles
as they did for those of later times. On the contrary,
they were called for according to the older model of femininity which still dominates the narrative portions of
the completed epic. But they also may have furnished a
remarkable opportunity for later redactors, for whom they
would have furnished evidence of Draupadī's frailty as a
woman. The inherent inequality between the two protagon-
ists, suggested by means of their respective sexual identifications, creates an impression of inherent inequality
in the arguments. The conflict between a *kṣatriya dharma*
of power and protection and the eternal *dharma* of truthful-
ness and honored obligations most probably could not have
been settled at the level of argument alone. But on the
level of narrative with its endless opportunities for suggestion, subtle coloration, the issues might be sufficiently muddied to create an illusion of resolution.

[1]Pratap Chandra Roy, trans., *The Mahabharata of Krishna-Dwaipayana Vyasa*, Vol. IV, Udyoga Parva (Calcutta: Oriental Publishing, 1883-96) 65. I regret that the size of the Mahābharata and very strict limitations on my available time have made it necessary for me to base this paper exclusively on English translations of the epic. I have used two translations: the literal and stilted but reputedly scholarly P. C. Roy translation cited above and the single volume that was available at the time of writing of J. A. B. van Buitenan's new translation: *The Mahābhārata* (Chicago: University of Chicago, 1973). The van Buitenan translation is based upon the Poona critical edition. This of course was not in existence when the Roy translation was produced; the latter was based on the popular version presented by the 17th century commentator Nīlakantha. I expect that far more thorough and accurate work can be done on problems in the epic when the van Buitenan translation is complete.

[2]Roy, op. cit., VIII, Santi Parva, Part I, p. 349.

[3]Ibid., IV, Udyoga Parva, p. 65.

[4]Ibid., II, Vana Parva, Part I, p. 1.

[5]Ibid.

[6]Ibid., IV, Virata Parva, p. 30.

[7]Ibid., II, Vana Parva, Part I, p. 34.

[8]Ibid., IV, Virata Parva, p. 33.

[9]Ibid., p. 31

[10]Ibid., p. 33

[11]Ibid., VII, Sauptika Parva, pp. 31-32.

[12]Ibid., VIII, Santi Parva, Part I, p. 25.

[13]Ibid., VII, Karna Parva, pp. 200-2.

[14]Ibid., IV, Virata Parva, p. 55.

[15]Ibid., p. 1.

[16]Ibid., p. 132.

[17]Van Buitenan, *Mahābharata* I, In the Beginning, p. 289.

[18] Roy, op. cit., II, Sabha Parva, p. 162.

[19] See the account of the Pāṇḍavas' birth, p. 6.

[20] Roy, op. cit., IV, Virata Parva, p. 5.

[21] Ibid., VII, Santi Parva, Part I, p. 2.

[22] Ibid., IV, Virata Parva, p. 5.

[23] Ibid.

[24] During an incident of the forest exile, Krishna's wife Satyabhāmā asks Draupadī to explain how she manages to rule so effectively the Pāṇḍava heroes. Draupadī responds with a long recitation of her own qualities as the ideal wife. Cf. ibid., III, Vana Parva, Part II, pp. 505-8.

[25] Her task of sustaining her band is made much easier through the sun-god's gift of a vessel that remains full until Draupadī has eaten from it (as a faithful wife, she must, of course, eat last). One day the holy man Durvāsas, known for his hot temper, arrives with his band of followers and demands a meal after Draupadī has eaten. The pot remains empty; but the quick-witted Draupadī calls upon Kṛṣṇa, who creates an illusion of full stomachs among Durvāsas' band, and hence averts the impending crisis.

[26] The most influential critical study of the Mahābhārata is still E. Washburn Hopkins, *The Great Epic of India* (New Haven: Yale University, 1913). Hopkins based his analysis on a number of factors: epic quotations from existing contemporary works, philosophical systems reflected in the epic, divergences in patterns of versification.

[27] Compare, for example, Shakuntala Rao Shastri's *Women in the Vedic Age* (Bombay: Bharatiya Vidya Bhavan, 1960) with her *Women in the Sacred Laws* (Bombay: Bharatiya Vidya Bhavan, 1953). Wendy Doniger O'Flaherty has recently published on an aspect of this problem in *Art and Archaeology Research Papers* (Winter 1976); unfortunately I have not been able to examine her paper.

[28] Hopkins went so far as to call these parts of the present poem the "pseudo-epic": op. cit., p. 381.

[29] Again, I am accepting the dating concluded by Hopkins, ibid., pp. 386-402.

[30] Op. cit., pp. 13-16.

[31] A common epic conception. The "field" is the wife; should a husband for some reason be unable to beget children, he can acquire a proper substitute--often, in the epic, a brahman or an ascetic. The offspring of the field

will then belong to the owner--i.e., the heretofore child-less husband. See the discussion in Johann Jakob Meyer, *Sexual Life in Ancient India* (Delhi: Motilal Banarsidass, n.d.) 168080.

[32]Kuntī had won the ability to call upon the gods for service as a boon for faithful service to a difficult Brahman. Her first attempt to use her boon resulted in a misadventure with the sun and the resultant birth of the Pāndavas' arch-opponent Karna. But later, at Pāndu's command, she finds heavenly progenitors for the five Pāndavas.

[33]See J. A. B. van Buitenan's argument to this effect in his "On the Structure of the Sabhaparvan of the Mahāb-hārata," *India Maior: Congratulatory Volume presented to J. Gonda*, J. Enskin and P. Gaeffke eds. (Leiden: E. J. Brill, 1972).

[34]The exact nature of the match is not clear in the present version of the epic; but it is clearly a match of skill rather than of chance.

[35]At least in its present form. The importance of this theme to the whole of the present epic has long been recognized. See, for example, R. C. Zaehner, *Hinduism* (New York: Oxford University, 1966) 102-24.

[36]Van Buitenan, op. cit., pp. 181-91.

[37]The match with *Devayānī* is explicitly recognized as miscegenation in the story (ibid: p. 187); Yayāti resists it as improper; but Devayani insists because Yayāti had previously taken her hand (a central rite of Hindu mar-riage) in order to help her climb from a well into which Sarmishthā had pushed her.

[38]Devayānī's father is Śukra--an ascetic Brahman of considerable power and hence a figure whom Yayāti would not disobey lightly.

[39]For the rights of the *rtu*, see J. J. Meyer, op. cit., pp. 220-24.

[40]The full impact of stories such as this one is real-ized when one remembers that the resolutions reached in them then become precedents in an Indian legendary equiva-lent of the Western common law. That is to say, Yayāti's choice becomes paradigmatic, as does also the later choice of Yudhisthira.

[41]Roy, op. cit., II, Sabha Parva, p. 148.

[42]Ibid., Vana Parva, Part I, p. 64.

[43]Ibid., Sabha Parva, p. 137.

[44] Ibid., pp. 139-40.

[45] Ibid., p. 141.

[46] It is licit for a man to have multiple wives, but the reverse is not the case. Draupadī is an exception, again as a result of conflict in the *dharma*. According to the epic, Arjuna won her in the course of a great contest for her hand. When he brought his prize home and called to his mother Kuntī to come and see what he had won, she, without seeing, instructed him to share it equally with his brothers. A mother's commands are inviolable--hence the resultant multiple marriage, accomplished over the protests of Draupadī's father and society in general.

[47] See examples in Nancy E. Falk, "Wilderness and Kingship in Ancient South Asia," *History of Religions* XIII (August 1973) 9.

[48] For menstrual prohibitions see Meyer, op. cit., pp. 225-28.

[49] See examples, ibid., pp. 219-220.

[50] Roy, op. cit., XI, Anusasana Parva, Part 2, p. 205.

[51] Ibid., X, Anusasana Parva, Part I, p. 131.

[52] A number of epic stories tell how a woman in a single piece of cloth becomes an agent of seduction. See, for example, van Buitenan, op. cit., p. 266, where an *asparā* so clothed causes the sage Gautama to spill his seed and ibid., where the beautiful Tilottamā proves the undoing of two *daityas*. King Pāndu meets his death when his lust is aroused by the sight of his second wife Mādrī walking in a single sheer skirt, ibid., p. 259. Also Roy, VII, Salya Parva, p. 117 and ibid., Vana Parva, Part 2, p. 265.

[53] So Damayantī follows Nala into exile, wearing a single piece of cloth: ibid., II, Vana Parva, Part I, p. 129. And Draupadī herself wears a single garment both when leaving for exile, ibid., II, Sabha Parva, p. 164 and when applying for service as *sairamdhri* at Virāta's palace: ibid., IV, Virata Parva, p. 16. Similarly the single piece is worn by the dead heroes' wives weeping for their husbands after the carnage of the great war, ibid., VII, Stree Parva, p. 16.

[54] Ibid., II, Sabha Parva, p. 140.

[55] Ibid., VI, Drona Parva, p. 454.

[56] Ibid., p. 460.

[57]Van Buitenan, op. cit., pp. 217-18. When the goddess Gaṅgā sits on the right thigh of King Pratīpa, intending to seduce him, he refuses her advances, saying "You embrace me while sitting on my right thigh, beautiful woman, but that is the place for children and daughters-in-law, shy girl. The share of a mistress is on the left." Instead he takes her as daughter-in-law.

[58]Roy, op. cit., IX, Santi Parva, Part 2, p. 337.

[59]Ibid., IV, Virata Parva, p. 30.

[60]Ibid., III, Vana Parva, Part I, p. 31.

[61]Ibid., p. 57.

[62]Van Buitenan, op. cit., p. 167.

[63]Roy, op. cit., Anusasana Parva, Part 2, p. 323.

[64]"A wife attains to those regions which are acquired by her husband." Ibid., XII, Aswamedha Parva, p. 40.

[65]Ibid., X, Anusasana Parva, Part I, p. 116.

[66]Ibid., pp. 6-11.

[67]Van Buitenan, op. cit., p. 240.

[68]Roy, op. cit., IV, Udyoga Parva, p. 256.

[69]He says, "I hope, without yielding to that uncleansed understanding which is natural to persons of thy sex, thou hast, during my absence from home, been firm in the observance of the duties of hospitality." Ibid., X, Santi Parva, Part III, p. 633; the full story is on pp. 633-36.

[70]Mothers, of course, have a similar responsibility--and the epic is even richer in stories of their efforts to check or to energize their failing sons. Gāndhārī, failing with Dhṛtarāṣtra, tries to check Duryodhana herself--and again fails. Kuntī on several occasions speaks words to the Pāṇḍavas that echo those of her daughter-in-law. In one of the most powerful passages of the epic Kuntī cites her own precedent, a woman named Vidula who calls her defeated and self-pitying son a eunuch and a no-account. Kuntī also reprimands Karṇa, who, as only she and he know, is her oldest child. The river Gaṅgā tries to dissuade her own son Bhisma from a foolish fight brought on by his own lack of sensitivity to the women's *dharma*.

[71]See examples given throughout this paper.

[72]Usually such conflicts occur between husband and wife or between mother and son. In the latter, the mother usually has the last word. This is consistent with the veneration of son for mother as reflected in all portions of the Mahābhārata.

[73]It further suggests to me that during the early development of the epic the sexes were very likely free of the associations described here.

[74]See n. 69.

[75]See for example, Shrirama Indradeva, "Correspondence between Woman and Nature in Indian Thought," *Philosophy East and West* 16 (July-October, 1966) 161-68.

[76]See for example, Roy, op. cit., X, Santi Parva, Part 3, p. 426.

[77]Of course, this is not the only technique by which the narrative is allowed to cite a preference that is not afforded by the argument itself. Consider, for example, Yudhiṣthira's identification as "son of Dharma" in the story of the substitute fathers.

[78]Roy, XI, Anusasana Parva, Part 2, p. 130.

[79]On at least three occasions, which stand out from the remainder of the epic because they seem so uncharacteristic of Draupadī. Twice during the forest exile she places Bhīma in terrible danger in response to apparent whims: first, when she sends him to gather celestial lotuses from a lake sacred to Kubera (ibid., III, Vana Parva, Part I, pp. 310-26) and second, when she asks to see the peak of the Gandhamādana mountain (ibid., pp. 338-43). Again, when she has been assaulted by the general Kīcaka in the court of Virāṭa, she literally seduces Bhīma into taking a revenge that seriously threatens to betray their mutual disguise (ibid., IV, Virata Parva, p. 32).

[80]See the story of Draupadī's marriage, n. 46. Draupadī's partiality is the reason given by Yudhiṣthira for her early collapse during the final walk--see below; the story is told in ibid., XII, Mahaprasthanika Parva, pp. 275-79.

RĀMAKRṢṆA PARAMAHAṀSA:
A Study in a Mystic's Attitudes Towards Women

Arvind Sharma
University of Queensland

I

Rāmakrṣna Paramahaṁsa (1836-1886) is, as is well-known, one of the leading mystics of modern India.[1] He has left a deep impression on the attitude of modern Hindus towards other religions.[2] This aspect of his life and religious experience is quite well-known. This paper delves into a rather less well-known aspect of his life--his attitude towards women.

The attitude of a mystic towards women is, needless to say, of great spiritual and social significance, especially for a religion like Hinduism. Yet the study of the attitude of mystics towards women in Hinduism has been handicapped by the absence of first-hand accounts of their attitudes and behaviour towards women. For this reason alone, Rāmakrṣna is deserving of serious study, for his case provides a striking exception to this dearth of, first-hand documentary material.[3] One of Rāmakrṣna's disciples, a certain Mahendranath Gupta, recorded the conversations of Rāmakrṣna along with the circumstances in which they took place "from March 1882 to April 24, 1886,"[4] till only a few months before Rāmakrṣna's passing away. This diary, kept in Bengali, fills five volumes and has been available in English translation at least since 1942 under the title: "The Gospel of Sri Ramakrishna." This source, coupled with Swami Saradananda's well-known biography[5] of Rāmakrṣna called "Sri Ramakrishna the Great Master," provides abundant material for a study of Rāmakrṣna's attitude toward women.

115

II

As one surveys this material one is struck by the
fact that Rāmakrṣṇa's attitudes towards women do not seem
to be, at least at the first glance, entirely consistent.
One might even say that he seems to have been ambivalent
in his attitude towards women. Let us look at the evidence first.

In several contexts, Rāmakrṣṇa conveys a rather negative assessment of women. For Rāmakrṣṇa the purpose of
life was God-realization. And what was his advice for
those who wished to realize God?

> Those who wish to attain God or make progress in
> their devotional practices should particularly
> guard themselves against the snares of lust and
> wealth. Otherwise they will never attain perfec-
> tion.[2]

The English words lust and wealth lack the colour of
the original expression used by Rāmakrṣṇa--Kāminī-kāñcana
or "woman and gold."[7] According to Rāmakrṣṇa, "the two
obstacles to spiritual life are woman and gold."[8] And
since Rāmakrṣṇa also said that, "It is woman that creates
the need for gold,"[9] we are in the end left really with
only one obstacle to spiritual salvation--women. Thus
Rāmakrṣṇa told his followers and disciples on one occasion:

> "Woman and gold" is the cause of bondage. "Woman
> and gold" alone constitutes saṃsāra, the world.
> It is "woman and gold" that keeps one from seeing
> God.

At this point he held a towel in front of his face
and then asked his disciples:

> Do you see my face any more? Of course not. The
> towel hides it. No sooner is the covering of
> "woman and gold" removed than one attains Chidān-
> anda, Consciousness and Bliss.

Then he went on to say:

> Let me tell you something. He who has renounced
> the pleasure of a wife has verily renounced the
> pleasure of the world. God is very near to such
> a person.

The devotees listened to the words in silence.

Master (to Kedar, Vijay and other devotees):
He who has renounced the pleasure of a wife
has verily renounced the pleasure of the world.

It is "woman and gold" that hides God. You
people have such imposing moustaches, and yet
you too are involved in "woman and gold." Tell
me if it isn't true. Search your heart and
answer me.[10]

And then he went on to remark, "I see that all are
under the control of woman."[11] Elsewhere he compares being
under a woman's influence to being under a ghost's influence;[12] he also compares "woman and gold" to "the hog
plum--all stone and skin. If one eats it one suffers from
colic."[13] He advises those who wish to develop true renunciation to "keep themselves at least fifty cubits away
from women,"[14] he states that "'woman and gold' alone is
the world; that alone is māyā."[15] He describes sitting
with or talking with a woman for a long time as a "kind of
sexual intercourse;"[16] he testifies to the "betwitching
power of women;"[17] and he claims that, "I have never enjoyed a woman, even in a dream."[18] Ramakṛṣṇa's marriage
with Śārāda Devi was never consummated.

It is clear from these statements that on several occasions Rāmakṛṣṇa shared the view, traditional in certain
sections of Hinduism, that women constitute the major obstacle to God-realization.[9]

III

However, having said this, it would be unfair to
Rāmakṛṣṇa to stop here, for when one turns from these
conversational snippets with his disciples to the biographical details of his life the picture changes. The spiritual discipline or *sādhanā* of Rāmakṛṣṇa, which spanned
twelve years, has been divided into three periods, from
1856-1859; from 1860-1863 and from 1864-1867.[20] In each
of these three phases, "women" in some form played a key

role in Rāmakṛṣṇa's spiritual progress. It is well known
that in the first phase of *sādhanā*, the major mystical
experience of Rāmakṛṣṇa consisted of a vision of Kālī[2]--
the Mother Goddess, an experience from which Rāmakṛṣṇa
came out uttering "repeatedly the word 'Mother' in a plain-
tive voice."[22] Not only that, it took place in a temple
which had been built by a low-class but rich widow.[23] In
the second phase of his spiritual progress Rāmakṛṣṇa was
instructed by a lady called Bhairavī, also known as Brāh-
maṇī, whose coming Rāmakṛṣṇa had foreseen in a vision,[24]
and who instructed him in Tāntrika practices,[25] one of
which involved the following procedure as described by
Rāmakṛṣṇa himself.

> On one occasion, I saw, that the Brahmani had
> brought at night--nobody knew whence--a beauti-
> ful woman in the prime of her youth, and said
> to me, "My child, worship her as the Devi."
> When the worship was finished, she said, "Sit
> on her lap, my child, and perform Japa." I was
> seized with fear, wept piteously and said to
> Mother, "O Mother, Mother of the universe, What
> is this command Thou givest to one who has taken
> absolute refuge in Thee? Has Thy weak child the
> power to be so impudently daring?" But as soon
> as I said so, I felt as if I was possessed by
> some unknown power and an extraordinary strength
> filled my heart. And uttering the Mantras, no
> sooner had I sat on the lap of the woman, like
> one hypnotized, unaware of what I was doing,
> than I merged completely in Samadhi. When I
> regained consciousness, I saw the Brahmani
> waiting on me and assiduously trying to bring
> me back to normal consciousness. She said,
> "The rite is completed, my child; others restrain
> themselves with very great difficulty under such
> circumstances and then finish the nominal Japa
> for a trifling little time only; but you lost
> all consciousness, and were deep in Samadhi."
> When I heard this I became assured and began to
> salute Mother again and again.[16]

From the third phase of Rāmakṛṣṇa's spiritual pilgrimage comes even more striking evidence of how "woman" can
participate in spiritual life. Indeed, even womanhood
itself may be embraced as a part of one's comprehensive

spiritual seeking. This is known as Madhura Bhāva[27] in Bhakti *sādhanā*, in which the male devotee adopts the role of a female worshipper of God. When Rāmakṛṣṇa adopted this mode he was criticized for doing so but he disregarded the criticism and, adorned in feminine dress and ornaments, his biographer tells us,

> the Master gradually merged so much in the mood of the women of Vraja desirous to have the love of Krishna, that the consciousness that he was a male person disappeared altogether and every thought, word or movement of his became womanly. The Master, we were told by himself, was thus in a woman's dress for six months under the faith that he was the spiritual consort of God.[28]

There is some evidence to suggest that during this period Rāmakṛṣṇa began to menstruate.[29]

Not only did women play an important role in the spiritual practices of Rāmakṛṣṇa, but even after Rāmakṛṣṇa had completed his *sādhanā* and had won recognition as a spiritual figure, women continued to play a part in his life.[30]

It is clear, then, that Rāmakṛṣṇa's attitude towards women is somewhat puzzling. On the one hand woman is condemned as the greatest obstacle to God-realization; on the other hand not only does he undergo a transvestite transfiguration himself to experience God, he sees God as inhabiting a woman's body. Can this ambivalence be reconciled?

IV

The situation does seem to this writer to be capable of reconciliation from a particular standpoint.[31] Although Rāmakṛṣṇa's attitude to women is a variable and not a constant--it seems to vary predictably in relation to a central referent--that of God-realization. Thus all his criticism is directed against women when they seem to present an obstacle to God-realization, as in the case of most men of the world; on the other hand, whenever woman stands in a positive relationship to God-realization, whether as an aspect of the Godhead itself, as Kālī, or as one assisting in God-realization as a Teacher or Guru, or as a devotional mode or as herself striving for God-realization, Rāmakṛṇṣa has nothing against her.

The following conclusions can thus be drawn about Rāmakṛṇṣa's attitude to women:

(1) His attitude varies from time to time and is thus a variable;

(2) Although his attitude is variable it is not arbitrarily so--it is not unpredictable;

(3) It is predictable in relation to a central referent--namely, God-realization; and

(4) If women relate positively to the prospect of God-realization his attitude towards them is positive[32] and if they relate negatively to the prospect of God-realization, his attitude is negative.

Or to conclude in Rāmakṛṣṇa's own words:

As there are women endowed with *vidyāśakti*, so also there are women with *avidyāśakti*. A woman endowed with special attributes leads a man to God, but a woman who is the embodiment of delusion makes him forget God and drowns him in the ocean of worldliness.[33]

NOTES

[1] See R. C. Zaehner, ed., *The Concise Encyclopedia of Living Faiths* (Boston: Beacon, 1959) 257.

[2] Ibid.

[3] See Aldous Huxley, 'Foreword' to Swami Nikhilananda, *The Gospel of Sri Ramakrishna* (New York: Ramakrishna- Vivekananda Center, 1942).

[4] Swami Nikhilananda, op. cit., p. viii. Aldous Huxley describes him as Rāmakṛṣṇa's Boswell! (p. v) HIM.

[5] Swami Saradananda (trans. Swami Jagadananda), *Sri Ramakrishna the Great Master* (Madras: Sri Ramakrishna Math, 1952).

[6] *Sayings of Sri Ramakrishna* (Madras: Sri Ramakrishna Math, 1965) 45.

[7] Ibid., p. 53, n. 1.

[8] Swami Nikhilananda, op. cit., p. 247.

[9] Ibid., p. 166.

[10] Ibid., pp. 438-9. Rāmakṛṣṇa sometimes drew a distinction between the householder and the *saṁnyāsī* when it came to women. "One cannot obtain the knowledge of Brahman unless one is extremely cautious about women. Therefore it is very difficult for those who live in this world to get such knowledge. However clever you may be, you will stain your body if you live in a sooty room. The company of a young woman evokes lust even in a lustless man. But it is not so harmful for a householder who follows the path of knowledge to enjoy conjugal happiness with his own wife now and then. He may satisfy his sexual impulse like any other natural impulse. Yes, you may enjoy a sweet meat once in a while." On the other hand sex "is extremely harmful for a sanyasi. He must not even look at the portrait of a woman. A monk enjoying a woman is like a man swallowing the spittle he has already spat out" (ibid., p. 387).

[11] Ibid., p. 439. "Worldly people are in a state of chronic intoxication--mad with 'woman and gold;' they are insensible to spiritual ideas. That is why I love the youngsters, not yet stained by 'woman and gold.' They are good receptacles and may be useful in God's work" (ibid., p. 781).

[12]Ibid.

[13]Ibid., p. 817.

[14]Ibid., p. 603.

[15]Ibid., p. 670.

[16]Ibid., p. 701.

[17]Ibid., p. 748.

[18]Ibid., p. 832. It must be kept in mind, however, that even in the course of this generally denigratory attitude, Rāmakrṣna makes exceptions. (1) He points out that one way to overcome passion is to be like a woman--a technique later suggested by Mahatma Gandhi as well. "How can a man conquer passion? He should assume the attitude of a woman. I spent many days as the handmaid of God. I dressed myself in woman's clothes, put on ornaments, and covered the upper part of my body with a scarf, just like a woman. With the scarf on I used to perform the evening worship before the image" (p. 603). (2) He accepts that some women could lead man to God (p. 216). (3) He regards all women as the "embodiments of Sakti" (p. 336). "Again I saw a woman, wearing a blue garment, under a tree. She was a harlot. As I looked at her, instantly the ideal of Sītā appeared before me. I forgot the existence of the harlot, but saw before me pure and spotless Sītā, approaching Rāma, the Incarnation of divinity, and for a long time I remained motionless. I worshipped all women as representatives of the divine Mother. I realized the Mother of the Universe in every woman's form" [*Memoirs of Ramakrishna* (Calcutta: Ramakrishna Vedanta Math, 1957) 172-3].

[19]It has been said that just as Rāmakrṣna warned men against women he also warned women against men, that he "advised them to renounce lust and wealth and warned them against the snares of men" [*Life of Sri Ramakrishna* (Almora: Advaita Ashrama, 1924) 524]. It has also been pointed out that when Rāmakrṣna talks of "woman and gold," "one must specifically bear in mind that the Master is propounding no cult of woman-hatred. The study of his sayings in their entirety...will show that his attitude towards womankind was one of profound respect bordering on worship. For he saw in them a symbol of the Divine Mother of the universe in a special sense. It was in this light that he viewed all women, and he wanted his devotees also to cultivate the same attitude. But at the same time he impressed on his disciples that, when viewed with a sensual eye, 'woman' was the greatest danger to the spiritual aspirant. Of course, by 'woman' he meant 'sex' or 'carnality,' but the

great teacher that he was, with deep insight into the workings of the human mind, he preferred to use the concrete
for the abstract and always spoke of the bondage of 'woman'
and not of 'sex.' His motive must have been purely psychological, for speaking on the same subject to his women
devotees, he used to warm them against the dangers from
'man.'" [*Sayings of Sri Ramakrishna* (Madras: Sri Ramakrishna Math, 1965) 43, n. 1].

[20] Swami Saradananda, op. cit., p. 153.

[21] Ibid., p. 140.

[22] Ibid., p. 141.

[23] Ibid., chap. IV.

[24] Ibid., pp. 185-6.

[25] Ibid., chaps. X, XI.

[26] Ibid., pp. 195-6.

[27] See Swami Nikhilananda, op. cit., p. 115. Also see
T. M. P. Mahadevan, *Outlines of Hinduism* (Bombay: Chetana,
1960) 91.

[28] Swami Saradananda, op. cit., p. 234.

[29] Ibid., p. 238.

[30] See, *Life of Sri Ramakrishna* (Almora: Advaita
Ashrama, 1924) 528, 539, etc.

[31] There are at least two other ways in which some sort
of a reconciliation between the two bodies of evidence presented earlier could be effected. (1) It could be effected
by recognizing a discontinuity between the levels of the
Master and the disciples. Most of the criticism of "woman"
is met with in the didactic material about Rāmakṛṣṇa; on
the other hand, their spiritual acceptance is reflected in
the biographic material about his life. It could then be
argued that as a Teacher he need have no scruples about
mixing with women, but the disciples, being spiritually
less advanced, had to be careful. There is some evidence
to support this (see Swami Nikhilananda, op. cit., p. 595,
626, etc.,) and there is a possible parallel here with that
of the Buddha who advised Ānanda, a disciple monk, not even
to look at women but was himself visited by lay women devotees on some occasions at "odd hours." Nevertheless the
reconciliatory power of this model is womewhat limited by
the fact that even after Rāmakṛṣṇa had become the Master
he continued to be alert when it came to women. He said:

"I am very much afraid of women. When I look at one I feel
as if a tigress were coming to devour me. Besides, I find
that their bodies, their limbs, and even their pores are
very large. This makes me look upon them as she-monsters.
I used to be much more afraid of women than I am at present. I wouldn't allow one to come near me. Now I per-
suade my mind in various ways to look upon women as forms
of the Blissful Mother." He went on to say: "A woman is,
no doubt, a part of the Divine Mother. But as far as man
is concerned, especially samyasi or a devotee of God, she
is to be shunned. I don't allow a woman to sit near me
very long, no matter how great her devotion may be. After
a little while I say to her, 'Go and see the temples.' If
that doesn't make her move, I myself leave the room on the
pretext of smoking" (pp. 593-4). Not only that, as a disciple he himself accepted instructions from a lady, hence
this model only goes so far. (2) Another way to reconcile
the two bodies of evidence would be to maintain that what
the Master was opposed to was "sex" which for a man is
symbolized by women and for a woman by men. But as most
of his disciples were men, and those who kept records of
his life and teachings only men, most of Rāmakrṣna's statements seem to be directed against women. This model again
is helpful in understanding the situation somewhat but
leaves unanswered the question: then why does he sometimes
make positive statements about women (pp. 336, 425, 432)
and why does he recommend adopting a woman's ways to overcome passions (p. 603)?

[32]Even sex, the great no-no of the spiritual path, is
acceptable in the realm of God-realization, according to
Rāmakrṣna. Thus when Rāmakrṣna was asked: "When one sees
God does one see him with these eyes," he said:
God cannot be seen with these physical eyes. In
the course of spiritual discipline one gets a
"love body," endowed with "love eyes," "love
ears," and so on. One sees God with those "love
eyes," One hears the voice of God with those
"love ears." One even gets a sexual organ made
of love.
At these words, M. Brust out laughing. The
Master continued, unannoyed, "With this 'love
body' the soul communes with God."
M. again became serious.
[Swami Nikhilananda, op. cit., p. 115]

[33]Ibid., p. 216.

DIONYSUS, CYBELE, AND THE "MADNESS" OF WOMEN*

Jack T. Sanders
University of Oregon

An understanding of Dionysus and of his worship is highly important for the study of female religiosity, for Dionysus is preeminently the god of women. In the literature of antiquity, his divine entourage was made up almost entirely of women, and those men who ventured to join his predominantly female worshippers often dressed in women's clothes for the occasion. Frequently, Dionysus himself wears female garb and dances in the midst of his attendants, and his hair flows down and out in ringlets like theirs; only his beard marks him as male. The women who followed Dionysus to the forested mountain for the raw orgies that so characterized his worship were seen by their husbands, sons, and kinsmen as conforming to the stereotype of woman as inscrutable ninny and wanton. Euripides, in his famous play, the *Bacchae*, has portrayed this attitude in detail.

> (Pentheus speaks)
> It chanced that, sojourning without this land,
> I heard of strange misdeeds in this my town,
> How from their homes our women have gone forth
> Feigning a Bacchic rapture, and rove wild
> O'er wooded hills, in dances honouring
> Dionysus, this new God--whoe'er he be.
> And midst each revel-rout the wine-bowls stand
> Brimmed: and to lonely nooks, some here, some there,
> They steal, to work with men the deed of shame,
> In pretext Maenad priestesses forsooth,
> But honoring Aphrodite more than Bacchus.[1]

A god who appeals almost entirely to women, and who seems himself to express something essentially and subliminally female demands an explanation that accounts especially for these phenomena. While most students of the complex of phenomena that make up Dionysus and his worship have tended to offer his origins as the primary explanation for Dionysiac "oddities," which origins they find to be removed from Greece proper (Thrace, Phrygia),[2] only--to my knowledge--Walter Otto has attempted to provide a strictly phenomenological explanation.[3] Correctly perceiving that mere explanations of origins explain nothing, Otto left all evidence of such entirely out of account, and, at the same time, he virtually ignored temporal distinctions and pooled all his sources, from Homer to Nonnus, together as one body of raw material. From this matrix he was able to mine one of the most fascinating sketches that exists of any god, ancient or modern: that of a god who is mad, mad in the absolute power of raw nature. "He is life," writes Otto, "which, when it overflows, grows and in its profoundest passion is intimately associated with death."[4] Thus is to be explained, according to Otto, the dual nature of the god: that he brings both joy and sorrow, that his rites are celebrated both in the winter and in the spring and summer, that he embodies both life and death, and that he engenders the two masks of the theater: that of comedy and that of tragedy. To this explanation he adds, what is especially important for our interest here:

> We should never forget that the Dionysiac
> world is, above all, a world of women. Women
> awaken Dionysus and bring him up. Women accom-
> pany him wherever he is. Women await him and
> are the first ones to be overcome by his mad-
> ness. And this explains why the genuinely
> erotic is found only on the periphery of the
> passion and wantonness which make their appear-
> ance with such boldness on the well-known sculp-
> tures. Much more important than the sexual act
> are the act of birth and the feeding of the
> child....The terrible trauma of childbirth, the
> wildness which belongs to motherliness in its
> primal form, a wildness which can break loose
> in an alarming way not only in animals--all
> these reveal the innermost nature of the Diony-
> siac madness: the churning up of the essence of
> life surrounded by the storms of death.[5]

Intriguing as this possibly correct explanation is-- and the topic, "Dionysus and women," has yet to receive

a fully satisfactory discussion--Otto's explanation rests
upon a base which contains a major flaw of method--that
is, in rejecting a consideration of the origins of the
worship of Dionysus, Otto shut out the possibility of
understanding the original meaning of that worship and
thus of giving a truer picture of its meaning for the Hel-
lenic period. As he put it, "We must not inquire into the
reasons why [the women] are distraught and wild, but we
must ask, rather, what *divine madness* means."[6]

It is my contention that no proper explanation of the
Dionysiac worship can be given that does not take into
account its origin in the pre-Hellenic culture of Greece,
whose primary deities were goddesses related to the earth
and to grain and a god of annual vegetation--an *eniautos
daimōn*--and whose society, which the pantheon reflects,
was matriarchal. An earth mother religion in pre-Hellenic
Greece is, of course, no new idea, and some of the best
known scholars in the fields of Greek religion, ancient
religion, and history of religions have argued for the
existence of such a religion. I have been particularly
persuaded of the correctness of this view by the work of
Marija Gimbutas, *The Gods and Goddesses of Old Europe 7000
to 3500 B. C.*,[7] who has shown convincing evidence of such
a religion in the neolithic and chalcolithic periods over
an area that extends from the western Ukraine to southern
Italy to western Asia Minor, including Crete and the les-
ser islands; and by the work of Axel Persson, *The Religion
of Greece in Prehistoric Times*,[8] who has demonstrated, on
the basis of Minoan and Mycenaean signet rings, the exis-
ence of such a religion in Greece and on Crete during the
period of high Minoan culture. It is further Gimbutas's
view that, when the patriarchal Indo-Europeans came into
Greece with Zeus Pater and his pantheon, the new religion
did not eradicate the old but sought accommodations with
it in various ways, producing the complex and confusing
mosaic of ancient Greek religion. These accommodations

invariably took the general form of masculinization.[9] I
consider this position valid and do not intend to debate
it further at this time. Thus, in order adequately to
understand the Dionysiac women's religion, one must first
trace the process of masculinization from the oldest written records down to the present--a period of nearly 3000
years!--and then attempt to understand the role of women
in the religion in each successive period. In the space
remaining, I should like to make a beginning of this procedure, sketching the progressive masculinization of the
worship of Dionysus in the historical period and then confirming and supplementing that sketch with another sketch,
the progressive masculinization of the worship of Attis,
which was a parallel development.

The worshippers of Dionysus may well have been, in
times before the *Iliad*, all women. In that oldest known
Greek literary work, there appears a brief reference to
Dionysus, surrounded by his "nurses," who is purused by a
man, one Lykurgus. When Dionysus sees defeat, he takes
refuge in the sea and is sheltered by another female, the
sea-nymph Thetis.[10] While the *Iliad* does not call the
nurses maenads, mad women, it does state that Dionysus was
"possessed by madness," and one of his female attendants is
compared to a maenad, a fact which reveals that readers of
the *Iliad* would have had to know what one was.[11] I believe
that I am correct in saying that, in myth, Dionysus is in
fact never portrayed as being attended by men. Satyrs are
not infrequently and Sileni are occasionally portrayed in
paintings of Dionysiac scenes, but it is not clear that
they should be called attendants or worshippers.[12] This
absence of men from the retinue of Dionysus in myth may
well point to their absence in cult as well, and that possibility is considerably strengthened when one remembers
that, even in Plutarch's time, there was still an official
group of women worshippers of Dionysus at Delphi, called
thyiads, "raging women," whose main function seems to have
been a trieteric Bacchic rout on Mt. Parnassus.[13]

By Euripides' time, at any rate, male participants might be expected in the Bacchic routs, although they were expected to wear women's clothes, and only such classes of men as prophets and retired men were likely to partici- pate.[14] Persson thinks that men worshippers of the tree goddess are shown in women's clothes on some of the Minoan signet rings,[15] but I am not entirely persuaded; the fig- ures there look Sumerian to me, and Mesopotamian influence on Crete is recognized. Thus it appears that the Indo- European Greeks fell heir to an old indigenous cult in which only women participated, and that men only attained access to the cult gradually over a period of centuries; and even then they had to appear like women.

No historical reconstruction, of course, can be that neat, and the fly in the ointment here is the phallic procession known as the rural Dionysia. Here men are the main participants.[16] I think that this festival is prob- ably subject to explanation within the framework that I am outlining, but perhaps for the present it is best to let it remain as evidence that no historical development fol- lows an entirely uniform and linear pattern.

When one turns from the ancient to the modern scene, however, the contrast is marked; for now women remain en- tirely in the background. In films of Dionysiac festivals in Serres produced by the University of California Exten- sion Media Center,[17] and in a film of similar festivals on the island of Skyros produced privately by Maria Maurikou, a graduate student at U.C.L.A., one has a good view of vir- tually uncorrupted Dionysiac festivals still being prac- ticed, but the women are only observers! In the case of the Yugoslavian festivals, this may be no more than a con- tinuation of the rural Dionysia, since phallic symbolism is pronounced. (The *kalogeros* does, however, carry some- thing vaguely resembling a thyrsus.) But the festival on Skyros is a different matter, for here we clearly have the Bacchic rout. Men don animal skins, as did Dionysus and

the maenads in the vase paintings of old; men dress as
women; men dance wildly through the streets and out the
town, playing, like their female predecessors over 2000
years ago, wooden flutes and tambourines, while women
watch from doorways and windows, laughing. The triumph of
the Indo-European patriarchal culture over the aboriginal
matriarchal culture is here complete.

An ancient god who was an equivalent of Dionysus was
Attis, and a development parallel and complementary to the
one just sketched may be traced in his worship. Attis
comes definitely into Greece and Italy from western Asia
Minor, where he was the little darling and consort of the
earth-mountain-mother goddess, Cybele. Hugo Hepding, who
in his 1903 monograph, *Attis seine Mythen und sein Kult*,[18]
collected all the literary sources for a study of Attis,
has listed Attis-Dionysus parallels.[19] (I have some doubt
about some of these.) The idea of the immortality of the
soul exists in connection with both gods, and connected
with this is the annual Bacchic rout; the worship of both
knows the dendrophoria, especially of pine trees;[20] both
gods are related to water, Attis to rivers and Dionysus to
the Sileni, who are "originally daimones of springs,"[21]
(Hepding might have mentioned the frequent connection between Dionysus and the sea); their worshippers may be
called reborn, and union with the deity is a feature of
the worship of both, to the degree that priests of Attis
were called Attis and priests of Sabazius (who is another
variant of Dionysus) Bacchus; Dionysus was closely associated with the bull and Attis with the ox; the Hilaria,
the joyous spring festival in honor of Attis, probably
entailed a marriage to the Great Mother and so was comparable to the hieros gamos of Dionysus at the festival of
Anthesteria, in February. So far Hepding. I should like
to strengthen Hepding's case by mentioning other--to me
prominent--points of comparison.

For one thing, both gods die a tragic and violent
death. In Orphism existed the myth of the rending of
Dionysus-Zagreus by the Titans, and this theme may be compared with the several literary references to the fact
that women sometimes rent their own sons in Bacchic madness. Attis, for his part, dies of self-castration, or
from the attack of a wild boar, or is put to death by the
parents of Cybele, to whom he was untrue.[22] For another
thing, something like a Bacchic rout of women was proper
to the worship of Attis. A number of the texts assembled
by Hepding show this to be the case, but the clearest is
the sixty-third poem of Catullus:

> (Cybele sings)
> 12 Come away, ye Gallae, go to the mountain
>   forests of Cybele together,
>   together go, wandering herd of the lady
>   of Dindymus.
> . . . .

A few lines later Catullus refers to the place

> where the Maenads ivy-crowned toss their
>   heads violently.[23]

Finally, both Attis and Dionysus are the male deities
who go through the successive stages of life--infancy,
vigorous young manhood, old age--who are closely associated
with the earth-mother goddess. For Attis that is clear,
Cybele is the earth-mountain-mother goddess; but for Dionysus the case must be argued, since, in historical times,
such a divine personage appears nowhere in myth in relation
to Dionysus. I am convinced, however, that Dionysus was
originally related to such a goddess, whom the Greeks
called simply Semele, earth. According to the myth, Semele was a mortal who bore Zeus's son, Dionysus, and for
her pains was thunderbolted by Zeus: but the word "semele"
is an Indo-European word for earth. It is related to
Slavonic zemlja, earth, and to Lithuanian žemýna, the earth
goddess; and there are Phrygian inscriptions which place

together *diōs zemelō*, the god and the goddess.[24] Furthermore, Semele was worshipped as a goddess in many places.[25]
How has she become a mortal in the Greek myths? She has
become so, one may conjecture, by the fact that the Indo-
Europeans, with a male-dominated pantheon, triumphed in
the region that had been her domain; and the conquering
god did to the indigenous goddess what conquerors have
normally been wont to do, he thunderbolted her. Thus the
masculinization of the worship of Dionysus began at the
moment when the warlike, patriarchal Indo-Europeans over-
ran the more peaceful matriarchal Old Europeans in the
Aegean region. They eliminated the goddess and turned
her worship into the worship of a god, who now became
Zeus's son (as Athena now became his daughter); but the
worship of the goddess was not eliminated, it was only
now thought to be the worship of the god alone.

There remains only to sketch briefly the progressive
masculinization of the worship of Attis and Cybele. Originally, both priests and priestesses served the divine
pair, as was logical. As late a writer as Dionysius of
Halicarnassus, in describing the early Roman rites of
Cybele, states that "a man, Phryx, and a woman, Phrygia,
performed for her the priestly rites";[26] and the evidence
assembled by Hepding seems to show that, as would be expected, since the goddess was primary and the god secondary, the majority of the various priestly functionaries
was one of priestesses.[27] For the Roman period generally,
however, the worship of both Cybele and Attis was marked
especially by the maenad-like frenzies (recall Catullus's
sixty-third poem) of the castrated Galli. (For a vivid
account of the frenzied act of castration, see Lucian,
De dea Syria 51.) These castrated Galli seem to represent
a certain development, however, and not to be original;
Hepding, at least, has presented a convincing argument
that the rite of castration was not original. He offers
the following observations: The oldest literary reference

to Phrygian cult practices does not mention it;[28] there
are three different versions of Attis's death, as was noted
above; and the inscriptions regarding the orgeon of Cybele and Attis at Piraeus make no mention of such a practice.[29] These castrated Galli, then, who wear women's
clothes, would appear to be an example of the way men
moved into a basically female cult in order to participate
in the orgies of the Great Mother. Such a movement would
thus parallel the phenomenon of men's taking over originally female roles in the worship of Dionysus (and Semele).
In the worship of Attis and Cybele, however, the movement
will have been carried to its painful conclusion; the men
have become women. The reverse of this development, however, is that they then took over, so that, by the time
of Lucian, the worshippers of the goddess and her consort
were predominantly male, albeit altered males.

NOTES

*This essay is offered here in a form only slightly different from that in which it was presented in the Women and Religion Section of the 1975 AAR meeting. It represents a preliminary analysis, and I am aware that further analysis and clarification remain to be done. Thus, the essay should be read as programmatic and, perhaps, as provocative, rather than as definitive. Further analysis, leading to a more definitive statement, is planned for the coming months.

[1]Euripides, *Bacchae*, 11.215-25, in *Euripides*, Vol. 3, Loeb Classical Library, trans. Arthur S. Way (New York: Macmillan, 1912).

[2]Cf. Jane Harrison, *Prolegomena to the Study of Greek Religion* (New York: Meridian, 1955; 1st publ. 1903) 364-79; Martin P. Nilsson, *Geschichte der griechischen Religion* 1. (München: C. H. Beck'sche Verlagsbuchhandlung, 1967³) 564-68, 578-80; cf. further the discussion in Walter F. Otto, *Dionysus. Myth and Cult*, trans. Robert B. Palmer (Bloomington and London: Indiana University, 1965; 1st publ., 1933) 52-64, and Marija Gimbutas, *The Gods and Goddesses of Old Europe 7000-3500 B. C. Myths, Legends and Cult Images* (Berkeley and Los Angeles: University of California, 1974) 227: "Discussions about the Greek Dionysus—whether he came to Greece from Thrace, Crete or western Asia Minor—are pointless, since all these lands belonged originally to the same Mother Culture."

[3]Otto, *Dionysus. Myth and Cult.* I intend, by the term "phenomenological," a total functional approach, which is to be distinguished from the "historico-religious" approach. (For this distinction, I am, of course, indebted to Mircea Eliade, "The History of Religions in Retrospect: 1912 and After," *The Quest. History and Meaning in Religion* (Chicago and London: University of Chicago, 1969) 12-36.

[4]Otto, p. 141.

[5]Otto, p. 142.

[6]Otto, p. 135.

[7]Gimbutas, the work cited in n. 2.

[8]Axel W. Persson, *The Religion of Greece in Prehistoric Times,* Sather Classical Lectures 17 (Berkeley and Los Angeles: University of California, 1942).

[9]Gimbutas, "Mythical Thought in Pre-Christian Europe," University of Oregon Department of Religious Studies Distinguished Visiting Lecturer Series, 1975.

[10]*Iliad* vi.136.

[11]Cf. Otto, p. 54.

[12]Cf. Otto, p. 176, who points out that often Dionysus seems to be contrasted to the satyrs.

[13]Cf. the references given by Nilsson, p. 573, as well as the discussion there.

[14]Cf. the evidence of *Bacchae*, ll.170-89, 248-54.

[15]Persson, pp. 89f.

[16]Cf. Nilsson, pp. 591f.

[17]*Anastenaria* and *Kalogeros* (Berkeley: University of California Extension Media Center, both 1969).

[18]Hugo Hepding, *Attis seine Mythen und sein Kult*, Religionsgeschichtliche Versuche und Vorarbeiten 1 (Gieszen: J. Ricker'sche Verlagsbuchhandlung [Alfred Töpelmann], 1903).

[19]Hepding, pp. 213-16.

[20]Cf. "Dionysus δενδρεύς, δενδρίτης, ἔνδενδρος," Hepding, p. 214.

[21]Ibid.

[22]Cf. the discussion of the variant forms of the myth in ibid., pp. 121, 218, and the other evidence cited there.

[23]*The Poems of Gaius Valerius Catullus*, trans. F. W. Cornish (New York: Macmillan, 1912) 90-91, 92-93; cf. further, Hepding, pp. 17, 136.

[24]Cf. Nilsson, p. 568.

[25]Cf. the evidence in Otto, pp. 67-70; although, Otto argues for the originality of Semele's mortality, which was then converted into deity by her association with Dionysus. What Otto has rejected, however, again provides the explanation: the coming of the male-dominated Indo-European culture into the region of the old Aegean female-dominated culture.

[26]Dion. Hal. *Antiquit. Rom.* ii.19.3-5

[27]Hepding, pp. 133-9.

[28]Herodotus iv.76, discussed in Hepding, pp. 127f.

[29]Cf. Hepding, p. 138-39.

THE SACRAMENT OF SERPENT-HANDLING*

Mary Lee Daugherty
Morris Harvey College

Overview

The serpent-handlers of West Virginia have until very
recently come from among the simple, poor white Anglo-
saxon Protestants who have formed a group of small, independent Holiness-type churches. In the past few years
their incomes have changed radically as the energy crunch
in the U. S. has given a new birth to the coal industry.
Many are now employed with good incomes as miners. Other
jobs are also emerging as the coal industry lifts the
economy. Serpent-handlers base their particular religious
practices on the so-called "longer ending" of the Gospel
of Mark:

> "And Jesus said to them, 'Go into all the
> world and preach the Gospel to the whole creation.
> He who believes and is baptized will be saved, but
> he who does not believe will be condemned. And
> these signs will accompany those who believe: in
> my name they will cast out demons; they will speak
> in new tongues; they will pick up serpents; and
> if they drink any deadly thing, it will not hurt
> them; they will lay their hands on the sick, and
> they will recover." (Mark 16:17-18)

The handling of the serpent as the great act of faith
reflects as in a glass, starkly, the harshness of the en-
vironment in which most of these people live. The land is
uncompromising and produces little; unemployment and welfare were chronic companions. The deep pits of the dark
mines into which men daily go to work have maimed and
killed them for years. The rattlesnake and copperhead are
the most commonly found serpents in the rocky terrain. For
many years mountain people have suffered terrible pain and
many have died from snake bite. Small wonder that it is
considered the ultimate act of faith to reach out and take

up the serpent when one is filled with the Holy Ghost.
Old-timers here in the mountains, before the days of modern medicine, could only explain why one lived and another
died as somehow an act of God's inscrutable mercy and
favor.

Knowing serpent-handlers to be biblical literalists,
one might surmise that they, like other sects, have picked
out a certain passage of scripture and built a whole ritual around a few cryptic verses. While this is true, I am
persuaded that serpent-handling holds for them the significance of a sacrament.

Webster's Dictionary describes sacrament as "a formal
religious act that is sacred as a sign or symbol of a
spiritual reality; one believed to have been instituted by
Jesus Christ; the eucharistic elements."[1]

Tapestry paintings of the Lord's Supper hang in most
of their churches. Leonardo da Vinci's Last Supper is the
picture I have seen over and over in their churches and
homes. Here in West Virginia, the serpent-handlers whom
I know personally, with one exception, do not celebrate
the Lord's Supper, the Eucharist. Rather, it seems that
the ritual of serpent-handling is their way of celebrating
life, death and resurrection. Time and again they prove
to themselves that Jesus has the power to deliver them
from death here and now. Many have been bitten numerous
times, but few have died. Their continued life and their
sometimes deformed bodies bear witness to the fact that
Jesus still has power over illness and death. Even those
who have not been bitten know many who have and the living
witness is ever present in the lives of their friends. If
one of the members die, it is believed that God allowed it
to happen ever to remind the living that the risk they take
is totally real. Seldom have I heard one say that a brother or sister who died lacked faith.

I have offered my interpretation of their serpent-
handling experiences as sacramental to them and although

"They had not thought of it in exactly those words, they do agree that they are celebrating their belief that Jesus gives them life over death. It is important also to know that serpents are often handled at the funerals of believers either at their request or at the request of their families. This gives us another clue to the symbolic meaning it holds for them. Even as a Roman Catholic priest may lift up the host during a mass for the dead representing his belief that in the body and blood of Jesus there is life so I believe the serpent-handlers lift up the serpent in dance indicating that Jesus has power over death and that they have living evidence in their own bodies that the power of Jesus has lifted up most of them from death in the here and now.

Even for those of us who read and study Church History we must confess we know little enough about the last twelve verses of the Gospel of Mark. Much controversy apparently surrounded the omission of Mark 16:9-20 from some early manuscripts and their inclusion in others. Perhaps knowing this we can be more tolerant of the literal interpretation given to these verses by the serpent-handlers of Southern Appalachia who are able to read the Bible only in English and who read only the King James version. The rituals of serpent-handling, speaking in tongues, drinking of poisons and the laying on of hands have now become sacramental to them.

Past History

As recorded in the Gospel of Mark, verses 16:9-20 were known by Christians at least by the second century A. D.; William Farmer states in his recent book:

> "Celsus seems to have known Mark with the longer ending around 180 A. D. Irenaeus certainly knew Mark 16:9-20 at this time. So also did Tatian around 170 A. D. Justin Martyr probably knew these verses by 150 A. D. In fact external evidence from the second century for Mark 16:9-20 is stronger than for most other parts of the Gospel."[2]

The Alexandrian theologian Origen, who lived between 185 and 254 A. D., knew of verses 9-20. In Book II of his treatise *Against Celsus*, Origen quoted from Mark 16:9-20 as he sought to validate the resurrection of Jesus as witnessed by her.

Of the eight or nine Greek verbs in Mark 16:17-18—the crucial passage in question here—six (emphasized below: #1-4, 6-7) are future active indicative verbs:

1. Sēmeia de tois pisteusasin tauta *parakolouthēsei*:
   And these signs *will accompany* those who believe:

2. en tô onomati mou daimonia *ekbalousin*;
   in my name *they will cast out* demons;

3. glossais *lalēsousin* kainais;
   they will speak in new tongues;

4. [kai en tais chersin] opheis *arousin*;
   [and in their hands] *they will pick up* serpents;

5. kan thanasimon ti piōsin, ou mē autous blapsē;
   and if they drink any deadly thing, it *will not hurt* them;

6. epi arrōstous cheiras *epithēsousin*,
   on the sick *they will lay* their hands,

7. kai kalôs *hexousin*.
   and *they will recover*.

In some non-Biblical Greek literature and in certain verses of the Bible, the use of a future indicative active verb can be considered as a command.[3]

We know also from early church history that certain gnostic Christians called "Ophites" used the snake in the celebration of the Lord's Supper. Although we have no original documents from this group, Epiphanius, an early Church Father, says the serpent was released from a box and allowed to entwine itself around the sacred elements of the Eucharist. The serpent was considered by the Ophites to be the "enlightener" and benefactor of man. By the Parates and Sethians two other gnostic groups, the serpent was identified as the "Logos" or "Word" that "Became Flesh" (John 1:14) and thus was a symbol of Jesus. One ponders the question as to whether there was a type of magic

associated with the serpent and the Eucharist in these
early gnostic groups? If so could there be some linkage
between this and the argument over the ending of the Gospel of Mark? It is hard to know the full story of these
verses, since the records of history are so scarce. From
the Biblical record itself we have no evidence that serpent-handling as it is now practiced here in Appalachia
was practiced in the same manner in the early Christian
church. Paul unintentionally "picked up" a serpent while
gathering fire wood in Malta (Acts 28:1-6) but not as a
religious ritual.

Among West Virginia serpent-handlers the serpent symbol is, I believe, profoundly meaningful for their daily
life experiences. The serpent lives in the earth, in dark
holes, it crawls on its belly, it sheds its skin, and it
lives by its wits. Many of the serpent-handling men are
now and have been miners. They too enter the dark holes
of the earth each morning as they enter the mine shaft;
they often must lie in the dirt and pull and press the
levers of the automatic miner. This is especially true if
they work in a small 30 inch mine seam. They come out at
night and shed their skins or their dirty work clothes,
shower and are renewed. They too must often live by their
wits to survive in a harsh occupation where danger is ever
present. One might wish that many who live in the urban
centers of our region could find such a meaningful symbol
for their lives and rituals of worship.

Present History

The cultural isolation of their lives is also very
real. Few have traveled more than a few miles from home.
Little more than the Bible is read. Television is frowned
upon and movies are seldom attended; even a ball game is
the "devil's thing." No biblical commentaries are ever
read; church history is unknown. The Bible is communicated
primarily through oral tradition in the church or read at
home. This is true because most of the older members are

shy about their inability to read well in public. There
is no awareness of other world religions. Even contacts
with Roman Catholics and Jews are rare. Some of their
children may go to Sunday school at other churches since
they have no Sunday school curriculum. Most of their lives
revolve around the church and believers are in church
meetings two or three times per week for two to four hours
at a meeting. I know of only one among their group who
has received two years of college education and he is
being trained to take over the pastor's place in his local
church. Some are now holding important positions in the
mines. One minister is the mine Superintendent in his
community. Many of their young are now finishing high
school. However their exposure to the outside world is
still minimal and most still seek holiness above all else.
As they pursue holiness they believe that Jesus commands
them to try out his power and to trust Him for life as
they are obedient to His words in Mark 16:17 and 18.

It is recorded by Weston La Barre that "serpent-handling began in 1909 in Sale Creek, Tennessee."[4] George
Went Hensely of Grasshopper Valley, Tennessee, was reading
Mark 16:17-18. After climbing White Oak Mountain he found
a large rattlesnake. Several hours later, during an evan-
gelistic meeting which he was leading he took up the
rattlesnake to demonstrate his faith; then, he encouraged
others to do the same. Snake-handling is now practiced
widely throughout the Southern Appalachian regions and in
some urban centers of Ohio, Michigan and Indiana. It is
outlawed in all states now except West Virginia; but, it
is still practiced. The big question to ask is *WHY*?
These people are very "straight" and usually law abiding
in every way. What significance does this ritual have for
them? Why has it spread with such meaning? There are
many answers to these questions but one important answer
is, I believe, that it has become sacramental for them and
is their unique way of celebrating "life, death and resurrection."

Two women and a gentleman in their 80's who are currently living in Charleston, West Virginia remember attending a tent revival in 1933 in Charleston. Men from Cabin Creek were handling serpents during this meeting. This is the earliest date I have discovered from an interview in January of 1976. Serpent-handling began on a regular basis in 1948 when a local miner was taught serpent-handling by his mother-in-law of Virginia and Tennessee. The church at Big Creek and then Scrabble Creek, West Virginia became the center in 1949. Other churches then emerged. I have visited serpent-handlers in four locations in West Virginia. I am told there are about 20 churches with 1200 to 1400 persons attending. However as I travel the state I discover there are still other churches handling serpents. Often they do not know about each other. West Virginia decided in 1966 not to outlaw serpent-handling. Religious freedom is very important here.

There are thousands of small Holiness churches in the rural areas of this state. While four-fifths of all Protestants are members of mainline denominations, according to the records, no one knows just how many persons attend Holiness churches. Roles and records are not important to these people. They laugh and make jokes about churches which give you a piece of paper as you enter the door telling you when to pray and when to sing. They find it difficult to believe that you can order God's Spirit around by a piece of paper. Hence church roles are not important either.

Those who make up the membership of the serpent-handling churches are often former members of other Holiness churches or of Baptist or Methodist churches. Thirty to forty years ago these Protestant denominational churches were more highly emotional in their worship services than today. In the Holiness churches, the attainment of personal holiness and being filled with the Spirit is the purpose and goal of one's life. Members view the secular world as evil and beyond hope. Hence they do not take part in any community activities or social programs.

Fifty-four percent of all persons in the state of West Virginia still live in communities of 1,000 people or less. Thus, the small churches of these rural people are the rule rather than the exception. Freedom of worship and the "doing of your own thing" are the heritage of the Scotch-Irish who settled these mountains some 200 years ago. They had few ministers, and few could read. Thus oral tradition, spontaneous worship, and shared leadership were important years ago, as they are still today.

History shows that, when the Scotch-Irish forebears of many now living in Appalachia came to America, most of them were Presbyterians. Being too poor to buy land along the East coast, they moved toward the wilderness and thus into the mountains. At first they had clergy and possessed the skill of reading. But the life they lived here was harsh and difficult, and soon they were without clergy or church.

By the second and third generation the skill of reading was lost. Organized religion for the most part died out for a number of years. However, with the sweep of revivals in the 1800's, religion came back to the mountain people. This time it was highly emotional, without benefit of trained clergy or structure. The free style of the Holiness revivals took root in the mountains.

Description

Serpent-handling holiness church members live by a very strict code, and a large sign in the church at Jolo, for example, indicates that dresses must be worn below the knees, arms must be covered, no lipstick or jewelry is to be worn. No smoking, drinking, or other worldly pleasures are to be indulged in by "true believers." Some women do not cut their hair, others do not even buy chewing gum or soft drinks. Others do not allow television in their homes.

The church is the center of their lives; it provides for
all their needs. Many Holiness people with whom I have
talked indicate they will go to see a doctor for an oper-
ation or if they are in need of some other medical treatment, but never for snake bites or for the treatment of
poison taken in church, nor for any injury from fire used
in the church services. For years they have practiced
divine healing in the mountains, since medical facilities
are scarce. Four counties in West Virginia still do not
have a doctor, nurse, clinic, dentist, or ambulance service.

The "true believers" usually sit on the platform of
the church together. They are the members of the church
who have demonstrated that they have received the Holy
Ghost. This is known to them and to others because they
have manifested certain physical signs in their own bodies.
One sign is the picking up of serpents. If they are bitten,
as many have been, and have not died, they have thus proved
that they have the Holy Ghost. Those who have been bitten
many times and survived are the "real saints." The "true
believers" also demonstrate that they have the Holy Ghost
through the jerking of their bodies and their various
trance-like states. They may dance ecstatically for long
periods of time or may hit the floor and not be hurt. They
may drink the "salvation cocktail," a mixture of strychnine
and water or lye and water. They may also speak in tongues
or in ecstatic babblings. Usually this is an ecstatic conversation between themselves and God. However, sometimes
members may seek to interpret the language of tongues.
They lay their hands upon each other to heal hurts or even
serious cancer. They do pass their hands through fire. I
have witnessed this activity and no burn effects were visible, even though a hand remained in the flame for a brief
time. In the past they picked up hot coals from the pot-
bellied stoves and were not burned. They block out pain
totally while they dance in a deep trance.

One woman who attended church at Scrabble Creek experienced stigmata twice: blood coming out of her hands, feet,
side and forehead. This was witnessed by all persons
present in the church. When asked about this startling
experience, she said that she had prayed that God would
allow people to see in her body how much Jesus had suffered for them by His death and resurrection. This woman
is a practical nurse raised in Holiness churches. Her
experience is undoubtedly rare in Protestant denominations.
Holiness people tend to worship God with all their bodies.
Perhaps as we become more educated, we in the more mainline
churches have worshipped God with only our heads.

Small, independent Holiness churches scattered throughout the hollows of Southern Appalachia are usually not related to each other, and each group makes its own rules and
orders its own life. A church in any area may be known as
"Brother So-and-So's" or "Sister So-and-So's church" to
those who live around, but the sign over the door will
usually indicate that the church belongs to Jesus. Such
names as "The Jesus Church," "The Jesus Only Church," "The
Jesus Saves Church" and the "Lord Jesus Christ's Church"
are all common names. These churches do not form a denom-
ination, nor do they have a written doctrine or creed. The
order of the service is spontaneous and different every
night. Everyone is welcome, and people travel around to
each other's churches, bringing with them their musical
instruments, snakes, fire and poison as well as their tes-
timonies and messages from God about their gifts or healing
or interpreting of tongues.

When one sees the people handling serpents in their
services, the Garden of Eden story immediately comes to
mind. In Genesis 3, the serpent represents evil that
tempts and must be conquered. But it seems that the serpent means something far different to West Virginia mountain people than in the Genesis story. There is never an
attempt to kill the snake in Appalachian serpent-handling

services. Practitioners seldom kill snakes even in the
out of doors. They let them go at the end of the summer
months so that they may return to their natural environ-
ment or hibernate for the winter. They catch different
snakes each spring to use in their worship services. When
one asks why, they say quite simply that they do not want
to make any of God's creatures suffer. Therefore, it seems
that the handling of the serpent is also a way of confron-
ting and living with their own fears about life and the
harshness of life as they experience it here. The serpent
is handled with both love and fear in their services, but
never killed. The handlers may be killed by snake bites,
but they will not kill the snake. Neither do they force
the handling of the serpents on any other members, or on
any visitor. Only one man that I know here in West Virginia force feeds the serpents through the winter months
and in his church Serpent-handling may take place almost
the year around. In no way are they defanged or milked
of their poison.

Perhaps Paul Tillich offers us a helpful insight at
this point. In his book, *The Courage to Be*, Tillich seems
to imply that all human beings plagued by anxiety seek to
turn that anxiety into objects of fear. These objects can
then be met with courage. Perhaps serpent-handlers project
many of their anxieties about life onto the deadly serpent.
They become and are real objects to be feared. Hence it's
a real act of faith at many levels of the mind and soul to
conquer one's fear and take up the serpent.

Another observation which should be made is that the
snake is seldom handled in private, but usually in the
community of believers during the church service. The
members support each other as they take up the serpents
thus symbolically taking on life. It is almost a "rite of
passage." Children *are not* encouraged to pick up the serpents. Usually one is in one's late teens. Since many
marry young one is early an adult. The church is often

made up of many extended families and indeed, the church community itself represents a large extended family. They tend to marry among other families that believe in Serpent-handling. Thus they encourage each other to encounter life with all its dangers and struggles. They usually refuse medicine or hospital treatment for snake bite. They have usually refused welfare for the most part and are known to rely on welfare less than people in other Holiness churches who do not handle serpents. They revere and care for their elderly who have usually survived numerous snake bites. Each time they handle the serpents they struggle with life once more and once more survive the forces that tradition-ally have oppressed mountain people. The poverty, the unemployment, the yawning strip mines, the dark death wait-ing in the deep mines are all harsh, uncontrollable forces to simple people.

The person of the Holy Ghost, as they and their King James Bible call the Holy Spirit, enables them not only to pick up the serpents, but to speak in tongues, to preach, to testify, to cure diseases, to cast out demons and even to drink strychnine or to use fire on their skin when the snakes are in hibernation during the winter months. When a people need to "force the hand of God" to such dramatic extremes to prove that they are loved and filled with the Spirit, we begin to see how totally these people have been oppressed and how much in need of affirmation they are. Having internalized the message inside of myself for many years that I was "no count" because I have been born of "poor white trash" on one side of my family, I have in my own being a deep feeling and understanding of their need to ask God for the performance of miracles to indicate love with spectacular demonstrations. Thus they are as-sured of their own worth, even if only to God. They never get this message from the outside world, where they have been regarded as the undesirable poor, confined to their pockets of poverty. Television and government have told us this for the past twenty-five years.

The Holy Ghost is the great equalizer in the church
meeting. One's age, sex, years in school are all of little
import. Being filled with the Holy Ghost is the only cre-
dential one needs in this unique society. As a woman now
into feminist thinking and reading, I cannot help but notice that, when the service is over and the women go out
of the church, the same traditional stereotype of male-
female relationships reemerge. One wonders what would
happen if the Holy Ghost ever got outside the walls of the
church into the daily lives of these women. Would they
begin to take equal power unto themselves? What revolutionary effects would this have? We are now just beginning to
experience the changing roles of women in West Virginia.
For example, in 1974 a woman went into the mines to work
for the first time. She did so for reasons of economic
survival rather than from a thought-out feminist philosophy.
It was the only way to stay off welfare. She broke down
the old, old taboo that a woman in the mines would bring
bad luck.

The Holy Ghost creates a mood of openness and spontaneity in the serpent-handling services that is beautiful.
Even though there is not much freedom in the personal lives
of these people, there is a sense of power in their church
lives. The religion does seem to heal them inwardly of
aches and pains and even major illnesses. Dr. Ari Kiev of
Cornell Medical School, who also visited the snake-handlers
with me, observed that they enter into deep states of
trance--in which they can even block out the pain of fire-
handling. They believe Jesus can heal. The Holy Ghost
remains a spirit but Jesus is a real person to whom they
can relate.

One often sees expressions of dependency as both men
and women fall down before the picture of Jesus, calling
aloud over and over again the name, "Jesus...Jesus...Jesus
..." The simple carpenter of Nazareth is obviously a person with whom mountain men can identify. Jesus worked with

his hands, and so do they. Jesus was, by our standards, essentially uneducated, and so are they. Jesus came from a small place, he lived much of his life out of doors, he went fishing, he suffered and was finally done in by the "power structure," and so are they.

As I think about the mountain women as they fall down before the picture of Jesus, I wonder what He means to them. I cannot help but wonder if Jesus is not to them a kind of "lover." Here is a simple man who treated women with great love and tenderness. In this sense He is unlike some of the men they must live with. Jesus also healed the bodies of women, taught them the Bible, never told jokes about their bodies, and even forgave them their sexual sins. In the mountains there are usually only beatings for adultery. It seems that in this type of dialogue about Jesus, some of the ideas of feminism could take root in the hearts of Appalachian women.

The last symbol, the Bible, usually remains closed on the pulpit, as it did the last night we visited the church. Since most cannot read well and are usually shy about their meager education, they do not usually read the Bible aloud in public, especially if some educated are present. They obviously read it at home, and most remember it from tellings and from memory. It is the final authority for everything, even the picking up of serpents and the drinking of poison. The Bible is all literally true, but the New Testament is most often read.

The church gives these people the arena to act out their feelings. For a short time they can experience being powerful when filled with the Holy Ghost. Frustrated by all the things in the outside world that they cannot change, frustrated by the way the powerful people of the world run things, in their own churches they can run their own show. So they gather three of four times a week, for three to five hours at a service. Each night they can feel important, loved and powerful. As I have indicated before, the

church and its service seem to act as a therapy session
where they can give vent to their feelings and heartaches
as well as worship God with all their bodies and voices.
In almost catharsis--like ways they work through their
anger, fears and frustrations. At last emerges the simple
but beautiful love that is in the heart of all mountain
people, I believe. I am always struck by the healing love
that emerges at the end of each service when they all love
each other, embrace each other, and give the holy kiss.
They are free to love once more. Sometimes I feel I have
a glimmer of what the Kingdom of God will really be like
as we kiss each other--with or without teeth, rich and poor,
educated and uneducated, male and female.

Dr. Nathan Gerrard, formerly head of the department
of sociology at Morris Harvey College, did an in-depth
study of these people some ten years ago. With their permission, he administered the Minnesota Multiphasic Personality Inventory, familiarly known as the MMPI. He also
administered this test to a similar group of Christians in
a mainline Protestant Church nearby. The results of the
test were striking. Gerrard's study indicated that the
serpent-handlers were slightly more normal than members of
the conventional Protestant denominations in the mountain
churches. Old members of conventional denominational
churches were more neurotic, pessimistic, anxious and rigid.
Serpent-handlers seemed to have greater freedom from psychological stresses. God is very real to them, it seems,
and they are not afraid to die.

Gerrard's study also indicated that the young of the
conventional denominational churches and the young of the
serpent-handler churches are strikingly similar to each
other and have similar profiles to other adolescent groups.
Many young serpent-handlers may wander the hollows very
bored when out of school or out of a job, and they have no
plans for college. What seems to keep them from becoming
delinquent or demoralized is their wholehearted participation in a religious practice that functions as a catharsis

which drains off the malaise and strengthens self-esteem
by providing opportunity to achieve a "holy status."[6]

"Middle class church people tend to postpone immediate
pleasure for the sake of future pleasures. This tends to
kill one's capacity for spontaneity. The young serpent-
handlers are less defensive and guarded, and they have less
to lose in social image.

"Young serpent-handlers seem less alienated from their
parents, since few of them never expected until recently to
earn more money or have better jobs. They hope to attain
the same type of holiness of life as their parents, and
they respect them for what they have already achieved. Old
and young have the same view of the Bible. My own observation is that the serpent-handlers tend to marry very young
among each other and seldom travel far from where they are
born. Thus, they do not experience alienation from their
own roots and culture, as do many young people in other
churches who go off to college or to work in other parts of
the United States or the world. The serpent-handling
church service allows for great spontaneity, the full expression of fears and frustrations, love is also openly
expressed and one's whole body is brought into the worship
of God in singing, dancing and various trance-like states.
The participation by all and the unstructured service is
the heritage of their Scotch-Irish descendants.

I have often marvelled at the energy that is released
in the service and have wondered just what might happen if
the same kind of energy were taken outside of the wall of
the church and put to work on many of the social and economic problems of their lives, West Virginia being considered the most economically oppressed area of Appalachia.
Perhaps some will cry that this religion is an "opiate of
the people," and in some ways it is; but, it also has
"heart," it has "soul," and it gives them a sense of worth,
dignity and freedom.

I have learned much from them as I have visited in
their churches over the past six years. Perhaps I long

for a symbol in the modern technological world that would
have as much meaning for city dwellers. Serpent-handlers
practice faith, hope and love in a way which may strike
many as strange. But I am always impressed by their genuine love and warm acceptance of all who come to their
churches. Never do they insist that other Christians must
handle serpents as they do as an act of faith. Why do
many come to West Virginia during the warmer months to
practice their religious ritual openly. The answer lies
in understanding what the ritual of serpent-handling has
come to mean and what it symbolizes to them. It is I believe their own peculiar way of celebrating the Eucharist,
the belief that Jesus has the power to overcome death--
even death from the bite of a deadly serpent. This is not
to suggest that all Christians should take up serpent-
handling but does demonstrate the wide diversity of sacramental experiences in the Christian tradition. The
serpent-handlers joyously and ecstatically celebrate life,
death and resurrection as they handle the serpents. This
ceremony is, I believe, unique in the Christian world and
in the history of the Christian church.

NOTES

*Portions of this paper have appeared in *Things Appalachian* and in *Theology Today*, October, 1976.

[1] *Webster's New Collegiate Dictionary* (Springfield, MA, 1973) 1017.

[2] William R. Farmer, *The Last Twelve Verses of Mark* (London: Cambridge University, 1974) 31.

[3] Cf. Funk, Blass and Debrunner, *A Greek Grammar of the New Testament* (Cambridge/Chicago, 1961) §362 Herbert W. Smyth, *Greek Grammar* (Harvard University, 1959) §1917

[4] Weston La Barre, *They Shall Take Up Serpents* (New York: Schocken Books, 1969) 11.

[5] Paul Tillich, *The Courage To Be* (New Haven: Yale University, 1952) 38.

[6] Nathan Gerrard, *Scrabble Creek Folk*, Part II, Department of Mental Health Grant, available through Morris Harvey College Library, 1966, pp. 74, 77.

CLOISTER AND SALON IN SEVENTEENTH CENTURY PARIS:
Introduction to a Study in Women's History*

F. Ellen Weaver
University of Notre Dame

My God make me an *honnête homme* and never make me
an honest woman!
Ninon de Lanclos

Hélas! I am convinced (of the fruitlessness of the
efforts of the leaders) and am amazed that they
continue to make these sweet offers to us, because
(to accept) would be to sell our liberty and
right to the truth without gaining anything.[2]
Angélique de Saint-Jean Arnauld d'Andilly

No two women could have been further apart in life
style, in beliefs, in the traditions each had a part in
founding than Mademoiselle Ninon de Lanclos and Soeur
Angélique de Saint-Jean Arnauld d'Andilly. Of Ninon, that
remarkable libertine, friend of Saint-Evremond and most of
the other great seventeenth century freethinkers, Simone
de Beauvoir said in *The Second Sex*:

The Frenchwoman whose independence seems...the most
like that of a man is perhaps Ninon de Lanclos, seventeenth century woman of wit and beauty.

Ninon chose lovers and friends with as great discrimination
as abandon, and lived to a remarkable old age in which even
the wives and mothers of her discarded lovers sought entrance to her salon. She died peacefully, firmly refusing
to retract any of her disbelief in immortality or the existence of her soul, but providing for a decent, modest,
Christian burial for her long-cherished body.

Angélique de Saint-Jean was the niece of the famous
Mère Angélique who reformed the Cistercian monastery of
Port-Royal des Champs, and she was the youthful leader of
the recalcitrant nuns during the controversy into which the
women of Port-Royal were plunged by the theological debates
of their Jansenist friends, relatives and spiritual dir-
ectors. She was also historiographer of the monastery,

recording the reform movement from its beginnings in 1609
through the period of persecution (1664-1668), the uneasy
peace (1669-1679), and then the renewal of repression up
to her death in 1684. In her beliefs she was a fervent
Augustinian, in her life she was a determined ascetic, in
her rhetoric she was an ardent defender of conscience and
truth--the *Truth* with a capital 'T' of the Jansenists.

One could hardly imagine two women more diametrically
opposed. Yet a significant similarity unites them. Each
in her own way adopted as her own the modes of thinking,
expressing, and acting which traditionally had been the
restricted preserve of men. Each in her own way confronted
the rules (made by men) and the rulers (all of them men) of
her society, challenging them in a manner which had repercussions reaching down to our times.

The well-known saying of Ninon symbolizes well the
dilemma which faced these two women: there was no female
equivalent of the *honnête homme*--a term which persistently
confounds attempts to render it in English. The *honnête
homme* was that ideal French gentleman formed, ironically,
not in the Court or the university men's club (as in the
case of his English counterpart), but in the salons of the
influential women of Parisian society in the seventeenth
century. Larousse in the French definition stresses pro-
bity--adherance to highest principles and ideals, upright-
ness--as the dominant characteristic of the *honnête homme*,
and adds politeness, manners, and general *savoir faire*.
Honnête femme is just not the counterpart.

It was not in order to have lovers that Ninon rejected marriage. In seventeenth century society marriage was
no barrier to amorous dalliance, even for the most respected women. She remained single, in spite of great financial
and social difficulties, in order to maintain the independence of thought and style which she prized.

A similar obsession with independence of thought and
decision making drove Angélique de Saint-Jean to challenge

not only the official decision of the Church regarding the statements on the doctrine of grace said to be in the *Augustinus* of Jansenius, and the royal decree imposing the renunciation by signature of these alleged statements, but even the efforts of the male leaders of the Port-Royal group to achieve a compromise. The letter from which the opening quotation is taken was written in 1668 when the non-signers among the nuns were under interdict and virtual imprisonment at their country monastery, Port-Royal des Champs.[3] She is referring to a manoeuver of Antoine Arnauld, her uncle, the "grand Arnauld" of the history of Jansenism, and Pierre Nicole, along with the respected Jansenist bishops, calculated to work out a release for the nuns if they will sign the condemnation of the "five propositions" said to be in the *Augustinus* in a statement which makes no mention of Jansenius and does not state that the propositions are *in fact* in the book. Having signed a similar statement, which condemned the content of the propositions without admitting that they were contained in Jansenius' doctrine of grace, earlier and to no avail, the nuns are now leary of being led into another such empasse, and Angélique speaks for the majority when she expresses fear that once more they will compromise their freedom and right to truth and gain nothing in the end.

That two such opposite women are found to hold some very significant ideals in common is not entirely accidental. There are characteristics of the society of seventeenth century France which favored the existence of these strong independent women, and fostered close relationships among women of these seemingly oppositional worlds of cloister and salon. Not least among the characteristics is an almost obsessive concern with moral and religious reform.

Fascinating as Ninon de Lanclos is, I must bid her farewell at this point. Her story has been well told recently in English by Edgar H. Cohen.[4] The women of her

world of the salon who had close ties with the cloister
were those to whom she referred somewhat scornfully: "Les
précieuses sont les Jansénistes de l'amour." As a contribution to the present concern of women to recover their
past history, I propose to study these women, "précieuse"
and "Janséniste," and their world through concentration on
the correspondence between the nuns of Port-Royal and two
significant women in Parisian society, Madame de Sablé and
Madame de Fontpertuis.

Students of French literature of the seventeenth century cannot fail to note that there is a real sense in
which women dominate the culture of this era. Paris, in
particular, can be seen as a favored center of feminism.
Among the strong and fascinating women of that society,
not least influential were the nuns of Port-Royal. Their
struggle with ecclesiastical and royal authority was a
harbinger of a new era when freedom of conscience would be
respected, and the intellect of women also. An analysis
of the correspondence between these women of the cloister
and those of the salon reveals a powerful sisterhood forming a pervasive pattern in the fabric of seventeenth century French society.

The Role of Women in Seventeenth Century Paris

Orest Ranum in the "Acknowledgments" concluding his
very useful essay on *Paris in the Age of Absolutism* credits
the *Annales* school of French historians with important
contributions in the area of provincial history, but observes that it is possible that the subtle sociological
methods used by the *Annalistes* must still be tested on the
large urban societies.[5] Similarly, many young French historians are writing about minority groups of women--pros-
titues, witches, etc.,--[6]but there is very little written
from new perspectives on the small, but influential, group
of women who comprised salon society in Paris in the
Ancien Regime. This may be another case of an area that

to the French appears so overworked that there seems to be
nothing more to say. As a matter of fact, most studies of
the seventeenth century salon are made from the point of
view of their literary influence, and there are few anal-
yses of their sociological or religious significance. New
methods, and new points of view--especially the point of
view of the woman historian--might discover new values.
Each generation brings its own interpretation to the facts
of history. For example, we might evaluate much differently *les précieuses*, so maligned in their own time as well
as ours, if we raised one question: is it possible that
the criticism of the institution of marriage, advocation
of the limitation of births, and certain other feminist
echoes in the writings of some members of this group have
prejudiced the issue?[7] We might also discover that many
of the reforms in Catholicism mandated by the Council of
Trent owe their propagation in France more to the women of
the Salons than to the Bishops and priests of the society.

The material for such a study is almost too vast.
Besides the important literary contributions of women in
the seventeenth century,[8] these women have left copious
published and unpublished correspondence. The seventeenth
century was marked by the emergence of letter-writing as a
means of communication and as a literary genre. Letters
multiplied and became more and more literary. Often they
were written for the purpose of being read aloud in the
salons.

Besides the collections of letters like the great literary masterpiece of Madame de Sévigné and the correspondence of Madame de Sablé, significant collections of letters
can be found for many other seventeenth century women.
These women modeled their letters after the writers and
poets whose works they heard in the salons, and made great
use of letters. It is Madame de Sablé who is credited
with making the writing of letters for any and every--or
even *no*--excuse popular.[9]

The role of women in the society of seventeenth century Paris was significant and the freedom they enjoyed was far greater than in any other society of the time. In the Paris salons the subjugation under which women suffered in Spain and Italy was a standing joke.[10] The rise of the bourgeoisie gave feminism a "burning actuality." The education of women was no longer a question reserved to moralists and theologians, but was the subject of intense public opinion. The rapid increase in publication put in the reach of women a plethora of works on every subject, including orthography, philosophy, science and religion. Indeed, the question of woman, her dignity, her liberty, is posed from the beginning to the end of the seventeenth century, and preciosity gave unprecedented brilliance to this feminist movement.[1]

To understand preciosity, it is necessary to understand the development and importance of the salon. The salon began as the drawing room of fashionable women in court and parlementarian circles where famous artists of the day were gathered for intimate performance of their art. L. Clark Keating's *Studies on the Literary Salon in France, 1550-1615*[12] has quite well demolished the myth that the *chambre bleu* of Madame de Rambouillet which flourished between 1620 and 1665 was a totally new phenomenon, and that it was there that the art of polite conversation was born. As a matter of fact the origins of the literary salon can be traced back to the medieval courts of love and such figures as Eleanor of Aquitaine.[13] In the sixteenth century women like Marguerite of Navarre, sister of the renaissance monarch Francis I, championed the platonic ideal of identifying love with the desire for beauty and beauty with goodness, which raised love above the physical and emancipated it from carnal desire.

However, the renaissance in France was short-lived, and the passing of power by way of war and assassination from the Valois to the Bourbons was accompanied by a decided coarsening of the manners and morals of the court. It was to provide a refuge from the crude sensuality and course male chauvinism of Henry IV and his court that Madame de Rambouillet established her salon, recognized as the forerunner of those that flourished in Paris in the seventeenth century. Here the most famous literary figures of the century--Corneille, Molière, La Fontaine, La Rochefoucauld-- gathered with the men of affairs like Condé, Coligny and Cardinal Richelieu, and the women like Madame de Sablé and the Duchess of Longueville, Madame de La Fayette and Madame de Sévigné to read and discuss their poems and plays and fables. Here, too, a strict code of manners was developed. There was a return to the type of chivalric love ideal born in the court of Marguerite de Navarre but, nourished by the moral emphasis of the Tridentine Counter-Reformation which opposed spiritual love to carnal desire, this ideal was transmuted into one which retained the spiritual aspect while rejecting the romantic element and exalting the power of the will.

As this code of manners, politeness, culture and taste became more and more refined the result was preciosity. Yet the *précieuses* were not all "*ridicule*." It is true that in literature and conversation preciosity developed into a kind of art for art's sake, emphasizing style at the expense of meaning and exalting circumlocution in the name of modesty. But, as we have suggested, under this seemingly effete and empty-headed play with words there was often a serious note. Many among the *précieuses* (and *précieux*) were forerunners of modern feminists.

Thus the salon established the women as arbiters of social codes, of manners and morality, and preciosity gave style and luster to the movement. The *précieuses* could be ridiculed, but coming from a Molière such ridicule is a guarantee of attention and perhaps a subtle form of praise.

Nor was the world of the cloister lacking in striking women leaders. Reformation was in the air. The salon had reformed worldly manners and introduced a new moralism into

social interaction. The Catholic Church was also under-
going a rigorous reform. This was especially true of
religious orders: the old orders were recalled to the
practice of their ancient ascetic ideals and new orders
were founded. Among cloisters of both kinds women like
Saint Jeanne de Chantal who co-founded the Visitation nuns
with Saint François de Sales, Madame Acarie (Marie de
l'Incarnation) who established the Carmelites in France,
and Mère Angélique Arnauld who reformed the Cistercian
monastery of Port-Royal des Champs became the heroines of
a new generation of serious, stringently moral nuns.[15]

Women between Two Worlds

We often tend to think of the monastery as more separated from society in which it exists than it is--or ever
was. Certainly in Paris in the seventeenth century the
connections between cloister and salon were quite solid.
In the first place, the women within and without were related by blood and marriage. Although the population of
Paris was a quarter to half a million inhabitants, those
who formed the ruling class--primarily the Court and the
Parlement, the nobles of the sword and the nobles of the
robe--were probably no more than about two hundred families. There was a movement within the reform of religious
orders to do away with the dowry required for entry into
the monastery, but most monasteries still asked, directly
or by the subtle social pressure of custom, for a greater
contribution from the family of the candidate than any but
the members of the upper class could afford. It was still
the custom in the French noble families to place unmarried
daughters in "good"--i.e., rich--monasteries. Even where
there was strict adherence to the reform which required
careful testing of candidates to affirm the presence of a
valid vocation to religious life, it was common practice
for widowed mothers to retire to the monastery of their
nun daughters, and for sisters and cousins to continue

close childhood ties by entering the same monastery. Port-
Royal, the monastery chosen for this study, was no exception. At one time there were thirteen Arnaulds in this
cloister, representing three generations.[16]

Given this societal character of the cloister, it can
be understood that communication between the women's societies within and without the monastery was close and continual. In fact, since education of young women in upper
class families was often conducted by the nuns, many of
the women of the world of the Court-*Parlement* not only had
close relatives and friends in the cloister, but had spent
time there themselves.

It is certain that Port-Royal served many purposes
for these women. Young girls were sent there to receive a
good basic education as well as religious formation and
training in the arts of home and society. Widows retired
there to spend their last days in quiet and prayer. Society women attended mass in the lovely new Paris chapel,
and chose nuns of the popular community as spiritual
guides.

Close scrutiny of the relationships of these women
reveals, however, that the flow of services between cloister and salon was by no means one way. Madame de Sablé
and Madame de Fontpertuis provide examples of two general
types of women who linked the two worlds and the way that
this mutual exchange operated. Religion formed the bond
between the worlds, the matrix of the 'sisterhood,' but the
results had repercussions on culture and society as well.

Madame de Sablé's Port-Royal Salon: A symbiotic Sisterhood

Madame de Sablé is an example of a frequent phenomenon
in seventeenth-century Paris: a member of the most elegant
and frivolous circles who had close ties with a monastery
and ended her days in retirement there.

The Necrology of Port-Royal, given to long eulogies of
its benefactors, offers an unusually short notice concerning

the death of Madame la Marquise de Sablé.[17] The cool concise notice reflects the slight strain that often surfaced
in the nuns of Port-Royal and this *précieuse*.

Madeleine de Souvré grew up in the Court. In 1610, at
the age of twelve, she was a maid of honor to Marie de
Medicis who had just become the powerful regent of France.
Three years later, only fifteen years old, she was married
to the wealthy, much older, Marquis de Sablé. By all accounts the union was an unhappy one, and Madame de Sablé
was not at all bereft when the death of her husband in 1640
left her a well-to-do widow at the age of forty-two. Following the customs of the times, she had consoled herself
with lovers. Tallement des Reaux relates that the last of
her lovers, the grandson of the vicomtesse d'Auchy, visited
her nightly disguised as a woman. The Marquise placed the
daughter of this affair at Port-Royal to hide her while her
husband was alive because, said she, "After the great disdain I had shown for my husband I did not want anyone to
be able to say I was still sleeping with him."[18]

Contemporary accounts agree that Madame de Sablé was
one of the most urbane and charming of the women who formed
the inner court of the salon of Madame de Rambouillet.
When that famous *chambre bleu* closed the Sablé salon in the
fashionable Place Royale provided a continuation where the
Marquise received the elite among the *précieux* and *précieuses*.

Like many other women of this circle, as Madame de
Sablé aged she "took up religion" and joined another group,
les dévots.[19] The earliest incident that links this *précieuse*-become-*dévote* to Port-Royal is an important one for
the history of the monastery and the Jansenist movement.
It is the story of the argument between Madame de Sablé and
her friend, the Princess de Guemené, over the conflicting
advice of their spiritual directors--a Jesuit for the Marquise and a Port-Royalist for the Princess--over whether or
not one could receive communion on the morning after a

court ball. The Jesuit said "yes" and the Port-Royalist
(Jansenist) said "no" and their published arguments cata-
pulted the dispute which had been building up between
theologians directly into the public forum. The nuns were
immediately involved since Saint-Cyran, whose doctrines on
penance and communion were articulated in Antoine Arnauld's
response to the Jesuit, *De la frequent Communion*, had been
spiritual director of the monastery for some years. La
Rochefoucauld may have been correct when he laughingly referred to Madame de Sablé and the Princess de Guemené as
as the "founders of Jansenism."[20]

The incident indicates the element of ambiguity that
remained in the relationships between Madame de Sablé and
the Port-Royalists. She often played a diplomatic role
there, and partly because she simply did not want to give
up any of her friends and she had influential friends in
the camps of both Jesuits and Jansenists.

In 1653 the Marquise began to think of finding a convent in Paris near which she could spend her retirement.
Port-Royal was chosen and, despite the cool reception of
Mère Angélique, the aging foundress of the reform at Port-
Royal,[21] Madame de Sablé soon moved into her apartment
which was built over the chapter room of the monastery. A
window from the lodging of the Marquise opened into a little balcony which overlooked the sanctuary of the convent
chapel, so that the Marquise, a hypochondriac, could assist
at Mass without danger of contamination.

Now the world of the salon was truly rubbing elbows
with the world of the cloister. Madame de Sablé made of
her apartment at Port-Royal a Hotel de Rambouillet, very
aristocratic, "un peu galant et très bel esprit, d'une
dévotion élégante et peu severe."[22] Here La Rochefoucauld
spent hours discussing the varieties of love with her, and
here many of his Maximes were composed, often in collaboration with the Marquise.[23] Pascal may have written his
Discours sur les passions de l'amour for her. It is

certain that he was a frequent visitor at the salon, and the style of the *Discours* is that of the conversations recorded there.[24]

But it is above all her relationship with the nuns that is of special interest to a study of women in the seventeenth century. Like the Duchess of Longueville, whom she is said to have gained for Port-Royal, the Marquise lent her political support to the nuns during the period of persecution. And her support was not negligible. She was on good terms with the Queen, Anne of Austria, and one of the greatest mistakes made by the opposition in 1661 was to interfere with the living arrangements of the Marquise. The civil lieutenant had orders to close off all the entries between the house of Sablé and the monastery, which made her furious. Her letter to the Queen mother gained a royal ally for the nuns.[25]

The fact that she continued to be on good terms with many of the Jesuits, who visited her salon, enabled her to negotiate for leniency for the nuns. If, in the end, she chose to remain in Paris with the nuns whom the greater part of the community considered traitors for having signed the formulary, it was a decision that was probably influenced by love of comfort and an established circle of friends more than one arrived at out of conviction and sympathy for one party over another.[26]

On the other hand, she needed the nuns, if we are to judge by the volume of her correspondence with Mère Agnès, Mère Angélique, and later Mere Angélique de Saint-Jean. Although they never supported her whims, and in fact continually counselled her to overcome her hypochondria and to temper her gourmandise, still they listened sympathetically. No doubt just the fact of living next to--really, in--a house of women dedicated to a life of prayer and penance gave the aging worldling a tangible defense against the spectre of disease and death which haunted her last years and filled her with fear and neurosis.

Symbiosis is the best name I can find for the sisterhood between Madame de Sablé and the nuns of Port-Royal.
Indeed the image of the mistletoe clinging to the oak is
an apt one to portray the little apartment of the Marquise
de Sablé propped against the monastery of Port-Royal de
Paris.

The Missions of Madame de Fontpertuis:
Extension of Port-Royal into the World

The relationship between the nuns of Port-Royal and
Madame de Fontpertuis differs significantly from that of
the monastery and Madame de Sable. The widow of the *rob-
in*[27] exemplifies another type of sisterly relationship between cloister and world: the woman who does not enter the
monastery but who endeavors to live a life patterned on
the nuns' life while remaining active in society. A true
friend over a long period of time to both the nuns and
Antoine Arnauld, Pierre Nicole and other men who formed
the "Monsieurs de Port-Royal," Madame de Fontpertuis is a
much less colorful figure than the Marquise and far less
is known of her. In fact we know her only from passing
mentions of her connections with the *monsieurs* for whom
she provided safe and hidden quarters and with whom she
cooperated to smuggle in publications from the clandestine
presses in the Netherlands during periods of persecution,[28]
and the substantial collections of letters to her from
Arnauld and Angélique de Saint-Jean. None of her letters
to the Port-Royalists have come to light, so her character
must be constructed from one side only--for instance, from
the response of Angélique de Saint-Jean to events and needs
in the life of this woman, and the kinds of favors the nun
asked of her. However, even though one-sided, the material is so considerable that valid conclusions can be drawn.
In the last years of her life Mère Angélique de Saint-Jean
wrote over three hundred and fifty letters to Madame de
Fontpertuis, and there are about two hundred letters to her
in the published Arnauld collection.[29]

Angélique Crespin du Vivier, Madame Angran de Fontpertuis, was the widow of Jacques Angran, a member of the
Parlement of Metz. Her father had held a position analy-
gous to district attorney (*président aux enquêtes*), hence
she was firmly rooted in *robe* society. Her house in the
rue Sainte-Avoye served as a hiding place for Arnauld,
Nicole and Sacy during the difficult years of 1663-1668.
Later, when Arnauld had fled to Flanders, Madame de Fontpertuis made her way through the lines of the armies to
reach him. In 1682 she paid the cost of importing
Arnauld's work into France. It is also known that she
made frequent trips to Rouen, where there were several persons involved in smuggling these works into the country.
When Arnauld died in 1694 he made Madame de Fontpertuis his
executrix, and it was she who accompanied to Port-Royal des
Champs the heart of the great doctor of Jansenism which his
friends sent from Brussels.[30] Nicole also left all his
goods to Madame de Fontpertuis, charging her to take care
of the schools he had started.[31] From the correspondence
of members of Port-Royal with Madame de Fontpertuis over a
period of more than forty years emerges the portrait of a
faithful and almost formidable friend of both the men and
the women. She put all her resources--money, influence,
energy--at their disposal. In return what she seems to
have gained was a source of inspiration and counsel for her
spiritual needs.

Both Antoine Arnauld and Mère Angélique de Saint-Jean
write letters of spiritual direction to their friend, and
caution her not to tax her somewhat fragile constitution
with too much emphasis on physical austerities. But the
letters of the nun to the woman in the world (if not of it)
are, as one might expect, much more intimate and down to
earth than those of the great polemicist. Interspersed
with serious advice on the spiritual life are chatty comments about the hand work which the nuns have done for
Madame. Angélique de Saint-Jean does not hesitate to ask

that Madame de Fontpertuis do such errands for her as pur-
chasing silk to mend a chausible and Holland felt to make
the nuns' bonnets, or finding a position for a worthy
young woman who is in great need. She comments that these
favors are much less worthy of the good woman's efforts
than the "grandes commissions"--a reference, no doubt, to
the work of Madame de Fontpertuis to shelter the male leaders from the authorities, to finance their literature and
to smuggle it into Paris.[32]

It is also evident that Madame de Fontpertuis often
extended the work of the abbess into the secular world
which Mère Angélique de Saint-Jean could not enter. Several letters concern young women who entered the novitiate
of Port-Royal but were found unsuited for life in the monastery. Sometimes Madame de Fontpertuis is asked to act as
intermediary with the Bishop of Chalons in order to gain
acceptance for the young woman in the secular community established by Bishop Vialart, the *régentes de Chalons*.[33] In
other cases, the abbess expresses hope that her friend can
find respectable work in the home of other women friends for
the girl.[34] Here we recognize a very different kind of
sisterhood, one in which there is true mutuality.

Summary

The relationship of a woman like Madame de Fontpertuis with Port-Royal provides an interesting contrast to
that of a woman like Madame de Sablé. Through the salon
of the latter the religious ideals of Port-Royal penetrated
the literary circles of seventeenth century Paris. The
personal relationship of the Marquise and the nuns was ambiguous. Woman to woman the nuns sympathized with the
moody hypochondriac, and Mère Angélique did not hesitate to
mention her own migraine headaches. At the same time,
there was a continual effort on the part of the nuns to
convert their odd semi-inhabitant from the liaisons she
insisted on maintaining with the "enemy" to total adherence
to the circle of *les amis de Saint Augustine*, as the Jansenists preferred to be called.

Madame de Fontpertuis, by contrast, was a kind of extension of the sisterhood of the nuns into the world. She functioned as a sort of external sister whose range was not just to the bakery around the corner, but extended across the borders of cities and countries. She did all she could to live the life of a nun in the world, and her devotion to the community continued through good times and bad. Especially in the times of persecution she remained faithful at great personal risk.

Madame de Sablé lent her support to the nuns in the early days of the persecution, it is true. But it must be recognized that the persecution of Port-Royal in 1664 was a *cause célèbre* in Paris and the cream of the salon circle found it fashionable to be involved in the struggle of the nuns. After 1669, however, when the recalcitrant nuns in the country monastery were released from their interdict (due in large part to the intercession of the powerful Duchess of Longueville), the breach between this group and the few who had signed and remained in Paris was definitive. The Duchess of Longueville followed the controversial nuns and built a small chateau near the country monastery. Madame de Sablé did not imitate her friend. In the end she preferred her comfort to heroic defense of ideologies, and she remained in her Paris abode.

Madame de Fontpertuis was far less flamboyant than the Marquise and the Duchess. She never lived in or near the monastery. Yet in spirit she was much more a sister. Her loyalty to the original group, Port-Royal des Champs, never waivered. Up to and beyond the destruction of the monastery the members of that tragic group wrote to her as to one of their own.

Such relationships are not rare in seventeenth century Paris. Most of the women of the salon maintained more or less close ties with the cloister. Further examination will reveal the extent to which this bond between cloister and salon strengthened the position of the women, and contributed culturally, religiously and intellectually to the formation of modern French society. This, of course, will raise the question of how significant religion, per se, was in this development. At least it can be said that interest in religious reform provided a link--whether as conversational gambit or field of active dedication-- which connected cloister and salon and contributed to the formation of this dynamic sisterhood.

NOTES

[*]This article has appeared in the *Ohio Journal of Religious Studies* (Spring 1976).

[1]*Mon dieu faites de moi un honnête homme et n'en faites jamais une honnête femme.*

[2]*Hélas! c'est de quoi je suis parfaitement convaincue, et ce qui me fait admirer qu'on fasse si inutilement de si chères offres, puisqu'on vend sa liberté et les droits de la verité sans en rien attendre.*

[3]*Lettres de la Mère Angélique de Saint Jean.* Unpublished manuscript edited by Rachel Gillet. Bibliothèque de la Societé de Port-Royal, MS. Let. 358-361, No. CLIX (May, 1668) to M. Hamon. M. Hamon was the remarkable physician who, as a layman, was free to minister to the nuns when their priest-directors were prohibited from entering the monastery.

[4]*Mademoiselle Libertine* (Boston: Houghton Mifflin, 1970). A substantial bibliography of French sources and biographies is included.

[5](New York: John Wiley & Sons, 1968) 297-98.

[6]I refer here to a remark by Pierre Goubert, a leading French historian and pioneer in the *Annalistes* school, about theses on which students of his working. For his commentary on the school and a list of some of its studies see P. Goubert, *Louis XIV and Twenty Million Frenchmen* (New York: Pantheon Books, 1970) 329-31.

[7]See, for example, the *Introduction* of Georges Mongrédien to *Les Précieux et les Précieuses* (Paris: Mercure de France, 1963) 16-18; also the selections from Mlle de Scudéry and Abbé de Pure in the same work.

[8]For satyrical, allegorical descriptions of the society there are *Le Grand Cyrus* of Mlle de Scudéry or *La Relation de l'isle imaginaire et l'Histoire de la Princesses de Paphlagonie* of the Duchesse de Montpensier, "la grande Mademoiselle." Of great literary quality, as well as value for a study of mores of the society are the novels of Mme de La Fayette. Her *Princesse de Clèves* is significant for its rejection of the courtly love ideal in favor of the moral and spiritual love that was a frequent subject of discussion in the salon of Mme de Sablé.

[9]For an interesting discussion of this see René

Jasinski, *Histoire de la Littérature Française* (Paris: Nizet, 1965) I:238; Roger Lathuillère, *La Préciosité: Etude Historique et Linguistique* (Geneva: Droz, 1966) 637; Gédéon Tallemant des Reaux, *Les Historiettes*, ed. A. Adam (Paris: Gallimard, 1960-61) I:520, n. 1.

[10]*La plus grande des douceurs de notre France est celle de la liberté des femmes, et elle est si grande dans tout le royaume que les maris y sont presque sans pouvoir, et que les femmes y sont les souveraines,* is only one expression of this theme. Abbe de Pure, *La Prétieuse /sic/* (Paris: Droz, 1938) I:114.

[11]See the useful discussion of the role of women in Lathuillère, pp. 652-65.

[12](Cambridge, MA: Harvard University, 1941).

[13]It is true, as Mr. Keating points out, that there were medieval obstacles to free social intercourse between men and women which persisted well into the sixteenth century: "Women had to be freed from two sorts of bondage: that of the chivalric ideal which isolated them from an active share in social responsibilites, and that of the misogynistic philosophy found in the *Roman de la Rose* and similar works" (ibid., p. 7).

[14]This brief resume owes much to Lathuillère and G. Mongrédien, *La Vie Littéraire au XVIIe Siecle* (Paris: Tallandier, 1947). Mongrédien has provocative comments on the feminism of, for example, Abbé de Pure and Mlle de Scudéry.

[15]The finest study of this reform in religious orders is to be found in Louis Cognet, *La Spiritualité Moderne* (Paris: Aubier, 1966). The second part, *La Prépondérance Française* is indispensable for an understanding of the Counter-Reformation spirituality in France. Unfortunately, the book is not available in English translation.

[16]Lucien Goldmann bases his brilliant but controversial thesis, *Le Dieu Caché* (Paris, 1956) about Port-Royal, for which he uses marxist economic theory, on the fact that a large majority of member of the community of hermits, (including Pascal) formed around the monastery of Port-Royal in 1638 came from "robe families." A study of the family ties and social background of the members of the monastery would be fruitful, and would probably reveal that those nuns who came from lower classes became extern (lay) sisters, while the choir nuns were drawn from the upper classes.

[17]A translation would be: "This day [16 January 1678] marks the death of Dame Madeleine de Souvré, widow of

Messire Philippe de Laval, Marquis de Sablé, a very special friend and benefactress of our Paris house, where she
had a lodging built which is at the end of the choir, of
which the chapter room forms a part. In this apartment
she finished her days at the age of seventy-nine years.
She was buried in the cemetery of the parish of Saint-
Jacques-du-haut-pas, as her humility had prompted her to
arrange in her will." *Necrologe de L'Abbaïe de Nostre
Dame de Port Roïal des Champs, Ordre de Cisteaux, Institut
du Saint-Sacrement* (Amsterdam: chez Nicolas Potgieter Libraire, 1723) 34.

[18]"*...je ne voulois pas...apres le grand mépris je
tesmoignois avoir pour mon mari, qo'on me pust dire que
je couchois encore avec lui.*" Tallemant des Reaux, *Historiettes*, 3rd ed. (Paris: J. Techener Libraire, 1854) III:
130, n. 1.

[19]This pattern in the lives of women in Parisian society reflected the evolution of culture in the seventeenth
century. The relaxed mores of the renaissance courts of
Francis I and Henry IV had been criticized and refashioned
in the salons of women like Mme de Rambouillet. New
ideals, new moral patterns were emerging. Right in the
court of Louis XIV a remarkable transition occurs between
the days when the young monarch publically flaunted a
queen and two mistresses before the court, and the era
when his secret marriage to Madame de Maintenon formed
Louis into a respectable "business man" of a king.

[20]This incident is recounted in all histories of
Arnauld and/or Port-Royal. For the account in the major
history of Sainte-Beuve see *Port-Royal* (Paris: Editions
Gallimard, 1953) I:1634.

[21]See the letters of Mère Angélique to Mme de Sablé
in Edouard de Barthélemy, *Les Amis de la Marquise de Sablé*
(Paris: E. Dentu, 1865) pp. 110-11. This work includes a
good introduction, "De la Societé honnête aux XVIIe siècle"
which locates Mme de Sablé in these circles.

[22]"Le Salon de la Marquise de Sablé" in (Marie) Gougy-
Francoise, *Les Grandes Salons Féminins* (Paris: Debresse,
1965) 19-22. See also the excellent study by N. Ivanoff,
La Marquise de Sablé et son salon (Paris: Presses Moderne,
1922).

[23]Mme de Sablé's *Maximes et pensees diverses* (Paris:
S. Mabre, Cramoisy, 1678) are very similar in style and
content to La Rochefoucauld's and give witness to their
collaboration.

[24]See discussion of this in Victor Cousin, *Madame de
Sablé* (Paris: Didier, 1854) 93-99.

[25] Sainte-Beuve, II:627-28; Ivanoff, pp. 69-72.

[26] Ivanoff, p. 71

[27] A member of the '*Noblesse de robe*,' probably an attorney.

[28] For instance, F. Ravaisson, *Archives de la Bastille. Documents inédit recueillis et publiés par François Ravaisson* (Paris: A Durand & Pédone-Lauriel, 1876) VIII:41, 43-44, 56. These records of La Reynie concern the seizure of contraband books.

[29] The letters of Angélique de Saint-Jean are in the manuscript described in note 3 above. Arnauld's are published in *Oeuvres de Messire Antoine Arnauld* (Paris [Lausanne], 1775).

[30] *Dictionnaire de Biographie Française* (Paris: Letouzey et Ané, 1936) II: cols. 1233-34.

[31] Léon Séché, *Les Derniers Jansénistes* (Paris: Didier, 1891) I:102.

[32] *Lettres*, CCXCVI (April, 1675).

[33] This was a remarkable experiment for its time. The young women lived a very austere life, but took no vows and did not live in a cloister. They were directly responsible to the bishop alone. Their teaching to young women, done mainly in the homes, was primarily religious doctrine in the Jansenist tradition. For a description of a similar group in Alet founded by Bishop Pavillon, see Rene Taveneaux, *La Vie Quotidienne des Jansenistes* (Paris: Hachette, 1973) 77-79.

[34] *Lettres*, CCLXXXV (January 1675); CCVIII (August 1675) and others.

III. OUR FOREMOTHERS (AND FOREFATHERS) REVISITED:
Rereading the Biblical Narrative

WHO WAS REBEKAH?
"On Me Be the Curse, My Son!"

Christine Garside Allen
Concordia University

I. Comments on Methodology

The opportunity to enter into the mystery of Old Testament interpretation is a very welcome one. Like Jacob one is tempted to be afraid and say: "This is nothing less than a house of God this is the gate of heaven!" (Gen 28: 17). I would like to enter this house; but I shall enter from a door which has never been used before.

Hermeneutics of the Old Testament has passed through many different stages. Some interpreters have concentrated on the question: Who is or are the writers of the texts? With the help of careful examination of writing style and the use of computer programming, it has been possible to delineate four different groups of writers of Genesis delineated by the letters 'L', 'P', 'J', and 'E'.[1] This means that if one is attempting to uncover the original meaning of the text which records the story of Rebekah (Genesis 23-24), extensive historical data must be brought to bear upon the interpretation. For each line of the text one examines, a judgment must be made as to its source, context, and purpose. In this process some rather startling results occur. For example, Prof. Otto Eissfeldt claims that the two links between Abraham, Issac and Jacob, namely the wooing of Rebekah and the stolen blessing, are later additions to the text. They are "representations of the post-Mosiac people of Israel projected back into the pre-Mosiac age."[2] The purpose of this addition he claims was to develop firmly a patriarchal history. "For here the figures of the patriarchs, at first quite independent of one another are being put into family relationships."[3]

The reason this conclusion is startling at least for

this author is that I want to discuss the role of Rebekah
in Genesis specifically in reference to the extraordinary
function she plays as mediator between Abraham and Jacob.
It is my thesis that on the level of spiritual call she,
more than Issac, can be viewed as handmaiden, vessel,
prophet, sacrifical victim, suffering servant,--in short,
as the point where God's will became known on earth at a
certain crucial time in salvation history.

Is it possible for both Prof. Eissfeldt's thesis and
my own to be correct, or does the acceptance of one necessarily exclude the other? The answer to this question entails a brief look at what criteria one could use to determine the *truth* of the conflicting theses. The most obvious way would be to attempt to discover the *facts* which
would enable us to test the *correspondence* of each thesis.
And it is enjoyable to think ourselves into heaven searching out Rebekah and asking her: "Were you the sister of
Laban? Did you deceive Isaac: Why:" Etc. Unfortunately,
any such apodictic information is not immediately available. There are no facts within our grasp. There is,
however, a book.

One might ask, however, how can this book, the nature
of which is in question, *itself* be the criteria for affirming or denying an interpretation? And it is tempting at
this point to shift to a very loose theory of *coherence* to
account for the apparent conflicts in the two proposed
theories of interpretation. In this way, any theory which
holds together is as true as any other. There is however,
a certain relativity in this approach which is repugnant to
the scholar's heart. Furthermore, when *coherence* gets
stretched as a criterion, it represses innovation. Prof.
Eissfeldt's thesis, that Rebekah did not form a material
link between Abraham and Jacob, and my thesis, that she
forms a spiritual link, are in opposition to the main core
of Old Testament research.

Perhaps there is a solution by adopting what Wittgenstein describes in his later works as a *perspectival* approach to the text.[4] In this way the text serves as a
point where the interpretation begins and ends. One is
not free simply to develop just any theory at all about
the text without regard to the words and phrases stated
there, as one could if coherence were the only criterion.
On the other hand, a strict correspondence to a single interpretation is avoided. This means that there are many
possible perspectives from which a single text may be examined. In this way, a statement which is true within one
perspective might be considered false or irrelevant within
another. For example, it may very well be that Rebekah is
not the mother of the man who married someone called Rachel
and fathered Joseph, that Prof. Eissfeldt is correct historically that this is a later addition to the text. And
I am certainly not competent to judge the truth or falsity
of his claim within his framework of hermeneutics. And
yet, if we follow his suggestion we may think about the
role of God in creating salvation history, remembering that
we are not examining an ordinary book, but rather a sacred
one. Here we might allow ourselves to question why it
seemed important at a particular time in history to link
Abraham, Issac, and Jacob together. Why does God *want* us
to think of them as joined? It is at this point that I
would like to make a final point about methodology of interpretation. In addition to recognizing that one always
approaches a text from a particular perspective, it should
be made manifestly clear to the reader what exactly this
perspective is. When I mentioned God in the above paragraph it was implicit in my interpretation that a religious
perspective was being employed. I could have given a po-
litical-historical answer as well, by stating that the
Israelites wanted to recreate their roots in a national
identity. And probably there is some truth in this. What
interests me, however, in the story of Rebekah is not

primarily the question of the authenticity of her material
link between the patriarchs, or her role in the social
history of the Israelites. Rather, I am concerned to extract from her life a religious model which might play a
role in contemporary woman's spiritual quest. In doing
this I follow the suggestion of Prof. Martin Buss:

> One can argue that socio-psychological analysis--
> whether formal or informal--is needed or at least
> helpful to form a bridge from the text to the hearer
> and that it is a major task of the scholar to provide
> one. The aim of such a study would not be primarily
> to establish the original sense in a positivistic
> manner(...), but to open the human meaning of the
> text.[5]

This means that the insights of technical research in archaeology, philology, textual, literary, and form criticism
which have dominated hermeneutics this century must be
placed in a certain human and religious context.[6]

Another way to approach textual interpretation is to
consider who is the reader. It is helpful to note in passing that an interpreter is above all a reader. Attempts to
classify readers have used the division: Hebrew, Protestant,
and Catholic. Location in history, age, national identity,
cultural heritage, vocations, and of course sex also contribute to the perspective from which the reader comes to
the text. One might call these the threads of the perspectival pattern. At one point the thread of national identity may be predominant, and at another time the thread of
religious affiliation, and still another the thread of age.
This means that what a young person chooses to extract and
emphasize from a text could differ significantly from what
an older person may choose. Perhaps one of the most striking examples of this is the extraordinarily rich diversity
of interpretations of the *Song of Songs*.

It is interesting to speculate about the reasons the
reader or interpreter had for emphasizing a particular aspect of a passage. And we have just survived a period of

extreme Freudian auto-biographical explanation which often
served more to prove the total irrelevance of an interpretation than to make us sensitive to the perspective of the
interpreter. An obvious example of this sort of critique
is the claim that *all* Kierkegaard meant to do in *Fear and
Trembling* was to justify his refusal to marry Regina. The
teleological suspension of the ethical that Abraham was
called to make in his willingness to sacrifice Issac becomes merely a facade for Kierkegaard's inability to make
a marriage commitment. The superficial nature of such
psychoanalytic critiques tend to make people go to the
opposite extreme and claim that the social, psychological,
and religious context of the interpreter does not matter
at all. This, of course, takes us away from the perspectival thread pattern which appears to me to be the most
fruitful image to use in approaching hermenutics.

In this paper, I want to consider the thread of sex
identity as a determining factor in the perspective of the
reader, and if that reader is a writer as well, of interpretation. In *The Interpreters Bible* Robert Grant gives
the following description of the ancient period of interpretation:

> (In the ancient period) some of these methods of
> interpretation were traditional in the Judaism out
> of which Christianity arose; others were gifts of
> the Hellenistic schools; and others were standards
> of interpretation ultimately developed sithin the
> Church itself.[7]

It goes without saying that all these interpreters were
men. In the medieval period, according to John McNeill,
an interest developed in the moral sense of the Bible, conflicts arose between those who were interested in the Bible
as allegory and those who viewed it as history; new forms
of criticism emerged with Luther and Calvin.[8] It was also
the case that during the medieval period, women entered the
world of hermeneutics. St. Francis de Sales expresses this
fact in the following way:

> That we may realize that such writing issues with
> better results from the devotion of lovers than
> from the learning of scholars, the Holy Spirit
> has willed that many women should work wonders in
> it. Who has ever expressed the heavenly affec-
> tions of sacred love better than St. Catherine of
> Genoa, St. Angela of Foligno, St. Catherine of
> Siena, or St. Mechtilde?[9]

And he mentions as well the "most learned ignorance" of
the Blessed Teresa of Jesus who later was proclaimed Doctor of the Church.[10] The technique of interpretation of
these women consisted in mediation on the gospel and silent
prayer. In each case they attempted to uncover the meaning
of the passage in terms of the nature of God and of their
own vocation to sanctity.

In the modern period, women have begun to receive the
same formal education as men. It is not surprising then,
that they are entering the field of hermeneutics using the
same tools of interpretation as their male colleagues. The
question remains as to whether threads of sexual identity
will show in the pattern they weave. One rather marvelous
example of a vivid female thread is found in Cady Stanton's
book, *The (Original) Feminist Attack of the Bible*:

> It was certainly a good test of Rebekah's patience
> and humility to draw water for an hour, with a
> dozen men looking on at their ease, and none of-
> fering help. The Rebekah's of 1895 would have
> promptly summoned the spectators to share their
> labors, even at the risk of sacrificing a desir-
> able matrimonial alliance. The virtue of self-
> sacrifice has its wise limitations. Though it
> is most commendable to serve our fellow-beings,
> yet woman's first duty is to herself, to develop
> all her own powers and possibilities, that she
> may better guide and serve the next generation.[11]

Mrs. Stanton wrote her book first of all to win women to
the cause of sufferage, and as will be seen later on, this
political thread is interwoven with other threads of protestant ethical values and white racial values. She turned
to the Bible not to bring women closer to God but to break
the power of the Bible on their consciousness.

Another woman, Sister Emma Thérèse Healy, seeking to
explain and draw readers to the state of perpetual virginity, focuses primarily on Rebekah before the marriage.
"And in truth, Mary was, like Rebekah, an exceeding comely
maid, and a most beautiful virgin, and not known to man."[12]
And in the classic *All the Women of the Bible* we find a
very sympathetic interpretation of Rebekah "No young woman
in the Bible is so appealing." The author Edith Deen even
considers the religious dimension of her personality. However, her main tendency is to classify the women in terms
of the men who are closest to them. She divides the women
of the Bible into daughters, wives, mothers, widows and
other unnamed women. Of Rebekah herself she states: "Does
she not typify the mother down the ages who, weak in faith,
imagines herself to be carrying out the will of God?"[13]

Finally in contemporary women's writing we can deci-
pher general trends. The first is that of Mary Daly which
calls for a leap out of tradition and into a new form of
religion.[14] Unlike Lot's wife, she does not look back.
For her, there is nothing to be gained by re-examining
Rebekah. The other approach is seen in Rosemary Ruether's
collection of essays entitled *Religion and Sexism*. In this
book careful scholarship is combined with a feminist consciousness.

> "By looking back at these images, by establishing
> an autonomous subjectivity and standpoint from
> which to study, evaluate and judge these images,
> women today also shatter this mirror and, with it,
> shatter their own false mirror role. They estab-
> lish the basis for a new humanity beyond patriar-
> chy which must be based on dialogue and recipro-
> cal consciousness."[15]

Like Stanton, she is interested in studying tradition in
order to break out of it.

It seems to me that there is another approach one
might presently take which does not replace either of the
other two as worthy and valid experiments in research, but

which stands beside them as an authentic alternative.
This approach calls one back into the Bible as a sacred
book; it demands a reinterpretation and re-evaluation in
depth of the mysteries contained there. On the most obvious level, it seeks to uncover models for women and a
critical evaluation of the lives of those we find reported.
And there are some very interesting figures who have been
hidden in the background such as Rebekah, Esther, Judith,
the bride of the Song of Songs, Sophia, and so on. We can
learn from these female figures about sanctity. Secondly,
it involves uncovering the weak figures of women, such as
Sarah or Rachel, and examining how we can learn from their
lack of sanctity. Thirdly, it can include a symbolic reversal of some of the male models in specific reference to
what women can learn from their life struggles. Jonas,
Moses, and Isaiah come readily to mind. The hidden premise
of this approach to women's identity is that if God has
created women and men in His own image, then the sacred
work which records the slow painful revelation of His incarnation and call to salvation will contain within it
much that speaks to women who are on the spiritual quest.

II. Some Traditional Interpretations of Rebekah

Most interpreters of Genesis have considered Sarah,
Rebekah, and Rachel to be minor figures in the revelation
of God's call to Abraham, Isaac, and Jacob. And it is perhaps due to the fact that so few women have turned their
mind to Old Testament research that this view has been
maintained so consistently. For the most part, men were
just not interested in what women were doing. I would
like to consider the possibility that Rebekah more than
Isaac deserves recognition as the crucial link between
Abraham and Jacob as well as being an extraordinarily profound person in her own right. It is important to note
that I put forth this interpretation as a possbility, not

as an established fact. It is a perspective for edifica-
tion, one of many possible ways to think about Genesis,
which does touch down at several points in the text, but
also calls for a stretching of the imagination. The precedent I draw upon for this type of exploration is that
established by Kierkegaard's exegesis of Abraham in *Fear
and Trembling*.

The possibility I am exploring is that Rebekah consistently responded to God's commands in order that His
will might be accomplished. She responded to His call
(Gen 24:15-47), she willingly left her family to follow
her vocation (Gen 24:58), she immediately recognized Isaac
(Gen 24:64), she suffered from barrenness and then from a
painful pregnancy for which she sought God's guidance
(Gen 25:20-23), she allowed herself to pass as Isaac's sister to protect his life (Gen 26:5-16), she aided the plan
to secure the blessing for Jacob, God's chosen one (Gen 27:
7-10), she offered herself in reparation if the plan
failed (Gen 27:13), she protected Jacob from death and arranged for him to be sent to her brother (Gen 27:43-46),
and finally she brought about a reconciliation between the
members of her family.

An exegesis of Rebekah demands a close look at the
spiritual quality of her husband. We are told twice that
Isaac is granted God's protection because of *Abraham's*
obedience (Gen 26:3). There is no pattern of a direct
call, test, and eventual works of merit in Isaac's life.
As A. S. Herbert expresses it: "Isaac is in fact little
more than the one who transmits the blessing from Abraham
to Jacob."[16] And even stronger, it appears that Isaac had
no recognition whatsoever of the potential in Jacob for
becoming one of God's extraordinary servants and our first
recorded mystic. We are told: "Isaac preferred Esau, for
he had a taste for wild game; but Rebekah preferred Jacob"
(Gen 25:28). It may very well be that God had to use
Rebekah to overcome Issac's blindness and lack of spiritual depth.

The strongest impediment in the way of my interpretation is the commonly held belief that Rebekah started off
well, but ended up badly. The stumbling block is her in-
tentional deceit of Isaac in convincing Jacob to steal the
blessing by disguising himself as Esau. This had been described by different interpreters as follows:

> By S. R. Driver:
>
> The narrative tells how, instigated by his ambi-
> tious and designing mother, Jacob deceives his
> aged father, and wrests from his brother his
> father's blessing. That the action of Rebekah
> and Jacob was utterly discredible and indefen-
> sible, is of course obvious.[17]

By Walter Bovie in the text of the *Interpreter's
Bible*:

> (Rebekah's) love for Jacob was so fiercely jeal-
> ous that it broke loose from any larger loyalty.
> As between her twin sons, she wanted Jacob to
> have the best of everything, no matter how he
> got it; and to that end she would not scruple
> at trickery and unfairness both towards her
> husband and her son Esau. There was something
> of the tigress in Rebekah, instinctively pro-
> tecting the cub that by physical comparison
> was inferior.

He also compares her to Jezebel and Lady Macbeth in:

> "a study of character..., and of the way in
> which an emotion essentially beautiful may be-
> come perverted. It is instinctive and right
> that a woman should love passionately. But the
> greatest love must always be subject to a
> greater loyalty: loyalty to truth, to honour,
> to the relationship of life to God."[18]

It does not occur to Prof. Bovie that it might be precisely
due to Rebekah's love for God that she is asked to 'suspend the ethical' and deceive Isaac. Or rather, it does
occur to him, but he dismisses the thought in the following
way: "As a strange example of the way in which lofty ideas
may be made a motive for low acts, it may be that Rebekah
told herself she was carrying out the will of God. Had
not the divine voice said to her, before Esau and Jacob
were born, that the elder shall serve the younger?"[19]

Perhaps the most clear comment comes from A. S.
Herbert:

> Jacob's fraudulent acquisition of the Blessing...
> is one of the most unpleasant stories of the
> book of Genesis....Again, the conduct of Rebekah
> was such as to arouse the most vigorous condemna-
> tion in ancient Israel. For not only did she in-
> stigate this deception; she was, by her conduct,
> acting against her husband and so destroying the
> unity of the family.[20]

Could it be, one might ask, that the most serious error
that Rebekah committed in the mind of most male interpreters was to deceive her husband? Was Abraham held responsible for deceiving his wife and son? It is tempting to
answer in the affirmative, and some of the statements of
Clara Bewick Colby, coauthor of *The Original Feminist
Attack*, would tend to support this on the Bible:

> With all Rebekah's faults she seems to have had
> things her own way and therefore she did not set
> any marked example of wifely submission for women
> of today to follow. Her great error was deceiv-
> ing her husband to carry her point and this is
> always the result where woman is deprived in any
> degree of personal freedom unless she has attained
> high moral development.[21]

It is clear that in all these commentaries, moral or ethical laws and in particular the injunction to tell the
truth, carry more weight than the possibility that God
might from time to time call someone out of the law. Elizabeth Cady Stanton leaves no doubt on this question for
she discussed the "supreme wickedness of Rebekah in deceiving Isaac, defrauding Esau, and undermining the moral sense
of the son she loved."[22] She states further:

> It is a pitiful tale of greed and deception.
> Alas! where can a child look for lessons in
> truth, honour, and generosity, when the mother
> they naturally trust, sets at defiance every
> principle of justice and mercy to secure some
> worldly advantage.[23]

In studying these various commentaries, one must separate
several factors. The first is the identification of the

good with ethical values. In particular, in the story of
Rebekah the fact that she deceived Isaac seems to be held
by everyone to be bad or unethical. It is interesting
that even for the feminist Ms. Stanton this ethical, and
in her case Protestant, thread dominates her interpretation
of Rebekah's action as much as her white racist attitudes
unexpectedly rise during the suffrage movement when black
men are given the vote before white women.[24] The independence of Rebekah as a woman, admirable in itself, is destroyed when she deceives her husband "to secure some
worldly advantage."

The second factor that must be separated out of the
commentaries is the interconnection between the supposed
psychological and social aims of Rebekah and the transcendent plans of God. We find that Rebekah acted out of
"fiercely jealous love," like a "tigress protecting her
cub," "passionately perverted love," "from low moral development," "supreme wickedness," "greed" and so on. The implication here is that Rebekah's basic personality was unethical, but that God used this immorality for a higher
purpose. S. R. Driver summarizes this attitude in the
following way: "The writer weaves delicately into his narrative a religious motive; he notices, as he goes along,
the providence of God, as *over-ruling* the chief actors in
the transaction."[25]

This attitude is re-inforced even more by the interpretations of the response of Rebekah to Abraham's servant
as the well. Driver states that Rebekah "quickly, though
unconsciously, announces herself as his master's niece."[26]
And A. S. Herbert confirms the same interpretation: "The
truth of the story lies in the fact that God guides even
when men are *quite unaware* of his guidance."[27] It appears
that where the action is neutral or positive, God unconsciously controls the people, but where it is negative then
God overrules their conscious behavior. Why does it not
occur to most interpreters that it is possible that God

might have prompted Rebekah in a conscious way before both
the event at the well and the securing of the blessing, so
that she knew in advance how to respond? Herbert opens
the door a little to this possibility in interpreting her
reaction when the servant wants to depart immediately:"

> The family is unwilling, but Rebekah consents.
> Perhaps the suggestion is intended that she,
> already in intention and by law part of Abraham's
> family, has become sensitive to the God of Abraham.[28]

However, the door is shut when he considers the deception
of Isaac. "However *unworthy her purpose*, one cannot but
admire the skill and devotion with which Rebekah plans on
behalf of her favorite."[29]

Perhaps if we approach the question in another way
Rebekah's situation might become clarified. What is it
about the blessing that is so important that centuries of
condemnation should be passed onto this woman for helping
her younger son to receive the blessing in the place of
the elder? The actual blessing is an follows:

> May God give you dew from heaven, and the richness
> of the earth, abundance of grain and wine! May
> nations serve you and peoples bow down before
> you! Be master of your brothers; may the sons of
> your mother bow down before you! Cursed be he
> who curses you; blessed be he who blesses you!
> (Gen 27:28-9)

The key is the phrase "Be master of your brothers." By
the blessing the younger is placed in authority over the
elder. According to Cuthbert Simpson's notes in the
Interpreter's Bible, the fact that Esau had already sold
his birthright to Jacob for a bowl of lentil soup already
ensured Jacob's position as head of the family and a
double share of the inheritance.[30] The question then
arises as to why the Blessing had to be secured at all.
Cuthbert makes the interesting observation that the passage Gen 27:1-40 was a later insertion of J and E into the
original text. "This suggests that by E's time the tale
had come to be regarded as morally objectionable, so an

attempt was made to lessen the embarrassment it caused by shifting the blame from Jacob to Rebekah, who being a woman, might be expected to act in a questionable manner, and whose reputation, for the same reason, was of less concern to her descendents."[31]

There are two premises in this interpretation which need some correction; first that women are expected to act in a questionable manner and second that their reputation is of less concern to their descendents. I think it is clear that women's behavior is generally understood by women and that at last women are beginning to take a genuine interest in the reputations of their female ancestors. So while one might appreciate the attempt to explain the post-mosiac linking of what are now considered to be unconnected patriarchal studies of Abraham and Jacob by the invention of Rebekah as a woman in her own right, it may very well be that the time has come for a fresh look at what has for so long been considered 'questionable behavior.' In short, what were Rebekah's alternatives?

III. A New Approach to Rebekah

Consider then the following proposal: that Rebekah throughout her life gave evidence of sanctity in that she responded immediately to God's call several times, she was long suffering, and she was exceedingly generous in offering herself and even her life when necessary. She was the first woman in sacred history to respond fully to God's designs. Neither Sarah who laughed at the angel's prophecy and was driven by jealousy, nor Rachel who stole her father's household gods gave evidence of sanctity. Not until the books of Ruth, Esther and Judith do we again have such fully developed and admirable female saints.

In order to make this proposal convincing it is necessary to show that Rebekah's life consistently demonstrates the qualities of sanctity: a total response to a call from God, long suffering and sacrifice, and willingness to go beyond the expected to fulfill the Divine will. Many

Christian commentaries interpret figures of the Old Testament in terms of the degree to which they prefigure the life of Christ. Rebekah also contains many aspects which can be interpreted by later insights into the Divine plan. However, it is important to note that she can be considered in her own right as a potential saint without seeing her primary importance through Christian 'spectacles.' For this reason, I will include any comments on prefiguration in the footnotes for those who might be interested in this other interpretation.

The first words we have of Rebekah are "Drink, my Lord" (Gen 24:15). The servant of Abraham has reached the end of his search for a bride for Isaac. He had been bound by oath to find someone to be a mother to the chosen people. The servant had asked her for a "little water" from her pitcher and she had responded immediately and generously. Not only did she offer water to Abraham's servant but she added "I will draw water for your camels, too, until they have had enough" (Gen 24:20). She who is destined to bear the seed of Israel in her womb offers water from her pitcher to servants and animals. Her work is to continue to offer this source of life not until *she* is tired but until "*they* have had enough." Her will is to be of service to the creatures of God.[1']

The next words she speaks are to identify herself and to offer the hospitality of her home to the strangers. "I am the daughter of Bethuel, the son whom Milcah bore to Nabor....We have plenty of straw and fodder, and room to lodge" (Gen 24:25-6)[2'] The true purpose of this meeting is soon revealed, and Rebekah is seen to be the woman God has chosen for Isaac. The fact that she was chosen by divine guidance is emphasized several times in the text. Had not Abraham said: "*He* will now send his angel ahead of you, so that you may choose a wife for my son there" (Gen 24:7). The servant as well prayed to God for a sign so that "she (will) be the one *you* have chosen for your

servant Isaac" (Gen 24:14). The sign, the generous offering of water, was given. While Rebekah's response is
usually attributed to her natural qualities of spontaneity
and generosity, it could easily have been the result of a
private inspiration in prayer. God might have revealed to
her sometime before that she would be asked to leave her
home and follow him into the desert. He could easily have
indicated to her the way to recognize the servant who would
lead her to the fulfillment of her vocation. He would be
the one, a stranger, who asked her for a "little water."
If God had asked her whether she would accept His call at
that earlier time, then He could just as easily indicated
to her the sign she was to give to the servant.[3'] It is
important to consider the possibility of Rebekah's own inner sense of the religious significance of the event.

The fact that Rebekah is considered to be a free person is recognized both by Abraham and by her family. The
freedom does not extend to the marriage contract itself,
but to the decision to leave her family and follow Abraham
into the desert. As Kierkegaard interprets this symbol,
it is the decision to leave the understanding behind and to
enter the nomadic life of faith.[4'] Abraham had said: "If
the woman does not want to come with you, you will be free
from this oath of mine" (Gen 24:8). Abraham believed the
offer would be accepted, for he continued to hold fast to
the divine promise. Since the faith of the servant was not
as strong, Abraham gave him peace of mind by releasing him
from the obligation if the woman should refuse to come.
Rebekah's family recognized the sacredness of the marriage
offer. "Let her become the wife of your master's son, as
Yahweh has decreed" (Gen 24:52). They did not give Rebekah
the freedom to decide whether to marry Isaac. They did,
however, allow her to decide when she was willing to go.
Her family wanted her to stay for a while, but the servant
was anxious to depart immediately, perhaps fearing the
death of his master. "They called Rebekah and asked her,

'Do you want to leave with this man?' 'I do,' she replied"
(Gen 24:58). Rebekah not only accepted the call into the
desert, but she accepted it immediately. In this act she
chose God and her new family over her natural relatives.[5']
The description in the narrative continues quite simply.
After the blessing "Rebekah and her servants stood up,
mounted the camels, and followed the man" (Gen 24:61).

While in the Old Testament the saints most often were
taught directly by the spirit of God or by His angels,
sometimes spiritual direction came from the hands of other
human beings. It is interesting to speculate about Rebekah's situation and in particular about how she developed
religiously. It is possible that both the servant during
the long pilgrimage through the desert and later Abraham
himself spoke with Rebekah about the call and test and
promise that the first Patriarch received from God. Particularly, we can imagine the interest that Rebekah had in
the extraordinary acts that God sometimes asks people to
do. Had He not asked Abraham to murder his son? And even
more, had Abraham not believed it better to keep this information from Sarah and from Isaac until after the divine
plan was completed? Perhaps Rebekah kept these thoughts
to herself as she listened to the teachings of Abraham.[6']

We know that she did not learn from Sarah, for we are
told that when Isaac heard how Rebekah had been chosen, he
made love to her and was consoled for the loss of his mother. This means that Rebekah was the most important woman
in the household. Abraham might have recognized her potential for sanctity and taken time after the evening meal to
teach her the secrets of God. In any event, Rebekah
seemed to have a deep awareness of her calling. She recognized Isaac immediately: "And Rebekah looked up and saw
Isaac. She jumped down from her camel, and asked the servant, 'Who is that man walking through the fields to meet
us?'" (Gen 24:65). Further, it appears that Rebekah did
not doubt she would bear children. In fact, the only
prayer of Isaac that is recorded in Genesis is that his

wife might conceive (Gen 25:22). One could even say that
the roles of Abraham and Sarah were reversed in Rebekah and
Isaac. Here the man worried about the material blessing of
his descendents and the woman the spiritual blessing.

When one compares Rebekah with Sarah and Rachel other
differences than merely the specific quality of their religious calling emerges. Both Sarah and Rachel suffered extreme jealousy as a result of being barren wives in poly-
gamous marriages. This jealousy was so strong that it led
Sarah to desire the death of Hagar, and Abraham's son
Ishmael, and it made Rachel so callous of her sister Leah's
need to be loved that she could sell permission for Jacob
to sleep with her for some mandrakes. Rebekah did not suffer jealousy from the presence of other wives, for Issac
was strictly monogamous. Rebekah's suffering came as a result of being the mother of fighting children.[7'] In other
words, she did not suffer from barrenness, but from overly
full conception. One could even say, that Sarah and Rachel
were as spiritually barren as were their physical bodies
while Rebekah gave birth in abundance. And just as there
is a sort of suffering that comes from lack of sanctity so
there is one which comes through sanctity.

We are told that Rebekah's sufferings began once she
conceived. "The children struggled with one another inside
her, and she said, 'If this is the way of it, why go on
living?'" (Gen 25:23). The suffering was so acute that she
felt the temptation to suicide. Instead of giving in to
this temptation, however, she carried her suffering with
her, and went to "consult Yahweh" at some holy place. She
wanted to discover what meaning this could have in the plan
of God. She was told: "There are two nations in your womb,
your issue will be two rival peoples. One nation shall
have the mastery of the other, and the elder shall serve
the younger" (Gen 25:23). The conflict occurs on at least
three levels: The first is the struggle between Jacob and
Esau for priority. The second is the political conflict

between the Israelites, descendents of Jacob, and the Edomites, descendents of Esau. And the third is the struggle
between the children of nature and those of God. St. Paul
expresses the third level of conflict as follows:

> Not all those who descend from Israel are Israel:
> not all the descendents of Abraham are his true
> children. Remember: 'it is through Isaac that
> your name will be carried on,' which means that
> it is not physical descent that decided who are
> the children of God; it is only the children of
> the promise who will count as the true descen-
> dants....Even more to the point is what was said
> to Rebekah when she was pregnant by our ancestor
> Isaac. but before her twin children were born
> and before either had done good or evil. In
> order to stress that God's choice is free, since
> it depends on the one who calls, not on human
> merit, Rebekah was told: the elder shall serve
> the younger, or as scripture says elsewhere: I
> showed my love for Jacob and my hatred for Esau
> (Rom 9:7-13).

The Apostle is concerned to show the free workings of grace
here and to de-emphasize the belief that good works or mere
physical worth are enough to be chosen by God. St. Francis
de Sales in considering the same theme adds another dimension to the conflict. Not only does God call whom he wills,
but he also decides who will have final authority over
another.

> It is not without mercy that among these sets of
> brothers it is the youngest who thus holds advant-
> age over their elders. Love of God is assuredly
> the lastborn of all the affections of the human
> heart, for 'that which is natural is first; after-
> wards that which is spiritual,' as the Apostle
> says. But this last-born inherits complete auth-
> ority, while self-love, like another Esau, is
> assigned to its service.[32]

Therefore, one could say that the third level of the narrative implies that the children of God come into conflict
with the children of nature, but that the result is a reversal of the order of authority with the children of God
as conquerers.

The political conflict between the Israelites and the Edomites is discussed in the book of Malachi.

> Was not Esau Jacob's brother,--it is Yahweh who
> speaks; yet I showed my love for Jacob and my
> hatred for Esau. I turned his towns into a
> wilderness and his heritage into desert pas-
> tures. Should Edom say, "We have been struck
> down but we will rebuild our ruins," this is
> the reply of Yahweh Sabaoth: Let them build!
> I will pull down. They shall be known an
> Unholy Land and Nation-with-Yahweh-is-angry-
> forever.
>
> (Mal 1:2-5)

The implication of this passage is that the people of Edom have offended God and therefore deserve to be punished. No effort on their part will change the decision God has made. The statement in further passages is that the Edom- ites sinned by offering blemished animals instead of their purest ones for sacrifice. In the same way their self-of- fering was half-hearted, keeping the best part for them- selves and giving what is useless to God. The conflict between the Israelites and the Edomites then has the same character as the third and first level of conflict. There is a struggle with an eventual triumph of the religious over the natural.

In this way, a forth level of interpretation can be seen in the story of the struggle between Isaac and Esau. Within each person there are natural born tendencies which sometimes come into conflict with a divine call. This can be seen in the moment when Abraham was asked to sacrifice his beloved son. In a more general way it is considered to be the struggle between the spirit and the flesh. In this sense Jacob symbolizes the spiritual dimension of the soul and Esau the natural dimension. Does not Jacob, a shepherd, live peacefully and close to home, while Esau loves to hunt wild animals? Furthermore, the struggle to gain priority over the natural involves two phases. In the first the person makes an act of will to grasp the priority. Jacob steals the birthright. In the second the spiritual

consecration must be given by God. The blessing is given
from another. Here the soul is passive or receptive to
divine grace whereas in the first phase it actively pursues its goal.

Rebekah's function in this twofold religious struggle
is to make it possible for the divine blessing to be given
to the one who was chosen by God. Before this is accomplished however, we are told of three different events which
add more information to the developing characters of Isaac,
Esau, and Rebekah. Isaac was spoken to twice by God and
told: "It is to you and your descendents that I will give
all these lands, and I will fulfill the oath I swore to
your father Abraham....All the nations in the world shall
bless themselves by your descendents *in return for Abraham's obedience*; for *he* kept my charge, my commandments,
my statutes and my laws" (Gen 26:2-6). And then: "I am
the God of your father Abraham. Do not be afraid, for I
am with you. I will bless you and make your descendents
many in number *on account of my servant Abraham*" (Gen 26:
24-5). The important point to note here is that Isaac is
being blessed by God because of what Abraham did. Nowhere
in Genesis does Isaac himself receive a direct call, pass
through a test of faith, or give evidence of any willingness to go beyond his duty. This does not necessarily mean
than he was not a saint, but rather that his own form of
spirituality was very ordinary. He did as he was told, but
would not have broken out of the natural order to give a
blessing to the younger son. We are told that he, like
Esau, was a lover of wild animals. It is even possible,
therefore, that Isaac was not a saint but an ordinary man
who preferred the natural to the spiritual. In any event,
it is clear that God was blessing him because of Abraham
and not because of anything he did himself.

Esau's ignorance of the divine was manifested in two
events: his willingness to trade his birthright for a bowl
of lentil soup and his marriage to two Hittite women. In

the first incident, the commentator observes: "Then Jacob
said: 'First give me your oath,' he gave him his oath and
sold his birthright to Jacob. Then Jacob gave him bread
and lentil soup, and after eating and drinking he got up
and went. *That was all Esau cared for his birthright*"
(Gen 25:32-4). One could interpret Esau's sacrifice of
the birthright as a spiritual disposition towards poverty
for in it he relinquished his claim to a double share of
the inheritance. However, it appears more likely that it
was due to a need to satisfy his natural appetites as soon
as possible; while the death of Isaac was far off, his own
hunger was immediate. As a man who loved the natural; distant rewards held no value. Furthermore, his decision to
marry two women who were close by instead of travelling the
necessary distance to find a wife from those chosen to be
God's children is another indication of his love of the
immediate. Even when he decides he does so out of the
recognition that Isaac and Rebekah approve of this than
out of any personal realization of the spiritual dimension
of such a union. Esau then is revealed to be a man who
prefers the immediate and natural to the distant and spiritual.

Rebekah is asked to pass through a test before the
ultimate act which will secure the blessing for Jacob.
She must detach herself from her body and offer it to a
stranger to save Isaac's life. She allowed herself to be
passed off as Isaac's sister "in case they killed him"
(Gen 26:8). Abraham had asked the same sacrifice of Sarah,
although he was careful to point out that they were indeed
brother and sister (Gen 20:12). As in many cases where a
sacrifice is offered, but not considered necessary for God,
Rebekah did not have to carry out the consequences of the
sacrifice. This in no way detracts from the seriousness
of the offer. She is seen to be willing to give her body
to save a life.

The situation is ready for the final wrenching from the natural to the spiritual. We learn "Rebekah happened to be listening while Isaac was talking to his son Esau." And as promptly as she had said to Abraham's servant 'Drink my Lord,' she calls Jacob to her side: "Now my son, listen to me and do as I tell you. Go to the flock, and bring me two good kids, so that I can make the kind of savory your father likes. Then you can take it to your father for him to eat so that he may bless you before he dies" (Gen 27:5-10). Two aspects of this situation must be considered: What were God's alternatives? What were Rebekah's alternatives?

Why did God not reveal His plan directly to Isaac? This certainly would have been preferable from the ethical point of view. Deceit would have not been necessary and family harmony would have been maintained. We are given some hints in the text. It states: "Isaac had grown old, and his eyes were so weak that he could no longer see" (Gen 27:1). Does this indicate a complete blindness in faith? Was it impossible for him to 'see' the will of God? Had he pursued the natural to such an extent that it destroyed his spiritual potential? We know that "Isaac preferred Esau, for he had a taste for wild game" (Gen 25:28). He loved the results of the hunt for the animal. And in fact, he made it a necessary condition for his blessing that some game be prepared for him to eat. If he had not made that request Jacob would never have been able to deceive him. It was his love for the animal which made it possible for the deception to occur. "Take your weapons, your quiver and bow; go out into the country and hunt me some game...so that I may eat" (Gen 27:4). One could say that Isaac placed the demands of earthly food before those of heavenly food.

If the above interpretation is correct then Isaac's blindness would be due to his love of the animal. This would place the blame for God's use of Rebekah on Isaac's shoulders. There are, however, other possibilities as well.

Kierkegaard suggests in one of his interpretations of the
sacrifice of Isaac that the sight of Abraham holding the
knife and his willingness to sacrifice his son could have
led to a loss of faith in Isaac.[33] In this way one could
say that Isaac had never had a deep faith although he followed the divine orders out of fear. His blindness would
then be the responsibility of Abraham. The sanctity of
the father indeed would have demanded the sacrifice of the
son.

There is also a third possibility. Instead of considering either Isaac or Abraham responsible for Issac's
blindness, one could view it as the result of a direct act
of God. We are told that God often hardens hearts when he
wants to in order to better show his glory. The most obvious example is found in the narrative of Moses and the
Egyptians. Here the hearts of one people were hardened so
that the slaves, the oppressed might be shown to be favored by God. It is possible then that a direct act
brought about the blindness of Isaac in order for the
divine action to be shown in a woman. In this way, the
first story of faith in Genesis would reveal the sanctity
of a particular man Abraham and the second of a particular
woman Rebekah and then the third of a man Jacob. The act
of blinding Isaac would be in order to reveal the richness
of the grace of God, that it calls both women and men to
its service, and that it overturns all natural expectations
and order to accomplish its plans.

The text itself does not give enough information to
definitively establish who is responsible for Isaac's
blindness. It is clear, however, that he is blind and that
he would have passed his blessing onto Esau unless something had intervened. There is yet another alternative
that God could have chosen. He could have allowed Jacob
to overhear Isaac and given him the courage to steal the
blessing in exactly the same way as he stole the birthright. It is clear, however, that Jacob was afraid of such

a move and in particular he feared receiving a curse instead of a blessing. As we shall see, it was only after he became freed from the potential curse that he was able to act. It appears also, that Jacob's courage developed only after his own call. It became so strong then that he was able to wrestle with an angel and refuse to let it go until it blessed him. Again while it is not clear why Jacob was not chosen to carry out the second phase of the struggle by himself, one could say that the double affirmation of two people working together for the same end makes the presence of the divine will more obvious. Jacob needed Rebekah's strength and she was willing to give it.[8']

It is at this point that Rebekah's alternatives must be considered. Rebekah could have been blind as well and then there would never have been any patriarchal link between Abraham, Isaac, and Jacob. She might have allowed that her vocation ended with the material birth of Esau and Jacob and care of Isaac. This would have been the model Sarah had bequeathed her. Or she might have recognized that Jacob was the chosen one but believed that she had no part in making this possible herself. In this case, she would merely wait for the prophecy she had received during pregnancy to work itself out. Still another alternative would have been to recognize Jacob's call, to observe Isaac's blindness, and to decide to speak directly with her husband in the hope of dissuading him from blessing Esau. This course is later followed by Esther. If, however, after prayer Isaac's blindness continued she might have considered running away with Jacob to her brother Labin. In this way she could have arranged for the wedding of Jacob and Rachel which ultimately produced Joseph. However, she would have forfeited the patriarchal blessing of Jacob and in this way broken the spiritual link from Abraham. Because of the patriarchal structure of the society at the time, she could not as a mother pass the blessing on to Jacob. And it is significant that Jacob

received his first call from God *after* he had received the
blessing from Isaac (Gen 28:14-5). Furthermore, Isaac was
old and ill; and it would not be a holy act to desert her
husband in time of need.

Rebekah then chose an alternative which used deceit.
Another holy woman, Judith, later on used deceit to murder
an enemy. Rebekah's deceit was to fool Isaac into believ-
ing that Jacob was his elder son Esau. Can it be that God
asked this *particular* deceit of her? There is no record
of any request, and yet it is certainly possible. In this
case, Rebekah would not merely be acting on her own to fulfill the prophecy during her pregnancy, but she would be
responding to a specific call to help the divine plan. Had
not Abraham been asked to sacrifice Issac? Could she not
be asked to sacrifice her marriage trust? Had not Isaac
been given back? Could not the marriage be reunited?
Would God not 'suspend the ethical for teleological reasons?'[34]

One can imagine the 'fear and trembling' that this
possibility must have aroused in Rebekah. Had she not left
her family to serve Isaac? And now God was asking her to
leave Isaac to serve Him. If the act was unsuccessful, or
the suggestion of an evil force, what would be the consequences? Had she not been told that woman from Eve was
prone to be deceived by the devil, and that God had placed
woman under the subjection of her husband as punishment for
the transgression? And yet it appeared to her that God was
asking her to go against her husband. How could she be
certain? The only certainty would be the success of the
act itself and of Jacob's vocation.[9'] This she could not
know before the act was committed. It would have to be an
act in the dark. If Isaac decided to send her into the
desert to die as Abraham had done to Hagar, she would accept the consequences. She would offer her life so that
the divine will might be done. She would risk humiliation,
ill repute and death so that the grace of God might descend
on Jacob.

Furthermore, she would protect Jacob from harm by taking upon herself the full responsibility of the deceit. When Jacob was afraid that he would receive his father's curse instead of his blessing, Rebekah answered simply: "On me be the curse, my son!" (Gen 27:13). In these words we have a strong clue that the decision to deceive Isaac was a holy act. Rebekah offered herself as a victim. Jacob was freed to receive the benefits of the blessing but not the punishment of the curse. As Abraham had to carry the weight of the knife he intentionally raised above Issac, Rebekah had to carry the weight of the words which would come from her husband. Abraham was willing to sacrifice his beloved son, and Rebekah was willing to sacrifice her life. Even with a profound certainty that the deceit was divinely called for, she must have felt some fear before the act was completed.

One could say then that God needed Rebekah in order to complete his work, and that she freely accepted the call to serve him. More than that, she offered herself as victim if the plan should fail. To be cursed would mean to be cut off from God and from his blessings for the rest of her life.[10'] In this way, the divine call cooperated with a human response, Rebekah met the test. And as in the case of Abraham, the sacrifice was transformed and Isaac given back. The feared curse was not uttered and Jacob became the son consecrated to carry out the ancestry of the chosen people. Rebekah was not sent out into the desert to die, but remained with Isaac until the end. There is even some reason to believe that Isaac's blindness was finally lifted. When he recognized his error at first he "was seized with a great trembling" (Gen 27:33). This trembling could be taken as a sign that he recognized his blindness. In fact he added an apology for placing his trust in natural foods. "Unsuspecting I ate before you came; I blessed him, and blessed he will remain" (Gen 27:33). He blames neither

Rebekah nor Jacob, but accepted the responsibility himself.
And one could even say that Isaac's sanctity, if it existed,
consisted in forgiving those who had wronged him, out of
love of God.

Rebekah brought about a further reconciliation between
Isaac and Jacob when she arranged for him to receive Jacob's
blessing before departing to her brother's home. She said
to her husband: "I am tired to death of the daughters of
Heth. If Jacob marries...one of the women of the country,
what meaning is their left in life for me?" (Gen 27:46).
It is interesting to note that even at this point Isaac did
not suggest that Jacob leave to marry a woman of the chosen
people as Abraham had done before. It is through Rebekah
that the divine will manifested itself. Instead of sending
Jacob away secretly, however, she led Jacob to Isaac where
he received another blessing and order to marry a woman
from Paddam-aram. And as Esau noted, Jacob left "in obedience to his father and mother" (Gen 28:7).

It is also possible to consider Rebekah's role in
bringing about a reconciliation between her two sons Esau
and Jacob. After Esau had realized that Jacob had received
his father's blessing he cried: "Is it because his name is
Jacob, that he has now supplanted me twice? First he took
my birthright, and look, now he has taken my blessing!"
(Gen 27:36). Esau 'burst into tears,' 'hated Jacob,' and
thought of killing him. Rebekah recognized this and decided to separate them by sending Jacob away. In this way
she protected Jacob from death and Esau from murder. During the years of Jacob's absence it is possible that she
was able to explain to Esau what had happened and why.
The extraordinary way in which Esau met his brother years
later suggests a change of heart. "Esau ran to meet him,
took him in his arms and held him close and wept" (Gen 33:
5). The entire family became reconciled to one another
and we are told that "Isaac was one hundred and eighty

years old when breathed his last. He died and was gathered
to his people, an old man who had enjoyed his full span of
life. His sons Esau and Jacob buried him" (Gen 35:27-9).

It we view the complete circumstances of Rebekah's
life in the above way it is clear that her sanctity was
evident in a most profound way. Not only does she serve
as a model of courage, immediate acceptance of grace, long-
suffering and willingness to die for God, but she can also
be seen as the *first* woman in the Bible to be a saint. In
this way she stands on her own, regardless of the role she
plays as mother or wife. Her primary significance is her
own response to God. In addition, however, she is also
the mother of the faith. As Abraham became the father of
the faith through meeting the test, so Rebekah became the
mother of the faith. More concretely, she is the mother
of Israel. Jacob was told: "Your name shall no longer be
Jacob, but Israel, because you have been strong against
God, you will prevail against men" (Gen 32:28). And if
one could break the chain of patriarchy a more proper
blessing would be "in the name of Abraham, Rebekah and
Jacob."

<u>Notes on the Christian Pre-figuration of the Rebekah
     Narrative</u>

1'   Rebekah is the first to offer water to assuage thirst.
In this way she pre-figures the Church which offers the
waters of Baptism. The vessel in her arms, like Christ,
becomes the Way through which the waters of life are be-
stowed. The Samaratian woman had said to Christ: "Are you
a greater man than our father Jacob who gave us this well
and drank from it himself with his sons and cattle?" She
was told: "Whoever drinks this water will get thirsty
again; but anyone who drinks the water that I shall give
will turn into a spring inside him, welling up to eternal
life (John 4:11-14). As Rebekah will *draw* water until all
the men and animals are satisfied, so Mary serves as a way
to the living waters until the end of time."

2'   In addition to receiving a stranger like Christ, Rebekah indicates that her father's house is large enough to
contain all who wish to enter. "There are many rooms in
my Father's house; if there were not, I should have told
you" (John 12:2).

3'   In a similar way an angel prepared the hearts of Mary
and Joseph for the miraculous birth of Christ. "In the
sixth month the angel Gabriel was sent by God to a town in
Galilee called Nazareth to a virgin betrothed to a man
named Joseph" (Luke 1:26). "He had made up his mind to do
this when the angel of the Lord appeared to him in a dream
and said, 'Joseph son of David, do not be afraid to take
Mary home as your wife, because she has conceived what is
in her by the Holy Spirit!" (Matt 1:20).

4'   Rebekah's immediate acceptance of the call is a recognition of one of the central teachings of Christ: "Anyone who prefers father or mother to me is not worthy of
me" (Matt 10:37). "I tell you solemnly, there is no one
who has left house, brothers, sisters, father, children or
land for my sake and for the sake of the gospel who will
not be repaid a hundred times over" (Mark 10:29-30).

5'   In her immediate response Rebekah indicates her total
acceptance of the call. She does not find some reason to
wait until later. "There was a man who gave a great banquet, and he invited a large number of people. When the
time for the banquet had come he sent his servant to say
to those who had been invited 'Come along: everything is
ready now.' But all alike started to make excuses" (Luke
14:16),

6'   Like Mary when she was confronted by the mystery of
God's work in the world, Rebekah could have kept what she
had seen and heard in her heart. "His mother stored up
all these things in her heart" (Luke 2:51).

7'   As Mary is described being in pain, giving birth to
the children of the world--children who war with one
another, Rebekah pre-figures this eternal struggle by her
suffering from fighting infants in her womb. "Now a great
sign appeared in heaven: a woman, adorned with the sun,
standing on the moon, and with the twelve stars on her head
head for a crown. She was pregnant and in labor, crying
aloud in the pangs of childbirth" (Rev 12:1-2).

8'   In the Rule of St. Benedict the responsibility of the
spiritual directory is described in terms of the Abbot's
role in the monastery. "Let him always bear in mind that
he has undertaken the government of souls and that he will
have to give an account of them" Chapter 2, And similarly
the disciple must follow orders without fear: "As soon as
anything has been ordered by the Superior, receive it as
a divine command." Chapter 5, Rebekah in taking responsibility before God for her command to Jacob shows the first
example in the bible of spiritual direction. Jacob's willingness to carry out the command, once he recognized that
he was freed from its possible negative consequences by
his obedience to Rebekah indicates his recognition of the
nature of the spiritual relationship of direction. *St.
Benedict's Rules for Monasteries*, trans. Leonard Doyle,
(St. John's Abbey, MN: The Liturgical Press, 1948).

9'   Rebekah saw the hidden sanctity of Jacob before Jacob
himself recognized it as Mary recognized the moment for
Christ's revelation. "The mother of Jesus said to him,
'They have no wine.' Jesus said, 'Woman why turn to me?
My hour has not come yet.' His mother said to the ser-
vants, 'Do whatever he tells you'" (John 2:6).

10'   This extraordinary offer was repeated by St. Paul:
"What I want to say is this: my sorrow is so great, my
mental anguish so endless, I would willingly be condemned
and be cut off from Christ if it would help my brothers of
Israel, my own flesh and blood" (Rom 9:2-3).

11'   Those who bring peace are especially close to God.
"Happy are the peacemakers: they shall be called sons of
God" (Matt 5:9).

NOTES

*This paper was written in connection with the Seminar on Form Criticism for the AAR (1975). It is expected that she collected papers from this seminar that will be published in a volume concentrating on interpretations of *Genesis*, ed. Prof. Martin Russ, Dept. of Religion, Emory University, Atlanta, Georgia within the next year.

[1] Otto Eissfeldt, *The Old Testament, An Introduction*, trans. Peter R. Ackroyd, (Oxford: Basil Blackwell, 1965) 188-212.

[2] Ibid., p. 42.

[3] Ibid., p. 41.

[4] Ludwig Wittgenstein, *Lectures and Conversations on Aesthetics, Psychology, and Religious Belief* (University of California Press, 1960).

[5] Martin Buss, Book Review of *The Bible in Human Transformation* by Walter Wink in "Union Seminary Quarterly Review" 29 (1973-75) 137.

[6] Reference from the Ecumenical Study Conference held in Oxford in 1949 and recorded in *The Interpreters Bible*, Vol I Genesis (New York: Abington, Colesbury) note p. 141.

[7] Ibid., Robert Grant p. 106.

[8] Ibid., John McNeill, pp. 121-26,

[9] St Francis de Sales, *On the Love of God*, Vol. I. (Garden City: Image Books) 38-39.

[10] Ibid., p. 40.

[11] Elizabeth Cady Stanton, *The (Original) Feminist Attack on the Bible* (New York: Arno Press, Harper and Row, 1974).

[12] Sister Emma Thérèse Healy, *Women According to Saint Bonaventure* (Eric, PA: The Congregation of the Sisters of St. Joseph, 1956) 221.

[13] Deen, Edith, *All the Women of the Bible* (New York: Harper & Ros, 1955) footnote p. 21, 26, and 14-17.

[14] Mary Daly, *Beyond God the Father* (Boston: Beacon Press, 1973).

[15]Rosemary Ruether, *Religion and Sexism* (New York, Simon and Shuster, 1974) Preface pp. 12-13.

[16]A. S. Herbert, *Genesis* (London, SCM, 1962) 69.

[17]S. R. Driver, *The Book of Genesis* (London: Methuen, 1916) 255.

[18]Walter Bovie, *The Interpreter's Bible*, op. cit., p. 668.

[19]Ibid., p. 681

[20]A. S. Herbert, op. cit., pp. 76-77.

[21]Clara Bewick Colby in *The Original Feminist Attack on the Bible*, op. cit., pp. 53-54.

[22]Stanton, op. cit., p. 52.

[23]Ibid., p. 53.

[24]Eileen Kraditer, *Ideas of the Woman Suffrage Movement* (Columbia, 1965).

[25]S. R. Driver, op. cit., p. 230 (my emphasis).

[26]Ibid., (my emphasis).

[27]A. S. Herbert, op. cit., pp. 59-60 (my emphasis).

[28]Ibid., p. 64.

[29]Ibid., (my emphasis).

[30]Cuthbert, Simpson, *The Interpreter's Bible*, op. cit., note Genesis 25:31, p. 668.

[31]Ibid., note Genesis 26:34-5, p. 679.

[32]St. Francis de Sales, op. cit., p. 65.

[33]Søren Kierkegaard, *Fear and Trembling*, trans. W. Larvi (Princeton, NJ: Princeton University, 1970) Preamble IV, 29.

[34]Ibid.

All Biblical references taken from *The Jerusalem Bible*, Reader's Edition (New York: Doubleday, 1968).

THE LEGACY OF ABRAHAM

Carol Delaney
Harvard Divinity School

Take your son, your only son Isaac, whom you
love, and go to the land of Moriah, and offer
him there as a burnt offering upon one of the
mountains of which I shall tell you. (Gen 22:2)

By faith, Abraham when he was tested, offered
up Isaac, and he who had received the promises
was ready to offer up his only son. (Heb 11:17)

The story of the "sacrifice of Isaac" is not just one
story among others, it is "central to the nervous system
of Judaism and Christianity."[1] Not only does it establish
Abraham as the father of faith, but provides the model and
the metaphors for the description and interpretation of
the Crucifixion. Abraham is considered the father of the
three Western religions; Judaism, Christianity and Islam.
Whether or not we belong to one of these religions our
values, laws, institutions as well as literature and art
have been deeply affected by them. Many of us are beginning to question the values, institutions and laws of our
culture, and therefore it seems fitting to look again at
the story of the founding father.

The Biblical scholar, E. A. Speiser says "the break
between Primeval History and the Story of the Patriarchs
is sharper than is immediately apparent."[2] It is important to bear this in mind for the remainder of the paper.
Although the Bible begins with Creation the history of our
culture rightly begins with Abraham. Therefore a word
about time and place. Abraham, if such a person actually
existed, is thought to have lived in the early centuries
of the second millenium B. C. During this time Haran, his
home, was a major crossroad on the ancient trade routes
connecting the south and the east with the north and the
west. Not only would articles for trade and technological
advances been transmitted, but customs, beliefs and stories.

Profound changes were taking place in the ancient Near East during the period between 2500 and 2000 B. C.[3] It is my view that among other things there was a change in the beliefs about pregnancy and human conception. I think there was a shift from the understanding that the male had a role in conception to the assumption that it was the primary role. I suggest that Abraham is a symbol of this change.

My purpose in looking at the story of the "sacrifice of Isaac" is not to reinterpret it to suit present needs, to make it relevant, but rather to use present concern as a basis for asking new questions of the story.

Shalom Spiegel says the Akedah, as this story is called, "renews itself in every time of crisis"[4] when people are suffering from oppression. It is meant to fortify them, to give them courage in their trials as Abraham displayed in his.

But is this the kind of model we need now? Why is the theme of child sacrifice *the* theme chosen by Biblical writers to express devotion to God? Why is Abraham's willingness to kill Isaac seen as an expression of great piety? Why is Sarah's point of view noticeably absent? Does the story have the same meaning for women, or is it a symptom of masculine culture?

Many people feel the story was intended as a prohibition against child sacrifice. When I turned to traditional interpretations of the story I found that most commentators focused on Abraham's piety. And his piety is based not on the fact that he put an end to the practice but on the fact that he was willing to kill Isaac. He is extolled precisely because he was able to suppress his compassion in order to perform God's will with a perfect heart.[5]

One commentator says "it was desired to show that Abraham's devotion to the God he worshipped was capable of going to the farthest point religion could reach....If men worshipping pagan deities could carry their religion to

that terrific cost"[6] how could Abraham do less? He cites
as evidence the fact that in the time of Elisha (850 B. C.)
the king offered his son.

This commentator in trying to find a rationale for
Abraham's deed has confused his history and his terms.
What should be immediately apparent is that Abraham's deed
is supposed to have occurred as much as 1,000 years earlier
than those of the so-called pagans with whom he is seen in
competition. Furthermore, the term pagan would have been
meaningless in Abraham's time.

The crucial question is whether child sacrifice as a
religious ritual[7] was already an established practice in
Abraham's time, or was it introduced then, practiced spor-
adically, only to reach its full expression at a much later
date? It was at this later time that Biblical writers,
gathering and compiling material, were desirous of making
a distinction between themselves and other Canaanites.
The linear and progressive view of history inherent in the
Bible supports the interpretation of the element of child
sacrifice in the Abraham story as a relic or fossil sur-
viving from some more primitive and barbaric people. The
Bible as well as those who take a developmental evolutionary stance toward history and culture would lead us to believe that child sacrifice was a primordial custom which
was modified only with the advance of civilization. The
evidence does not support this view. When it has occurred,
child sacrifice has appeared in highly civilized and advanced societies, and the evidence for the practice in the
ancient Near East is confined to the first millenium B. C.[8]
Developmental evolutionary theory when applied to culture
is dangerous in its assumptions, and tends, because of its
seeming truth, to inhibit questions. Those who argue that
the story symbolizes the prohibition of an ancient cultic
practice have occasionally recognized the inconsistencies
in the story and their theory. It is perhaps for this
reason that they turned instead to an exposition of

Abraham's piety. I find this exegesis equally unsatisfactory for I do not see why the willingness to kill a child should be considered a test of piety and the prime example of it. The object of this paper is to see what other possibilities of meaning are latent in the story.

The story of Abraham begins with the call from God to abandon the land and religion of his fathers. Implicit in the story is the idea that the religion of his fathers included child sacrifice.

Philo of Alexandria, one of the earliest commentators on the story, tells us that "in Babylonia and Mesopotamia and with the nations of the Chaldeans with whom he (Abraham) lived the greater part of his life the custom of child slaughter does not obtain."[9] In other words, at least in Philo's view, child sacrifice was not a feature of the religion of Abraham's ancestors. In order to skirt the enormity of the implications, Philo turns to Abraham's piety thus setting the direction that all future commentary would take.

Philo says "Abraham concedes nothing to the tie of relationship but his whole weight is thrown into the scale on the side of acceptability with God...he did not incline partly to the boy and partly to piety, but devoted his whole soul through and through to holiness and disregarded the claims of their common blood."[10] Philo is earnest to distinguish Abraham from others who have sacrificed their children "for their country to serve as a price to redeem it from wars or drought or excessive rainfall or pestilence."[11] There was no motive save the love of God, and but for this, Philo says Abraham "would have been the first himself to initiate a totally new and extraordinary procedure."[12]

The points that Philo makes are precisely those that Søren Kierkegaard takes up in *Fear and Trembling*. The "knight of faith" is, because of his extraordinary devotion, able to suspend the categories of the human ethical

realm. His "faith is a paradox which is capable of transforming a murder into a holy act well pleasing to God."[13]
Abraham is not a tragic hero, as are Agamemmnon or Jephtha,
for his deed was not done "for the sake of saving a people,
not to maintain the idea of state."[14] The hero, according
to Kierkegaard, could rest his conscience in the universal
ethical realm; but this is the very category Abraham has
had to suspend. Abraham "acts by virtue of the absurd,"
he is "either a murderer or a believer."[15] In order that
Abraham be absolved of murder, Kierkegaard, as Philo before
him, has had to transform him into someone super-human.
Kierkegaard's idolatry of the individual has gone to the
farthest reach, his "knight of faith" acts in a moral vac-
uum where there is no reference for judgment.

What becomes clear is that the love of God or duty
(heroism) comes before the love of people. In fact love of
God is placed in opposition to love of kin rather than the
fulfillment of it.[16] This theme is continued in the New
Testament in the requirements for discipleship. For example, Jesus says: "If anyone comes to me and does not hate
his own father and mother and wife and children...he cannot be my disciple" (Luke 14:56). Notice that he does not
permit the wife the same right against the husband. The
line that shocks us even more is when Jesus is told that
his mother has come to see him, and he turns to the people
he is addressing and says: "Who is my mother?" (Matt 12:48).
He goes on to say that whoever does the will of God is his
brother, sister and mother. Notice that he does not say
father. This leaves the position of the human father highly ambiguous.[17]

But let us return to the subject of child sacrifice.
The Bible is itself ambivalent on this subject. "Conse-
crate to me all the first born whatever is the first to
open the womb of the people Israel" (Exod 22:29). And "Do
not give any of your seed to Molech and so profane the
name of your God" (Lev 18:21) can be interpreted more as a

prohibition against the worship of other gods than against the practice of child sacrifice.

The ambivalence goes deeper. The slaughter of innocents receives quite a different valuation depending on who does it. When Pharoah decrees that all the first born sons of the Hebrews shall be cast into the Nile it is an abomination, yet when God slaughters the first born sons of the Egyptians it is justified. Abraham's willingness to kill Isaac is seen as an act of greatest piety, yet a comparable willingness in a Canaanite is reprehensible.

The Bible tells us that a ram was substituted for Isaac, and it does give evidence that first born sons were redeemed from their fate by the substitution of animals, the payment of money or dedication into the Levitical priesthood. However, the ambivalence between the practice and the substitution was never really resolved, for the Bible also gives evidence that the practice of child sacrifice continued throughout early Israelite history.[18] The substitution obscures but does not entirely erase the original intention. One is still left with the uneasy feeling that the child was considered the *appropriate* sacrifice.

This is confirmed by the uses to which the story has been put at various times in history. I can give only a few examples. In the 9th century A. D. children planted seeds in baskets which they swung round their heads with the incantation: "This be in lieu of me, this is my substitute and my exchange" and threw the baskets into the river.[19] During the Middle Ages the Akedah story was reinterpreted by some European Jews so that Abraham did kill Isaac. And when they were suffering persecution from the Crusaders, they considered it their sacred duty to kill their own children for the Sanctification of the Name.[20]

During the 20th century A. D. the story was invoked not only to give courage to parents as they sent their sons off to war, but to inspire heroic passion in the young men.

Wilfred Owen, aware of this use of the story, wrote "The
Parable of the Old Man and the Young" which ends with the
following:

> When lo! an angel called him out of heaven,
> Saying, Lay not thy hand upon the lad,
> Neither do anything to him. Behold,
> A ram, caught in a thicket by its horns,
> Offer the Ram of Pride instead of him.
> But the old man would not so, but slew
> his son--
> And half the seed of Europe, one by one.[21]

And this summer when I was doing research in the area of
Haran, I met a woman who had just given birth to her first
child after a long period of barrenness. She had traveled
to this place to offer a ram sacrifice in the name of
Abraham in order that her child might not die.

The legend goes on, the ambivalence continues. But
where did the idea that the first child belonged to the
deity come from, what was its motivation? Some would like
to see an analogy between the offering of first fruits and
the sacrifice of the first born. But is the offering of
fruits and vegetables from one's abundance motivated by
the same impulse as the taking away of life?[22]

To interpret the story of the "sacrifice of Isaac"
only within the Judeo-Christian tradition is somewhat
tautologous. However if it can be placed in a context and
seen in relation to other stories we get a completely new
perspective. Not only can we begin to see common themes
but are in a better position to evaluate the differences.

While there are several stories one could choose, I
would like to focus on Hesiod's *Theogony*, because it, like
Genesis, is a story of origins and the establishment of a
new religion.[23] Zeus, like Abraham, is the father of a
new faith; admittedly one is reputed to be an historical
human figure, the other a god. The "succession myth" recounted in the *Theogony* seems to have been known in various forms throughout the ancient Near East in the second

millenium B. C.,[24] although the *Theogony* is a late version.
It is thought to have been written down in the 8th century
B. C. and the source for the story of Abraham is thought
to stem from the 9th century B. C. But both refer back
to a time in the past that was roughly contemporary.

In the Greek story Ouranos is jealous of his sons and
so...

> from the beginning, and every time each one
> was beginning
> to come out, he would push them back again,
> deep inside Gaia...
> Ouranos exulted
> in his wicked work; but great Gaia
> groaned within for pressure
> of pain.[25]

Kronos, one son who escaped, devised a plan to castrate
his father and assume his position. From the blood of the
castration came the Erinnyes whose "original function (was
to) avenge injuries inflicted only on a mother."[26] We
shall meet them again later. Kronos, having established
his position with violence, must hold it with violence:

> Rheia, submissive in love to Kronos
> bore glorious children...
> but, as each of these children
> came from the womb of its mother...
> Kronos swallowed it down,
> with the intention
> that no other of the proud children,
> of the line of Ouranos
> should ever hold the king's position...
> For...it had been ordained...
> (that he would be) *beaten* by his *son*...
> therefore he kept watch and did not sleep
> but waited
> for his children, and swallowed them,
> and Rheia's sorrow was beyond forgetting.[27]

The castration deed, the son's aggression against the father, rather than the infanticide, is what has been remembered and elaborated. When Rheia is about to give birth
again, she wraps a stone in swaddling clothes and gives it
to Kronos instead of the infant Zeus. It is interesting

to note that in both the Greek and Hebrew stories the substitute is provided by someone other than the father; here
it is the mother, in the Bible the angel of the Lord stays
Abraham's hand which enables him to look up and see the
ram. This gives additional evidence that the mitigating
influence did not originate with the father.

The substitute became symbolic, for the stone[28] when
disgorged by Kronos became associated with the sacred
stone at Delphi in a later stage of Greek religion. We
might remember that the ram substituted for Isaac later
became associated with Jesus, the Lamb of God.

Stories of the infant Zeus are attached to Crete
where he is thought to be the son of the Mother Goddess,
and in these Kronos plays no part.[29] Stories of the adult
Zeus are thought to have accompanied the Indo-Europeans
who invaded Greece in the second millenium B. C. The
Theogony records the result of the combination of these
two traditions. Zeus is the last god in the "succession
myth" proper, and it is with him that the final transition
to the patriarchal way of life was effected.

Zeus did not become the chief god of the Greek pantheon without more violence. Those who stood in his way
were bound in Tartaros: there remained only one who threatened his position--Metis, the goddess who knew more than
all the gods or mortal people. Zeus had heard that she
would give birth to marvelous children, first Athena and
then a *son* who would *overthrow* him. So when Metis was
pregnant with Athena he swallowed her.[30] The only aspect
of this story remembered in our culture is that in which
Zeus gives birth to Athena by himself. Is this an example
of the incorporation of the worship a goddess into the
service of a patriarchal religion? In fact, are the infanticidal stories the means of demonstrating the authority
of the father?

Given the differences in tone, certain common themes
do emerge. What is striking is the association of infant-
cide and castration as the means of establishing the new

religion. To put it another way, the killing of a child
and the mutilation of the male sexual organ are the means
by which power is usurped. Kronos has been identified with
'El the great god of the Canaanites, and 'El is the name
of the god of Abraham. There is even one version in which
Kronos ('El) sacrifices his son and circumcises himself.[31]
If these stories in one form or another were known in the
ancient Near Eastern world, does it seem unreasonable to
suppose that there is at *least* a reflection of them in the
Biblical account of Abraham's "sacrifice of Isaac?"[32] Although there is no elaborated succession story in the Bible,
it is to Abraham's seed, namely Isaac and those who come
after, that the promises are given. And if one were attempting to make exact correlations between the Greek and
Hebrew stories Isaac, rather than Abraham, would be equivalent with Zeus, for he, like Zeus was the child redeemed by
the substitute. Yet Isaac, the child of promise, is
strangely not a very prominent figure in the Bible. This
fact has given rise to speculation that Isaac was sacrificed, and that the substitution rite was a late modifica-
tion. In the Bible, the "succession" has been circumscribed, perhaps artificially, and limited to one generation in the story of Abraham. However, my purpose is not
to make equivalencies, but to raise certain themes. Despite the fact that there is no proper succession story in
the Bible, Abraham is the founding father of a new religion,
a new way of life, for it is through him that God establishes his covenant with the chosen people. Once again,
the theme of killing a child and the male sexual organ (in
this case circumcision) are associated and are dominant
aspects of the story describing the establishment of the
new religion.

I suggest there is another standpoint one can take in
looking at these stories; they could be viewed as different
responses to a similar phenomenon, the responses varying in
accordance with the background and experience of the indigenous people. What then is the phenomenon to which they
point?

It would appear that maleness in the aspect of paternity forms the nucleus. Abraham means the father is ex-
alted; in relation to whom we might ask. His penis is the
holy place of the covenant. Zeus and 'El are to be regarded primarily as patriarchs and the "succession myths"
recount the battles in which they won patriarchal authority. Yahweh appears to mean the calling into being a
name, progeny.[33] The power of life and death over a child
is a demonstration of the power and authority of the father's right. Is the new order referred to the establishment of the authority of the father? What had been revealed?

I suggest that Abraham is the symbol of a change in
world view precipitated by the idea that men had come to
view their role in conception as primary. I am not so
naive to assume it marks the discovery of male participation in procreation, but rather marks the momentous shift
from the knowledge of participation to the assumption that
it was the primary role. The Biblical mind interpreted
semen as *seed*, the child in essence, the part for the
whole. In this understanding the child is fashioned solely by the impregnating principle provided by the father
while the woman supplies nothing of her essential being to
the child.[34] She serves merely as the *soil* in which the
seed is planted, her value becomes derivative.

This idea of conception is mirrored in the Greek stories. Clytaemestra is angry with Agamemmnon for tricking
her into sending Iphegenia to Aulis (supposedly to be married) and then sacrificing her. Clytaemestra kills Agamemmnon upon his return, and Orestes in his turn murders
Clytaemestra, his mother. The Erinnyes wish to avenge
her death by pursuing and tormenting Orestes, and there are
versions of the story in which they do. But in the play
by Aeschylus Orestes is absolved of guilt because:

> The mother is no parent of that which is called
> her child, but only the nurse of the new-planted

> seed that grows. The parent is he who mounts....
> There she stands, the living witness, daughter of
> Olympian Zeus, she who was never fostered in the
> dark of the womb.[35]

Athena did indeed have a mother, but Aeschylus chose to
ignore that fact. The Erinnyes are infuriated and out-
raged by what is going on; "Gods of the younger generation
you have ridden down the laws of the elder time."[36] Athena,
now under the power of her father, intervenes and black-
mails them into accepting a position in the new regime.
"I promise you a place of your own, deep hidden underground...where you shall sit...beside the hearth"[37] and "No
household shall prosper without you."[38] Originally to
avenge crimes done only to a mother, the Erinnyes have
been transformed into goddesses of marriage. They too
have been placated and put into the service of patriarchal
institutions. "Orestes' absolution records the final triumph of patriarchy."[39]

The view of conception in which the male is the primary engendering one sheds light on the alignment of the
powers of creativity and spirituality with the male principle and the *virtues* of receptivity and materiality with
the female. Prior to this view of conception it seems
quite likely that the *religious* power accruing from the
miracle of birth belonged to women regardless of whether
earlier cultures were truly matriarchies. As the idea of
male supremacy in conception took hold, not only did female deities and women themselves lose the power and status they had once enjoyed,[40] but the earth too became de-
sacralized, it too became merely soil. The earth and the
fruits thereof became the property of men, as did women
and children. The seed is the father's, the father and
the son are one,[41] the woman is merely the vehicle through
which this relationship is established.

What are the consequences of this view of conception?
The first problem that comes to mind is that of the so-
called legitimacy of a child. E. A. Speiser has this to

say: "The integrity of the mission must be safeguarded in transmission, the purity of the content protected by the quality of the container."[42] In other words, the container womb must be unsullied. Female virginity before marriage and fidelity after marriage became matters of utmost concern. If the tokens of virginity were not found in a betrothed maiden, "The men of her city shall stone her to death with stones, because she has wrought folly in Israel by playing the harlot" (Deut 22:21). And if the "spirit of jealousy" comes upon a man and "he is jealous of his wife...he shall bring her to the priest" (Num 5:14-15), who made her drink a mixture of holy water and dirt. If it made her sick it was assumed she was guilty of adultery and the penalty was death. One writer has said "No doubt many injustices were suffered in consequence of this practice which allowed the husband on the slightest pretext to level an accusation against his wife."[43]

Anxiety over the first born might naturally be higher, for the woman may have been pregnant at the time of her marriage or, as in Sarah's case, a long period of barrenness might be cause for suspicion.[44] The whole question of legitimacy was double headed, for not only did the father secure immortality through legitimate progeny, but the first born son stood to inherit from the father. Obviously it was not something to be trifled with. It is interesting to note in this connection that all first born sons in Genesis were passed over, for favor, inheritance or blessing, beginning with Cain.

If the life engendering ability is male then it is transferred from father to son. The son also possesses this ability and therefore as he matures he becomes a potential threat to the father's authority. This theme is the primary reason given for infanticide in the Greek stories, but is it also perhaps the rationale behind the command for obedience? The death penalty could be invoked for disobedience.

The authority of the father was taken to its extreme literal limit in Greek and Roman society where the father had power of life and death over his children. He could dispose of them with impunity provided it was done by the eighth day. Infanticide by the father was not considered a crime until the 4th century A.D., yet if a woman were found guilty of it she was tortured and put to death. Obviously it was an exercise of prerogative. Abraham, in taking Isaac without consulting Sarah, executed the prerogative of father-right.

The eighth day was significant. In Hebrew tradition it was the day for the sacrifice of the first born animals, and also the day on which circumcision was performed. Perhaps both might be seen as symbolic substitutions for the child. In Christianity it became the day of Baptism, being accepted into a family in which God was the father. Unbaptised children were thought to suffer eternal damnation in Hell; one might suggest that this is a projection of infanticidal impulses onto God. So-called illegitimate children have throughout our history suffered from the sins of the fathers by being stigmatized and ignored, and deprived of emotional and financial support.

David Bakan, a 20th century psychologist, has also seen a connection between paternity and the story of the "sacrifice of Isaac." But he sees in the story redemptive possibilities; for the symbolic substitutions mitigate and control infanticidal impulses. In fact, he says "The essence of Judaism and Christianity is the management of the infanticidal impulse...and a binding on the father against acting out the impulse."[46] I would suggest that it has been perpetuated on a grander scale. For what Bakan has not seen is that the impulse was provoked by and based on an erroneous conception of paternity, an erroneous view of conception. The symbolic substitutions, while surely a gain for humanity, do not really change but perpetuate the basic premise; that the child is the *appropriate* sacrifice.

Seed and soil, as a metaphor of conception, is deeply embedded in our culture. Not only has it been a powerful influence in shaping attitudes toward the sexes, but it has also been elaborated in sophisticated religious, philosophical and psychological speculation, from Aristotle to Freud. The ovum was not discovered until the 19th century; yet even today the metaphor of seed/soil is perpetuated in explanations of conception to children, in popular songs,[47] and in the media. The implications beyond the purely biological one have not even begun to permeate our consciousness.

Let me begin to sum up this discussion. I think the story of the "sacrifice of Isaac" is profound and central to our religious tradition and our culture. I think its meaning is to be found not in the ending of the practice of child sacrifice but rather in the establishment of father-right. I think the literal enactment and the symbolic transformations proceed from the same basic misunderstanding, the view of conception in which the father is the primary engendering one. I suggest the story functions to establish the authority of the father; this idea of paternity forms the basis of father-right, the foundation of patriarchy.

The genius of the Hebrew people could then be seen to lie in their powers of abstraction and symbolization. The idea of paternity was lifted from its concrete manifestation and transposed onto the symbolic plane—as the essence of God. The aniconic tendency of the Hebrews has long been noted as a distinguishing feature of their religion. But visual images and idols could be dispensed with. The metaphor or verbal image is far more powerful because it establishes meaning on two levels.

In the Bible Israel is identified either with God's first born or with woman. Israel's misfortunes are interpreted as God's punishment for disobedience or for playing the harlot. The metaphors imply that God is to be understood as husband and father. And in early Christianity,

at least, God's *seed* is the spermatic word, usually identified with his son the Christ. In the story of the "sacrifice of Isaac" it is not a human father nor a father god
(implying there might be mother gods, brother and sister
gods) but God the Father who demands the sacrifice and then
later offers his only son. The story functions to establish the authority of God the Father. The authority becomes omnipresent but invisible. This, more than anything,
legitimates the patriarchal way of life. Although the
revelation of paternity occurred at a particular time in
history, to the Hebrews it revealed the way things had been
from the beginning. The abstract idea of conception and
paternity was taken all the way back to Creation. No wonder there are no accounts in Genesis of the wars of the
new gods against the old in which patriarchal authority was
won. The revelation to the symbolic Abraham changed the
course of history in two directions--it colored the future,
which is our legacy, but clouded the face of the past. It
became the metaphorical framework for the re-interpretation
of primeval history as well as that within which history
would unfold.

I am tempted to speculate further and ask how much the
idea of seed, the transmission of the essence of the father
to the son, from generation to generation, had to do with
the development of the concept of history. For history as
we know it, has been primarily the record of the events of
one people, one religious tradition, and one sex.

[1]Shalom Spiegel, *The Last Trial*, trans. Judah Goldin (New York: Schocken Books, 1969) xvii.

[2]E. A. Speiser, *Genesis*, Anchor Bible (New York: Doubleday, 1964) LIII. The "break" means that the primeval stories were more general, deriving from Mesopotamia, while the patriarchal stories were more specifically the Hebrews own early history.

[3]Archaeological evidence indicates that "the end of the EB 2 period is marked in Southern and Western Anatolia by a catastrophe of such magnitude...that nearly every vil-liage was deserted and never again occupied" (*Cambridge Ancient History*, Vol. 1, Part 2, pp. 406-7). Furthermore, the earlier population "seems to have been of pre-Indo-European stock, or rather speech, practising a type of agricultural fertility religion in which a goddess played a predominant part" (*CAH*, p. 371). I suggest that many of the changes are due to the influence of these invaders both in the Near East and in Greece. The destruction is true also for N. Mesopotamia, Syria, and Palestine, though in the latter case because of invasion of nomads from the desert (3rd ed. [Cambridge: Cambridge University, 1971]).

[4]Spiegel, *Last Trial*, back cover.

[5]*Encyclopedia Judaica* (Jerusalem: Keter Publishing House, 1971) 2.482.

[6]See "Genesis," *Interpreter's Bible* (New York/Nash-ville: Abington-Cokesbury, 1952) 642.

[7]I wish to make clear the distinction between the re-ligious rite of child sacrifice in which the child victim, generally male, was required to be "without blemish" and taken from among the aristocracy, if not the king; and the practice of allowing deformed infants to die at birth, a custom some "primitive" peoples may allow. Infanticide has also been practiced as a means of disposing of excess pop-ulation in which case the victims are most often female. Needless to say, the latter practice has occurred in his-torical times in patriarchal societies and is known to have been practiced in India until the 19th century.

[8]Evidence for widespread practice of child sacrifice is confined to the first millenium B. C. This is not, how-ever, to deny that instances of it occurred earlier. Jephtha's daughter is a prime example.

[9] Philo, *De Abrahamo*, Loeb Classical Library, trans. F. H. Colson (Cambridge, MA: Harvard University, 1935) 7.93.

[10] Ibid., p. 97.

[11] Ibid., p. 89. This puts Abraham in a category apart from Agamemmnon or Jephtha; as well as Saul who would have sacrificed Jonathan had not the people protested (1 Samuel 14).

[12] Ibid., p. 95.

[13] Kierkegaard, Søren, *Fear and Trembling*, trans. Walter Lowrie (Princeton, NJ: Princeton University, 1941) 64.

[14] Ibid., p. 70. Kierkegaard also places Abraham in a separate category from Agamemmnon and Jephtha for reasons similar to Philo. It may be significant that Agamemmnon and Jephtha are more comparable in time, and both sacrificed daughters.

[15] Ibid., p. 67.

[16] To my mind, the idea of being devoted first to God or an ideal substituted for God and secondly to people provides a structure which allows for war.

[17] Either he identifies in some way with God or he is irrelevant. "There is something divine in the father...and something fatherly in God" (*Theological Dictionary of the New Testament*, ed. G. Kittel and G. Friedrich (Grand Rapids, MI: Wm. B. Eerdmans, 1967) suggests that the ambiguity is resolved most likely by identification.

[18] Mosca, Paul G., *Child Sacrifice in Canaanite and Israelite Religion*: a study in Mulk and (Molech), *Ph.D. dissertation, Harvard University, 1975. Mosca believes that the Bible doth protest too much in its desire to distinguish the Israelites from other Canaanites.

[19] *The Jewish Encyclopedia* (New York: Funk and Wagnalls, 1904) 7.436; see also entry for Kapparah rite in 14th century.

[20] Spiegel, *Last Trial*, esp. pp. XX, 24, 27, 104 and 138. It was during this time that the "ashes of Isaac" began to be worn on foreheads on fast days, implying that Isaac was indeed burned.

[21] Owen, Wilfred, *The Collected Poems of Wilfred Owen*, cited in Spiegel, *Last Trial* (see footnote pp. xii-xiii).

[22] I think not. I suggest that it is an attempt to combine two different traditions; one deriving from an agricultural society, and the other from a nomadic one. It is quite likely that this is behind the Cain and Abel story.

[23] I chose the *Theogony* precisely because it is a theological work and records how a new religion was inaugurated, although there are other stories which may appear to be more closely parallel; in particular that of Athamas who set to sacrifice his son Phrixis. At the last moment a golden ram flew down and rescued Phrixis, carried him off to Colchis at the east end of the Black Sea. Here Phrixis sacrificed the ram, hung the fleece on a tree guarded by a dragon. It was this fleece that Jason went in search of several generations later. This story, or that of Abraham in reverse order, could have traveled via Colchis, Boghaz-koy, Kültepe to Haran.

[24] West, Martin, *Hesiod's Theogony*, ed. and with Prolegomena and Commentary (Oxford: Clarendon Press, 1966) 20, 28.

[25] Hesiodus, *The Works and Days, Theogony, The Shield of Herakles*, trans. Richmond Lattimore (Ann Arbor: University of Michigan, 1959) 132.

[26] Graves, Robert, *The Greek Myths* (Harmondsworth, Middlesex, England: Penguin Books, 1973) 1.38.

[27] Hesiodus, op. cit., p. 150 (italics mine).

[28] The stone enshrined in the Kaa'ba at Mecca, is in Muslim tradition the stone upon which Abraham intended to sacrifice Ishmael. Previously, the stone was sacred to a female deity.

[29] West, op. cit., p. 290.

[30] Hesiodus, op. cit., pp. 176-77.

[31] Eusebius, *Preparation for the Gospel*, trans. Edwin H. Gifford (Oxford, 1903) Book I, Chap. 10, pp. 36-38.

[32] Cross, Frank Moore, *Canaanite Myth and Hebrew Epic* (Cambridge, MA: Harvard University, 1973) 26; see also n. 18.

[33] Cross, op. cit., pp. 65, 66.

[34] Mace, David, *Hebrew Marriage*: A Sociological Study, Philosophical Library (New York, 1953) 206.

236

[35] Aeschylus, "The Eumenides," third part of the *Oresteia*, trans. Richmond Lattimore (Chicago: University of Chicago, 1967) 158.

[36] Ibid., p. 163.

[37] Ibid., p. 163.

[38] Ibid., p. 166.

[39] Graves, op. cit., 2.70.

[40] Kramer, Samuel Noah, "The Goddesses and the Theologians: Reflections on Women's Rights in Ancient Sumer," paper delivered in Munich 1970, (personal pre-publication copy).

[41] The implications for the "mystery" of the Christian Trinity should be obvious.

[42] Speiser, *Genesis*, op. cit. pp. 93-94; see also "The Wife-Sister belief in the Patriarchal Narratives" in *Biblical and Other Studies*, ed. A. Altman (Cambridge, MA: Harvard University, 1963).

[43] Mace, op. cit., p. 248.

[44] Gordon, Cyrus, *The Common Background of Greek and Hebrew Civilizations*. (New York: W. W. Norton Co., 1965) 290.

[45] Langer, William, "Infanticide: A Historical Survey" (personal pre-publication copy).

[46] Bakan, David, "Paternity in the Judeo-Christian Tradition," in *Changing Perspectives in the Scientific Study of Religion*, ed. Allen W. Eister (New York: John Wiley, 1974) 208.

[47] A recent example is a 1976 song, "You're having my baby," by pop singer Paul Anka.

A MOTHER IN ISRAEL:
Aspects of the Mother Role in Jewish Myth*

Rachel Adler
University of Minnesota

The title "A Mother in Israel" suggested itself to me
in a mischievous mood. It is now a stock phrase in rabbin-
ical panegyrics on the traditional mother role. It is
amusing to reflect that the expression, within its original
context, and the mother role itself may have significance
which would startle a modern clergyman. Using evidence
from Biblical myth, rabbinic and post-rabbinic midrash and
halachic (legal) discourse, I will trace a strain within
Jewish tradition which subtracts the creative aspect from
the mother role in order to augment the power of a patriarchal deity and of the human father. Let me emphasize that
this is a single strain within the tradition, although it
seems to me a powerful, indeed, a dominant one. Jewish
tradition is not monolithic, and in mythic expressions it
is particularly flexible. In midrash, mutually exclusive
myths coexist side by side. At no time have Jewish scholars attempted to harmonize them. Instead, they were considered to represent different mythic perspectives. Moreover, the entire midrashic process, which is still ongoing,
permits myths to be reformulated, reinterpreted, retold,
each time a generation has outgrown its earlier meanings
or finds them insufficient. Hence, once having determined
the existence and the direction of a mythological strain,
we can add new elements to it, retell its stories, and
change its direction. That will be our final goal with the
strain we are going to trace in this paper.

A male god's assumption of the human female's role in
conception and parturition occurs in the myths of many
other Mediterranean and Near Eastern cultures beside ancient Israel. The accounts all wrestle with the difficulties involved in a concrete representation of this

237

accomplishment. These difficulties are well expressed in
a Hittite myth in which two gods, Kumarbi and Anu, battle
for supremacy.[1] Kumarbi bites off Anu's genitals, and Anu
triumphantly informs Kumarbi that he has been made pregnant. An arresting feature of Kumarbi's pregnancy is a
dialogue in which Anu and the fetal storm-god debate which
orifice of Kumarbi's body is to be the exit. Unfortunately,
the myth exists only in fragmentary form. Kumarbi collapses, complaining that his mouth hurts, and we learn only
that the deity comes forth from "the good place"--whatever
place that may be.

If I had to guess the storm god's point of egress, I
would speculate that it was some part of Kumarbi's head.
Anal birth, the closest analogy to vaginal birth, appears
in no known Near Eastern myth and I would therefore think
it less probable in Kumarbi's case. What may be substituted, as in the case of Dionysus' second birth from Zeus,
is a more decorous and esthetically pleasing birth from
the side or the thigh--a mythic Caesarian section.[2] But
it is more common for a male deity to give birth from the
head. The Egyptian god, Atum, creates by this method as
does Re.[3] Zeus brings forth Athena from his head.[4] Creation by the word is an etherealized creation from the head,
as is breathing into Adam the breath of life. In their
less ethereal forms, the pregnancy and parturition of male
deities seem monstrous, often ludicrous tales. One must
postulate an overwhelming theological need in order to explain them. In only one of these myths can birth-giving
be viewed as evidence of weakness. Kumarbi's pregnancy is
meant to signify his defeat in a battle which he could have
otherwise be supposed to have won. His is the only overt
role-reversal. In the other myths the god has not become
more feminine. Rather, he *augments* the male fertilizing
role with the female ability to conceive and give birth.
While remaining honorably masculine, he contains within
himself all that is valuable or unique about femaleness.
If he so desires, he can be utterly self-sufficient.

That being so, we should expect that in patriarchal
monotheism, where the self-sufficiency of the deity is of
the utmost theological importance, the creative aspect of
the female role will be claimed by the masculine deity,
and hence by his male worshippers, who know themselves to
be made in his image. For Judaic monotheism, however,
sexual creation myths have a grave drawback. They are
powerfully anthropomorphic. Anthropomorphism in myth is
always a question of degree. Yet it is true that Jewish
sources de-emphasize or moderate anthropomorphisms. In
none of the Biblical source documents, therefore, is God
male, although He is masculine in all. God gives birth,
therefore, only metaphorically, in poetry. Such an image
occurs in Moses' farewell song, where God is the womb who
brought forth the people of Israel: צור ילדך תשי, ותשכח
א-ל מחללך "You have neglected the rock who bore you; you
have forgotten God who labored with you."[5] In the P account, therefore, God creates solely by the word, while in
the more concrete J account He forms man out of earth and
blows breath into his nostrils.[6] But the role of birth-
giver, too important to be rejected yet too anthropomorphic
to be taken by God, is passed on by J to the creature
fashioned in God's image, and thus man gives birth to woman.

Many writers have recognized in this history an attempt to diminish the importance of Eve. The midrash which
alleges that Eve was created from Adam's vestigial tail is
a later reflection of this diminution.[7] Writers with axes
to grind are quick to identify Eve as a devalued mother
goddess, noting that her title "Mother of All the Living"
is a title of the goddess Aruru, whose priestess initiates
Enkidu sexually, thus making him "wise...like a god."[8] A
less biased scholar, Samuel Noah Kramer, suggests that
there are strong parallels between the Hebrew Fall and the
Sumerian myth in which the earth-goddess, Nin-hursag, cur-
ses the king of the gods, Enki, who has eaten her special

plants which, the text emphasizes, were born without pain or travail.[9] One of the deities Nin-hursag creates to heal Enki is Nin-ti, a pun on "the lady of the rib"/"the lady who makes live." The Biblical myth may be regarded as an inversion of this Sumerian myth in which the eater of forbidden vegetation is the Mother of All the Living. She is cursed by God the King and fated to be inferior to her consort and to bear children in pain. The Sumerian pun on "rib"/"make live" is transformed into a grimmer Hebrew pun on "rib"/"stumble."

Eve is the one who makes man stumble. She is an anticreator. God and Adam bring life into the world; Eve brings death into the world. This is implicit in the text. In midrashic terms one might say that God creates the light and Eve puts out the light. Exactly this image occurs in a medieval midrash collection, *Midrash Tanhuma*.

> Said the Holy One, blessed is He: Let her be given the commandment of menstrual impurity on account of the blood she shed. And the commandment of hallah. Why? Because Adam was the hallah offering of the world and she came and defiled him....And the commandment of lighting the Sabbath lights, because Adam was the light of the Holy One, blessed is He, as it says in Scripture, "The soul of man [lit. *adam*] is the light of God" [Prov 20:27], and she came and extinguished it. Let her be given the commandment of the lights to make her atone for the light she extinguished.[10]

The Hebrew myth contains a further reversal on the Sumerian myth of Enki and Nin-hursag. The goddess' ability to give birth without pain or travail is, in the Hebrew myth, assigned to Adam. He, and not Eve, gives birth in prelapsarian Eden. Eve's subsequent parturition is therefore devalued in two ways. First, it is not itself an original event but an imitation of the original event. Second, Eve and her daughters can never exactly reproduce the original childbirth. All they are capable of is an imitation which is messy and painful and thus inexact.

Eve's daughters duplicate only the consequence of Eve's sin, the clumsy version of Adam's cast-off accomplishment assigned her as a punishment.

When the Sumerian or Assyrian woman gave birth, she reproduced an act of cosmic significance. Her midwife recited the myth of the mother goddess' creation of humans, praying, "As the Bearing One gives birth,/May the mother of the child bring forth by herself."[11] The labor of the Jewish woman lacked such comforts. Biblical myth assured her, "I will make intense your pangs in childbearing,/In pain shall you bear children."[12] In the Mishnah the sages warn, "For three sins women die in childbirth: Because they are not observant of the laws of menstrual impurity, hallah, and kindling of the Sabbath lights."[13] Why particularly in childbirth? In the Gemara, the third-century sage Raba adds, "When the ox is fallen, sharpen the knife."[14] Childbirth, then, is viewed by this strain in the tradition in a punitive light. It is a time of agony, vulnerability and mortal danger.

What we have been observing is an effort to devalue the act of childbirth. Since the insurmountable fact is that women rather than men bear children, one way to annex this function to the male domain is to reinterpret childbirth as a cast-off male function passed on to women with some added disadvantages. Meanwhile, conception is identified as a purely male accomplishment and re-valued as the essential creative act. This second process culminates in the Talmud. The majority opinion in the Mishnah asserts that the commandment, "Be fruitful and multiply," is addressed exclusively to males.[15] The sole dissenter, an early second-century Tanna, Rabbi Johanan ben Beroka, cites the plural phrasing and context of the commandment in Genesis 1:28 to argue that Adam and Eve are both addressed. To counter his position, the sages of the Gemara tack on the next words of the commandment, "fill the earth and subdue it." They argue that subduing or conquest (כיבוש) is

characteristic only of males. Moreover, the word וכבשה,
meaning "and subdue it," without the Masoretic voweling
can be read as a masculine singular rather than as a plural. Having established that "subdue it" may be viewed as
an exclusively male commandment, they then generalize from
it to the earlier words, "Be fruitful and multiply." Re-
treating from this position, however, the Gemara then de-
rives the commandment from a later verse in which the re-
cipients are unambiguously male: "God blessed Noah and his
sons and said to them, 'Be fruitful and multiply and fill
the earth'" (Gen 9:1).

Now, usually, if a commandment is stated in full more
than once, either all of the statements are utilized in
legal exegesis or the first statement is used. Here, the
first statement is left without any exegetical function.
Moreover, there are only a few cases where exegesis overturns a clear statement of the law. Such a case is, for
example, "an eye for an eye," where the plain meaning of
the text became utterly unacceptable in the living common-
law of the Oral Tradition. Since the first instance of
"Be fruitful and multiply" clearly states that both man
and woman are addressed, only a powerful social reason
would explain why the sages sought an alternative source
for the command. Finally, where several proof-texts are
offered and then abandoned by the sages, it is usually because they are having difficulty in deriving the law. The
unusual and rather unsatisfactory methods utilized in this
Talmudic passage suggest that the sages were strongly motivated to assign men sole responsibility for human repro-
duction.[16]

Another evidence of the devaluing of the female creative role occurs in the mythological figure of Lilith, who
first appears as a demoness in Isa 34:14. References to
Lilith are fragmentary but frequent in Talmud and Midrash.
Amulets and bowls bearing incantations against Lilith date
from ca. 600 A. D.[17] Her evil personality was further
developed in Kabbalistic mysticism. In her apotheosis, she

is the slave-woman who replaces the Shekhinah as the consort of God. From this unspeakable union derive all the
agonies of the Exile.[18] Lilith, the beautiful and seductive, haunted the marriage bed tempting men to take pleasure in sex.[19] Red ribbons hanging around an infant's crib
are still used in some Hasidic homes to protect the child
against Lilith. The most complete account of the Lilith
myth is found in the early medieval midrash collection,
Alpha Beta d'Ben Sirach.[20] She is said to have been the
first wife of Adam and to have rebelled against the sub-
servient role demanded of her. In this account, Lilith
leaves Adam, pronounces God's name, flies up into the air
and makes her home by the Red Sea. Rejecting the nurturant role prescribed for women, she becomes a child-murder-
er. Lilith is a true counterpart of Lucifer, the first of
God's creations to fall. Like Lucifer, she sins through
rebellion and is sustained by her pride. Whereas Lucifer
sets himself up as the adversary of God, Lilith sets herself up as the adversary of man.

Part of Lilith's rebellion against patriarchal power
is her assumption of the "masculine" power of creativity.
She is extravagantly fecund, bearing hundreds of demons a
day. Her fecundity begins as soon as she is separated
from Adam and settled at the Red Sea, her own territory.
It is seen as terrifying, the outpouring of an alien and
uncontrollable energy. It is, moreover, significant that
the children produced by autonomous female power are demons. The woman who is autonomously fruitful is evil.

A virtuous and God-fearing woman is one who gracefully
accedes her creative role to the Deity, applauding His fertility when she is miraculously endowed with a child. An
extraordinary number of women in the Bible are barren:
Sarah, Rebecca, Rachel, the mother of Samson, Hannah, the
woman of Shunem in II Kings 4. The barren woman who receives a child from God is a favorite theme in Psalms. "He
turns the barren wife into a happy mother of children,

Hallelujah" (Ps 113:9). The עקרה, or barren woman, is
useful because she proves God's "fertility," so to speak.
Hence, midrashim from the Talmudic to the late medieval
collections industriously multiply the number of barren
women in the Bible and dramatize the miracle of their conception. According to a Talmudic midrash (Yebamoth 64b),
Sarah had no womb. Numbers Rabbah explains that the angel
who appeared to Samson's mother was careful to inform her
that it was she and not her husband who was the barren one
(Naso 10.5). According to Resh Lakish in Ruth Rabbah 6.2,
Ruth was forty years old when she became pregnant and had
Obed by a miracle. In Ruth Rabbah 7.14, moreover, he asserts that Ruth, too, lacked the main portion of her womb.
In late midrashim, even the ostensibly prolific Leah is
listed as a barren mother.[21]

We have established that man, in Jewish tradition, is
endowed with the primary creative role. In some views,
women bear no responsibility for generation other than
gestation and parturition. At his most god-like, however,
man can create self-sufficiently, utterly independent of
woman. This creation, like God's, utilizes both verbal and
craftsmanly techniques. All that is required is a sufficient degree of virtue to be worthy of creative power. The
result of the righteous man's creative power is the golem,
a humanoid created by magic, usually to serve its creator.
The first such creatures appear in the Talmud.

> Rava said: If the righteous wished, they could
> create a world,...for Rava created a man and
> sent him to Rabbi Zera. The rabbi spoke to him
> and he did not answer. Then he said: You must
> have been made by the colleagues [of the acad-
> emy]. Return to your dust.[22]

In the story which follows this, Rabbi Oshaya and Rabbi
Hanina utilize the Book of Creation to create a calf to
slaughter and eat for the Sabbath. The more righteous the
man, the more impressively he can duplicate the Divine
creation. There are, however, limits. Rava's golem is

mute, and although some later golems speak they lack souls.
"This creation of a golem," says Gershom Scholem, "is an
end in itself, a ritual of initiation into the secret of
creation....It confirmed man in his likeness to God."[23]
Originally an esoteric creature, the golem came into popular legend during the fifteenth and sixteenth centuries,
when great numbers of famous scholars were credited with
having produced golems.

Viewing the tradition from this vantage point, in
which God and man monopolize both natural and supernatural
creative powers, one must ask what function the mother role
would have in its framework. As many modern rabbis have
admitted, there is little concrete material in the tradition specifying exactly which roles are necessarily or consistently feminine. Part of the reason for this is that,
as tasks came to require much skill or became systematized
or industrialized, they were transferred from women to men.
This was the case with agriculture, pottery-making, weaving and bread-baking. The feminine tasks and roles in Jewish societies were those rejected by males. The other
problem is that we have fewer models and statements about
feminine roles in Jewish texts than about male roles.
Moreover, there seems clearly to have been a narrowing of
roles acceptable for women which began very early in Biblical history and proceeded through the Talmudic period.
Nevertheless, I think we can hypothesize that while the
emphasis on the creative aspect of the mother role was reduced, the emphasis on its nurturant aspect was greatly extended. Moreover, in the earliest Biblical sources, this
nurturant role involved much more than the cosseting of a
husband, children or dependents within the nuclear family.
We tend to forget that the Four Mothers--Sarah, Rebecca,
Rachel and Leah--were wives of wealthy chieftains. Their
machinations are attempts to secure for their sons the pre-
eminent rights to political power and riches, or, as in the
case of Rachel and Leah, struggles to become the more

powerful wife by having more sons and hence having access
to the political power of these sons in the future. Their
nurturance, therefore, contains a strong element of self-
aggrandizement as well as a powerful, even ruthless, protective capacity. Sarah casts Hagar out without a moment
of remorse. Rebecca hoodwinks her husband in order to dis-
possess her less favored son.

During the period of the First Temple, this role sheds
much of its protective aspect and becomes quite overtly a
political career available to a highly placed woman: the
g'virah.[24] Originally the g'virah was the mother of the
king. This was the role Bathsheba was seeking to secure
(or, conceivably, retain) for herself in I Kings 1, where
she allies herself with Nathan the prophet to extract a
promise from the aged David that her son Solomon would be
designated heir to the throne. Later in the history of
the monarchy, a sufficiently powerful g'virah might retain
her position without being at all related to the king.

Even when a woman possesses creative power, it is
usually her nurturance which is stressed. Hence, although
Miriam is identified as a prophetess during a period in
which a prophet is a miracle-worker, a source of new religious knowledge, and a poet, she is portrayed as the protector of her infant brother Moses and as the leader of a
women's victory chorus repeating a song sung by Moses.[25]

Although Deborah is also identified as a prophetess, what
is emphasized is her role as a quasi-military leader,
uniting, encouraging and reassuring the tribal armies. In
fact, the only woman in the Bible other than Deborah who
acts as a prophet is the obscure prophetess Huldah, who is
consulted by King Josiah in the Book of Kings. Much later,
the sages of the Gemara are puzzled by her assumption of
this "masculine" role. How could Josiah have consulted
her in preference to her contemporary, Jeremiah? The
school of Rabbi Shela replies, "Because women are tender-
hearted."[26] That is, her nurturant qualities will, he
thinks, ensure a more compassionate prophecy.

The Biblical expression which seems to exemplify this
powerful protective aspect of the mother role is אם
בישראל, "mother in Israel." The expression occurs only
twice. Deborah uses it to refer to herself during her
victory song.

> In the days of Shamgar son of Anath
> In the days of Jael
> Caravans ceased and travelers kept to the byways,
> The peasantry ceased in Israel, they ceased,
> Till I arose, Deborah, till I arose a mother in
>   Israel (Judg 5:5-7).

The other user of the expression is the wise woman of the
city of Avel of Bet Maacah (II Samuel 20). This city offers refuge to the rebel Sheva ben Bikri, who has challenged the monarchy of David. The city is besieged, and
the wise woman initiates a parley with David's general.
"You seek to destroy a city which is a mother in Israel;
why will you swallow up the inheritance of the Lord?" (II
Sam 20:1).

The term "mother in Israel," then, is an expression
used to describe a power which is institutional. Deborah
uses it to describe her protective abilities as a quasi-
military ruler, in contrast to her less effective pre-
decessor. The wise woman, who is herself a political con-
sultant, uses it to describe the rootedness and legitimacy
of a city. In reference to a city, moreover, the expression is probably related to the word אמה, "mother city, met-
ropolis."[27] Towns attached to the mother city were called
בנות, "daughters," implying some sort of protective relationship between them.[28] The ties were, in fact, economic,
administrative and military.[29] Which came first, the identification of mothers with city symbolism or the identification of cities with mother symbolism, is impossible to
say. However, Deborah's reference to herself as a "mother
in Israel" does demonstrate that the term is applicable to
persons and, by context, that it connotes powerful protection, and scholars agree that the song of Deborah is one
of the most ancient pieces of Biblical literature.[30]

In Jewish myth as well as in mythologized Jewish history, the woman who saves the Jewish people from catastrophe by her leadership or by some personal act of courage frequently figures. Jael, Deborah, Esther and Judith all fit this prototype. Jael is particularly interesting since both the Biblical text and later midrashic traditions portray her as a nurturant figure who suddenly turns on the man she is protecting. She repeats her words as one does in soothing a terrified child. "Turn aside, my lord, turn aside to me. Don't be afraid" (Judg 4:13). She gives him milk and puts him to sleep. A subsequent midrash asserts that Jael breast-fed Sisera.[31] The wise woman of Avel of Bet Maacah also illustrates the ruthlessness of an effective protector. Her task is to protect her city from siege while relinquishing as little autonomy as possible. She therefore stipulates that the hostage Sheva ben Bikri will not be surrendered alive, but that the citizens of the city will themselves execute him and throw his head over the city wall.

Another such character is Abigail, the wife of Nabal the Carmelite (I Samuel 25). Her husband, a wealthy landowner and an obnoxious drunken moral aborigine, offends David, who, still a king without a throne, is protecting the sheepfolds with his army. The servants, dismayed, go to Abigail, who immediately sends food for David's troops and herself goes to mollify him. David turns from his original intention of wiping out Nabal, his belongings and his employes, and Abigail returns home to find her husband drunk. She waits all night until he is cold sober and then tells him exactly what she has done. Nabal has a stroke and dies within two weeks time.

Jewish women who slaughtered their children rather than submit to conversion during the Crusades imitate this prototypic combination of nurturance and ruthlessness. One chronicler writes, "Tender mothers slaughtered with firm hand and heart their little children, and the little ones pronounced the unity of God as they gave up their souls on the bosom of their mothers."[32] Later militant mothers include resistance fighters of the Second World War, such as Tzviya Lubetkin, called, significantly enough, "the mother of the ghetto."[33] Marie Syrkin has an interesting account of this sort of mythologizing. "Of many young women who took leading parts in the resistance, I heard it said, 'She was called the mother.' Every ghetto apparently had its 'mother,' and sometimes more than one girl in the same ghetto was so addressed."[34]

We have, in summary, a powerful mythic strain with historical precedents as well, which depicts the mother role as a power-role involving leadership, daring and protectiveness on a societal rather than simply a familiar level. As Aviva Canter Zuckoff points out, this leadership role is usually permitted only in a time of crisis.[35] Nevertheless, the fact that women are considered to have such potential is significant. It certainly makes possible broader and more varied female roles than does the weak, family-devoted mother of Western stereotypes. Moreover, by making this broad protective role independent of biological motherhood, these traditional materials free women from narrow biologically-linked imagery: tedious comparisons with the earth of the moon and evocations ad nauseum of the miracles of pregnancy and birth.

While the mother in Israel seems to me a valid and useful prototype, it is nevertheless one-sided and incomplete, lacking in a creative aspect. We have much less mythic material to draw upon which depicts women or a feminine aspect of God as creators, either in the primary or in any secondary sense of the term. Woman is the created, not the creator, the named and not the namer. Seldom is she a poet, a prophet or a lawmaker.

In the materials we have traced, woman's creative aspect has been diminished while her nurturant has been greatly augmented. At the same time, we have an extension

of the masculine role to embrace the originally feminine
mysteries of creation and birth. It seems likely that this
extension stemmed from a sort of sexual imperialism, yet
however we wish to interpret it, the *range* of masculine
roles has unquestionably been broadened. It would be possible and feasible for us to reinterpret this role aggrandizement as a move toward human and divine androgyny. The
myths and images which stress God's mothering functions
could be the bases for new midrash in which God does not
arrogate these functions to His masculine self, but is
portrayed as possessing a feminine aspect. The same is
true of man. Here, for example, is a quotation from *Before There Was a Before*, a creation story ostensibly for
children, written by Arthur, David, and Shoshana Waskow.[36]
Their creation account, drawing upon two midrashim in
Genesis Rabbah, portrays the first human as an androgynous
being who importunes God to be separated into two sexes.[37]
God reluctantly agrees, but warns, "From now on, you, woman, will be the one who gives birth to children. That will
make it very easy for men to stop caring about children
and leave all childbirth and child care to women. I don't
want that. I want to be sure that people remember that
men are really part of giving birth too, and should care
about children. So maybe if I pass the word that the first
human was a man and that the first man gave birth, they'll
remember that men should learn to give birth. Imagine how
strange the story will sound! So they'll certainly pay
attention."

This seems to me an ethical contemporary interpretation of material which originally did not stress androgyny.
Rabbi Richard Levy uses a similar midrashic process when
he traces the word רחמים, "mercy," back to its root, רחם,
"womb, and therefore translates the phrase האב-הרחמן--
literally, the merciful Father--as "the motherly Father."[38]
From here it is a short step to viewing God as both mother
and father, lover and mistress, king and queen. Possibly

we may draw upon Kabbalistic mysticism for tools and images. The assumption is that the imagery we have is not unworkable but simply needs to be supplemented. Richard Levy supplies feminine imagery for describing the nurturant aspect of God. What is urgently needed are images and stories which emphasize the nurturant aspect of man.

The other great need is for midrash stressing the creative aspect of woman. Possibly the figure of the wise woman will give us a way to bridge the gap between nurturance and creativity. The difference between a wise woman and a prophetess seems less a matter of kind than of degree. Deborah seems to have functioned as both.[39] The point on the continuum at which the wise woman is most like the prophetess might be the proper context in which to portray characters like the Talmudic sage Beruria, or women who had access to an esoteric tradition like Adel, the daughter of the Baal Shem Tov, or Feige, the mother of Rabbi Nachman of Bratslav, or those women who functioned as Ḥasidic rebbes, such as Chana Rachel the Maid of Ludomir, or Malkele the Triskerin.

Another figure who bridges the gap is Hannah. Like the matriarchs, she is a barren mother, but she is also a poet and a great mistress of prayer. Traditionally she is credited with the invention of silent prayer. Hannah could be used to typify a spiritual creativity which is usually lacking in feminine roles.

Finally, it is important to remind ourselves that we have been discussing only the mother role and that, although traditionally it includes roles which we do not identify as related to motherhood, categorizing these roles as mother-roles may itself be limiting rather than liberating. I would hope that, whatever new midrash we do create, it will not conform only to one ideology or portray feminine roles by only one definition or in only one way. Because midrash has never been monolithic, it has been able to offer its students choices among truths as well as the

richness of paradox and conflict. Moreover, I would hope
that we can resist the temptation to write propaganda in
place of midrash. I have no use for a modern midrash which
cannot find a place for Rebecca the controlling mother,
Michal the bitch, and brutal Jezebel.

NOTES

*This article has appeared in *Davka* 17, pp. 20-28.

[1] Albrecht Goetze, trans., "Kingship in Heaven: Hittite Myths, Epics, and Legends," James Pritchard, ed., *Ancient Near Eastern Texts Relating to the Old Testament* (Princeton, NJ: Princeton University, 1955) 120-21. This text will henceforth be abbreviated *ANET*.

[2] Robert Graves, *Greek Myths* 1, rev. ed. (Harmondsworth, Middlesex, England: Penguin Books) 56.

[3] John A. Wilson, trans., "The Theology of Memphis" and "The Repulsing of the Dragon and the Creation: Egyptian Myths, Tales, and Mortuary Texts," *ANET*, pp. 5-6.

[4] Graves, 1, p. 46.

[5] Deut 32:18.

[6] Authorship assigned according to E. A. Speiser, ed., *Genesis*, Anchor Bible (Garden City, NY: Doubleday, 1964) 2:7, 1:26-27.

[7] Berakhot 61a.

[8] E. A. Speiser, trans., "The Epic of Gilgamesh: Akkadian Myths and Epics," *ANET*, p. 75.

[9] Samuel Noah Kramer, *Mythologies of the Ancient World* (Garden City, NY: Doubleday, 1961) 102-3.

[10] Midrash Tanhuma, Bereshit 59a.

[11] E. A. Speiser, trans., "Creation of Man by the Mother Goddess (Assyrian version): Akkadian Myths and Epics," *ANET*, p. 100.

[12] Gen 3:16.

[13] Mishnah Shabbat 2:6.

[14] Shabbat 31b-32a.

[15] Yebamot 65b.

[16] An amusing consequence is that women, having no obligation to reproduce, have no reason to refrain from using birth control as long as the method does not cause the man to commit the sin of spilling semen outside the vagina.

David Feldman, *Birth Control in Jewish Law* (New York: New York University, 1968) details the ingenious means used by later authorities to prohibit women from inviting men to exercise their obligation unilaterally.

[17] Raphael Patai, *The Hebrew Goddess* (New York: Ktav, 1967) 221.

[18] Patai, pp. 239-241.

[19] Gershom Scholem, *On the Kabbalah and Its Symbolism*, trans. Ralph Manheim (New York: Schocken, 1965) 157.

[20] *Alpha Beta d'Ben Sirach*, 47.

[21] Louis Ginberg, *Legends of the Jews* 5, iii; 6, p. 296 (Philadelphia: Jewish Publication Society, 1968) citing Aggadat Bereshit 52, 106-7 and Midrash Ha-Gadol I, 192, 468-469.

[22] Sanhedrin 65b.

[23] Scholem, p. 177.

[24] Roland De Vaux, *Ancient Israel* 1 (New York: McGraw-Hill, 1965) 117-9.

[25] Otto Eissfeldt, *The Old Testament: An Introduction*, trans. Peter Ackroyd (New York: Harper and Row, 1965) 211. Eissfeldt contends that the song at the Red Sea, which in Exodus 15 is attributed to Moses, is in fact a "secondary addition" to or "elaboration" of a far more ancient hymn by Miriam whose refrain is quoted in 15:21. He points out on p. 99 that victory songs are generally created by women. One may speculate that the text is seeking to de-emphasize the importance of Miriam by attributing her song to her brother.

[26] Megillah 14b.

[27] Francis Brown, S. R. Driver and Charles Briggs, *A Hebrew and English Lexicon of the Old Testament* (Oxford: Clarendon, 1966).

[28] Brown, Driver and Briggs cite numerous examples under בן, section 4.

[29] De Vaux, *Ancient Israel* 1, p. 228.

[30] Eissfeldt, pp. 100-101.

[31] Ginzberg, *Legends of the Jews* 6, p. 198. Ginzberg cites a medieval collection, *Rimzei Haftarot*, quoting an

aggadah to this effect. He further states that Niddah
55b and Tosefta Shabbat 8:24 presuppose the legend, which
would make its date as early as the second century C.E.
I have been able to check only the reference in Niddah,
which quotes Judges 4:19 in connection with a legal question about breast milk. This does seem to presuppose the
legend.

[32] Edmund Fleg, *The Jewish Anthology*, trans. Maurice
Samuel (New York: Behrman, 1940) 157.

[33] Rufus Learsi, *Israel: A History of the Jewish People* (Cleveland and New York: World Publishing, 1949) 654.

[34] Marie Syrkin, *Blessed is the Match* (Philadelphia:
Jewish Publication Society, 1947).

[35] Aviva Canter Zuckoff, "The Oppression of the Jewish
Woman," *Response* (Summer, 1973) 47-54.

[36] Arthur, David, and Shoshana Waskow, *Before There
Was a Before*, forthcoming.

[37] Genesis Rabbah 5:1.

[38] Rabbi Richard Levy, Director, Los Angeles Hillel
Council; from an unpublished speech.

[39] Conversely, the wise woman of Tekoa in II Samuel 14
is simply a skilled diplomat, a person experienced in
speaking and negotiating, brought in by a principal who
cannot afford to display his own hand in the business.

IV. THE WOMEN'S MOVEMENT AND FEMINIST THEOLOGY:

Nineteenth Century Arguments and
Twentieth Century Continuities

FROM MOTHERHOOD TO SISTERHOOD:
The Search for Female Religious Imagery in
Nineteenth and Twentieth Century Theology

Gayle Kimball
California State University, Chico

Western religion employs male images and symbols such
as God the Father, the Son, and the brotherhood of man.
American spokeswomen for at least two centuries have
sought to establish a place for women in religious termi-
nology, imagery and values. The reaction of women was
first to build on a primary female function--motherhood.
Harriet Beecher Stowe and Charlotte Perkins Gilman were
representative women who conceived a religious value system
based on motherly virtues of love and self-sacrificing service. Later thinkers, our contemporaries such as Mary
Daly, rejected an emphasis on motherhood, substituting
egalitarian sisterhood. This paper traces the search for
women's values defined as life-affirming, joyful, accepting
of the body and the earth, communal, sisterly.

Harriet Beecher Stowe was the most widely read novel-
ist of the nineteenth century and was a member of the prominent Beecher family of popular preachers. Her outpouring
of thirty books reflected and shaped the nineteenth century's glorification of the saving power of women as mothers. Mothers were like Christ in their loving self-sacri-
fice--a theme which was first developed by her older sister Catharine. Catharine Beecher explained that theories
about religion are "especially to be examined and decided
on by woman, as the heaven-appointed educator of infancy
and childhood."[1] Stowe added that mothers had a mediating
power; as one of her male characters said, "Mother, if I
ever get to heaven it will be through you."

In her Protestant Mariology Stowe stressed the role
of the mother of Jesus. In fact, since Mary was the only
earthly parent of Jesus, Harriet concluded that he had

more of the feminine than any other man. She spoke of
Mary as the teacher of Jesus, neglecting mention of Joseph.
Mary was also more insightful than the disciples, understanding more calmly and clearly what Christ's purpose was;
and she stood by him at the cross when his male disciples
had deserted him.

Stowe told her readers that without a good mother and
the wife who takes her place a man is lost; for, "We all
need the motherly, and we must find it in a wife" who
guides, cares for, tactfully teaches and catechises her
husband.[2] No altar is higher than the home altar; a serene
home heals those who come to it for succor. The home is a
mother's shrine, throne and empire, "more holy than cloister, more saintly and pure than church or altar."[3] Harriet
believed that women were special instruments of God's
grace. Their physical beauty is an inspiration to men and
their love has redeeming powers, for women are finer, more
tender and devoted, and less open to temptation than men.
Love is a sacrament and women are best able to love; therefore, "In matters of grace God sets a special value on
woman's nature and design to put special honor upon it"
and she urged the clergy to enumerate woman's influence
among the means of grace.[4]

In the twentieth century Aimee Semple McPherson and
Kathryn Kuhlman perpetuated Stowe's identification of wom-
en as oriented to the heart rather than to the mind and
saw women as closely tied to the role of nurturing loving
mother. McPherson defined herself as a "little mother
evangelist" preaching love and joy rather than the "mazes
of man's theology."[5]

McPherson's contemporary, feminist Charlotte Perkins
Gilman, disapproved of "modern motherolitry" but as a
transitional figure she retained much of the emphasis on
motherhood which she believed caused women to be altruis-
tic, loving, and concerned with social progress. She
explained that "the desire of the mother soul is to give

benefit rather than to receive it." Women see the word
"life" not as a noun but as "living," an active verb.
(This is also the theme of Mary Daly.) Gilman advocated
that mothers who carefully selected their mates could
"send forth a new kind of people to help the world...,"
instead of being used as servants and pseudo-mothers to
their husbands. She hoped for "the mother who is uprising,
whose deep, sweet current of uplifting love is to pour forward into service." She saw motherhood as the "supreme
power of the world..."[6]

In opposition to female emphasis on love, joy, and
service, Gilman condemned men for projecting a God of violence, wrath, vengefulness, pride and judgment. She believed that religion suffered from male domination and that
men's views were shaped by their experience as hunters
which caused them to focus on death and the afterlife. She
faulted male oriented religion for stressing obedience and
submission which is what men wish women to practice.

Present feminist theologians also react to male values,
what Sheila Collins calls the "demon of patriarchalism" or
what Mary Daly calls "demonic phallic morality," destructive machismo. Daly and Rosemary Ruether find that male
dominance leads to heirarchical dualities, splits between:
I/it, we/them, God/Devil, good/bad, humans/nature, and
feminine/masculine. Patriarchal religion emphasizes guilt,
judgment and death rather than the love, joy and life-giving attributes of God. Women from Stowe to Ruether agree
on this observation of the grimness and duality of male
religious expression.

Current feminist theologians still touch on the theme
of motherhood. Women have searched for historical models
and images. They focus on the Virgin Mary as one of the
few female symbols in Christianity. The Virgin must symbolically free and "save" the Son, writes Daly. While the
Virgin was traditionally important only in her relationship
to her son, "The New Being of antichurch is a rising up of

Mother and Daughter together, beyond the Madonna's image
and beyond the ambivalent Warrior-Maiden's image [of Joan
or Arc]."[7] Daly advocates that women draw on the potential
strength of Mary and Joan as important women, that women
bond together with their new sense of strength, and leave
the church which perpetuates women's subordinant position
to men. The keynote is no longer self-sacrifice for wom-
en but affirmation and acceptance of self.

Daly points out that the church honored Mary and
motherhood but no mortal woman could duplicate the the
feat of a virgin birth and that the church usurped mothers'
functions. Male priests, wearing skirts and caps, substituted baptism for birth, communion for feeding, baptism
for washing and extreme unction for consolation. The
church honored the motherly qualities of service, self-
abnegation, humility, charity and meekness but expected
them actually to be carried out by women and not by male
leaders of the church. Thus, Daly explains that "the traditional morality of our culture has been 'feminine' in
the sense of hypocritically idealizing some of the qualities imposed upon the oppressed."[8]

Reverend Letty Russell also utilized the theme of
motherhood, noting that God is called mother or wife in
the Old Testament, and described as a mother bird with
sheltering wings, as in the Psalms. She suggests that a
new model of ministry should include the role of mother,
advocate, and layperson. Both men and women would learn
to "specialize in this nurturing, enabling and mediating
role..."[9] The Virgin-Mother, the ancient goddess who had
no need of a consort, is an image also used by Penelope
Washbourn and by Beatrice Bruteau. The former explains
that women can use the model of the goddess as independent
and complete in her own being and the latter sees the Virgin as a symbol for unity and oneness coupled with the
concept of the Mother as creative multiplicity.[10] The
Virgin Mother provided a complementary image to God as the
Father.

The notion of motherhood also appears in feminist liturgies such as a worship service titled "Motherhood Reborn" celebrated at Graduate Theological Union in Berkeley which focused on grounding, creating, and delivery and defined God's presence as birthing that occurs within and among us."[11] Another feminist worship service referred to God as the "Lady of Birth."

For the most part, however, feminists have dropped the search for a female identity in the qualities arising from motherhood and have replaced it with the theme of sisterhood. A new mythology is being written as about the sisterhood of Eve and Lilith. Sisterhood stands for the opposite of male hierarchies and power structures of dominant and subordinate. It is associated with communal equalitarian values.

Sisterhood is a major theme for Mary Daly. She defines it as the revolutionary "bonding of those who have never bonded before."[12] She believes that sisters must form an exodus community to depart from the patriarchal church which offers no hope of reform. Women must form an anti-church, she states. Instead of artificial polarization, her aim is diarchy, of a "sisterhood of man" resulting in androgyny. Wholeness and androgyny are frequently reiterated feminist themes. To merge feeling and thought, the personal and political, to develop women who are full persons, adds to universal human becoming and thereby fulfills the Biblical promise that men and women are made in the image of God. That will be the Second Coming and is a transcendent spiritual event, Daly believes.

The Christa, the Coming of Women into actualization of their potential, is also looked for by Elizabeth Farians.[13] Letty Russell and Sheila Collins concur that women's liberation partakes of the numinous, as conversion to the women's movement is "structually similar to conversion to a new religious consciousness."[14] The liberation of women from their childlike status, their growth into maturity,

is a happening of such import, with such charge of new
energy, that it partakes of an awesome power and evolution.
Women are experiencing a "new way of seeing reality, which
might be likened by some to a conversion experience."[15]
These changes in the lives of women are signs of the Holy
Spirit at work, *subverting the church into being the
church*."[16] The community of support which frees women,
sends sisterhood on the way to servanthood, Letty Russell
believes, in the sense that newly maturing women are providing service to humanity. That women are developing a
new communal process is also asserted by an editor of
Women in a Strange Land.[17]

A new humanity is rising out of the woman's movement,
observes Ruether. The Judeo-Christian split between body/
soul, humans/nature, and self/other is being overcome.
Women have traditionally cultivated a communal personhood,
she notes; and are bringing about a new social ethic which
involves reconciliation with the garden earth and reconciliation of spirit and body.[18] Optimism about the ability
to change the human condition is part of the feminist
ethic.

In order to develop as persons who can manifest their
egalitarian values, women must search for their "stolen
identity," for past sources of strength and identity on
which to build. They are questing in many disciplines and
turning old images around. Traditional images of degrada-
tion for women are reversed: women find strength in Eve's
and Lilith's assertive acts and celebrate the "liberation
of the apples" in liturgy. They find delight in witches'
healing powers and rejection of the patriarchy.

Sifting through the history of religions women find
images such as the Hindu female Shakti as personification
of dynamic power and life-giving energy. The Old Testament
and Gnostic imagery of Wisdom as female, the Patristic view
of celibate female virgins as spiritual beings who formed
communities of women, and Shaker Ann Lee's and Mary Baker

Eddy's dual Mother-Father godhead are other examples of
what women find useful in self-definition. They return
often to the ancient mother goddess who Sheila Collins
finds has "transformative and integrative powers...equal
to that of the Christian Christ."[19]

Because there is such a paucity of female imagery in
Western religion, feminist scholars must be far ranging in
their pursuit for models, symbols and definitions of female
values. Literary images are a rich source as in the Heroine's quest for meaning in *Surfacing* by Marge Atwood or
Doris Lessing's *The Four Gated City*. Images in political
theory are found such as the nineteenth century French St.
Simonian expectation of a female messiah to redeem Western
society from excessive rationalism and sexual repression.
Themes from psychology are garnered by women such as Christine Downing, former president of the American Academy of
Religion.

Women are also thinking about the importance of their
own personal experiences as the source of definition of
female values. The consciousness raising discussion group
is the vehicle for sharing experiences. From these communal discussions emerges a theme for women's theology
which is the need for regaining the lost self. "The theme
of liberation and self-actualization which is found in the
concrete experiences of women thus forms the content of
feminist theology."[20] Not only is there the richness of
past history for women to draw from but also the content
of their own lives, is now seen as important and not trivial.

In feminist worship services and liturgies, women act
out the new imagery as in the passing of the apple from
which a bite is taken in commeroration of Eve's search for
knowledge. *Sister Celebrations* is a collection of liturgies which includes worship services such as "Sisterhood
Service on Mother's Day," combining nineteenth and twentieth century feminist images. In their rituals, women are

utilizing their sensuality and acceptance of the body, in dance, song, poetry, drama: these creative trans-rational activities have been described as right hemisphere of the brain functions which are more developed in females.

In addition to finding new sources of female imagery, women are asking for non-sexist language. Use the feminine pronoun for the Holy Spirit, says Letty Russell, for it is the Comforter and Reconciler. Search for the forgotten name of God, she asks, such as the plural meaning of Elohim. Mary Daly calls for the castration of language. She suggests that the world God may just be inherently oppressive, that, on the contrary, the concept of the Goddess is "loaded with healing associations."[20]

In conclusion, nineteenth century women used the traits of loving self-sacrifice projected on women by men to try to develop a sense of worth for subordinate women. Their strategy of giving pious women responsibility for converting souls was not realistic. Twentieth century feminist theologians are still attempting to rectify the problem of low status for women in the church. Some perhaps continue to make the error of exalting women as different from men in a female democratic cooperative spirit--which may only be a result of being oppressed. The concept of androgyny is an exciting one where women will be socialized, for example, to be assertive and men to be open with their emotions. The solution is, however, to have women's actual presence in religious leadership, not just female imagery. If change does not occur more rapidly, other conscious women will continue to follow Daly in her exodus from the patriarchal church, leaving it one sided in its expression of spirituality.

NOTES

[1]Catharine Beecher, *Commonsense Applied to Religion* (New York: Harper and Brothers, 1857) 25.

[2]Harriet Beecher Stowe, *My Wife and I* (New York: AMS, 1967, first published in 1871) 94-98.

[3]Idem, *The Minister's Wooing* (New York: Derby & Jackson, 1859) 566.

[4]Idem, *Dred* 1 (New York: AMS, 1967, first published in 1869) 357.

[5]Aimee Semple McPherson, *In the Service of the King: The Story of My Life* (New York: Boni & Liverwright, 1927) 89.

[6]Charlotte Perkins Gilman, *His Religion and Hers: A Study of Our Fathers and the Work of Our Mothers* (New York: Century, 1923) 92, 277, 279, 294.

[7]Mary Daly, *Beyond God the Father: Toward a Philosophy of Woman's Liberation* (Boston: Beacon, 1973) 130.

[8]Ibid., pp. 100, 195.

[9]Letty M. Russell, *Human Liberation in a Feminist Perspective--A Theology* (Philadelphia: Westminister, 1974) 180.

[10]Penelope Washbourn, "Differentiation and Difference--Reflections on the Ethical Implications of Women's Liberation," and Beatrice Bruteau, The Image of the Virgin Mother," *Women and Religion* (Missoula, MT: Scholars Press, 1974) 93, 127.

[11]Arlene Swidler, ed., *Sister Celebrations* (Philadelphia: Fortress, 1974) 11.

[12]Mary Daly, *The Church and the Second Sex* (New York: Harper and Row, 1975) 265.

[13]Elizabeth Farians, "The Coming of Woman: the Christa" (Pittsburg: KNOW reprint from *Seminarians for Ministerial Renewal*, April, 1971).

[14]Letty M. Russell, *Human Liberation in a Feminist Perspective*, p. 124 and Sheila D. Collins, *A Different Heaven and Earth* (Valley Forge, PA: Judson, 1974) 42.

[15]Collins, *A Different Heaven and Earth*, p. 202.

[16]Russell, *Human Liberation in a Feminist Perspective*, p. 159.

[17]Clare Fisher, Betsey Brenneman, Anne Bennett, eds., *Women in a Strange Land: Search for a New Image* (Philadelphis: Fortress, 1975) lx.

[18]Rosemary Ruether, *Liberation Theology* (New York: Paulist Press, 1972) 124.

[19]Collins, *A Different Heaven and Earth*, p. 143.

[20]Mary Daly, "The Qualitative Leap Beyond Patriarchal Religion," *Quest* 1 (Spring, 1974) 35.

FEMINISTS ON CHRISTIANITY:
Some Nineteenth-Century Parallels

Marilyn Chapin Massey and James A. Massey
University of Louisville

Simone de Beauvoir's classic study, *The Second Sex*,
developed what has become contemporary feminism's most
provocative and controversial category, that of woman as
"Other." She established that, because man has defined
women in relation to himself, woman has no self-definition,
no self-identity: "He is the Subject, he is the absolute--
she is the Other."[1] And the roots of this male-female
split in human society, indeed, the roots of all distortion of human relationships, are to be found in the nature
of human consciousness itself.

It is of interest to me that de Beauvoir turned to
Hegel for her definition of the alienating character of
consciousness: "We find in consciousness itself a fundamental hostility toward every other consciousness, the
subject can be posed only in being opposed--he sets himself
up as the essential, as opposed to the other, the inessen-
tial, the object."[2] The Hegelian philosophy has supplied
the categories for much of subsequent philosophical thought,
but my concern here is with its place in the nineteenth-
century in so far as it expressed the central motifs of a
movement that developed from a liberal Protestant interpretation of Christianity to an anti-religious humanism. I
find a remarkable parallel between the positions taken by
some of the leaders of this movement and what I consider
to be significant viewpoints among contemporary feminist
religious thinkers.

Specifically, I shall compare the nineteenth-century
religious thinkers, Friedrich Schleiermacher, David Friedrich Strauss, and Ludwig Feuerbach, with Letty Russell,
Mary Daly, and Sheila Collins, major representatives of

twentieth-century feminist religious thought. I shall
attempt to show in this comparison that twentieth-century
feminist thought reduplicates some of the most significant
trends in nineteenth-century religious thought.

I see structural similarities, which I shall explore
in this paper, between the thought of Friedrich Schleiermacher and Letty Russell, between David Friedrich Strauss
and Mary Daly, and between Ludwig Feuerbach and Sheila
Collins. Moreover, both sets of positions develop in
similar ways, beginning with attempts to face an important
cultural challenge to Christian faith with the resources
of Christian theology and then tending to take the side of
the culture against the original theological presuppositions.

David Friedrich Strauss (1808-1874) expressed the
central motif of his century's challenge: as long as human
reason is defined and experienced as limited, fallen, needing completion by a higher, supernatural wisdom, the biblical faith remains unchallenged as a bearer of truth. But
in the "present" age, with the power of the new scientific
consciousness, reason has asserted itself and has called
into question the very biblical world-view and religious
symbols that previously had limited it.[3] In a like way,
the raising of female consciousness to claim for itself a
full and equal citizenship in humanity brings into question the meaningfulness of biblical symbols. The woman
who no longer sees herself as "limited, fallen, needing
completion by a higher wisdom," who no longer is willing
to be circumscribed by the male of the species, is ready
to challenge biblical wisdom as a bearer of the truth because she sees that the predominantly masculine form of its
symbols is used to legitimate masculine dominance in the
church and in society itself. In this manner, both groups
will be found to question the relevancy of an historically
and socially determined biblical Word for a present cultural (or, in the case of feminism, counter-cultural) experience.

Moreover, the criticism of both groups involves anal-
yses of the subject-object split in human consciousness.
The nineteenth-century thinkers attacked what Rosemary
Reuther describes as the fundamental subject-object dualism of modern science, the Cartesian splitting of reality
"into a 'non-material thinking substance' and a 'non-
thinking extension' or 'matter'."[4] They all rejected the
Kantian thesis that an object cannot be known as it exists
independently of the knowing subject because, to them, it
produced an insuperable split between subject and object,
reason and being, knowledge and ultimate reality, religion
and reason. The overcoming of these divisions in human
consciousness could be accomplished only by means of an
understanding of the true nature of religion.

For contemporary feminists, the definition of the
subject-object split is drawn from the female's experience
of social oppression. The split is between the male as
Subject, as the human possessing economic, political, and
social power, and the female as Object, as the human lacking the power to shape individual or corporate destiny.
The goal of the feminist, as Letty Russell puts it, is to
overcome this split by advocating "changes that will establish political, economic, and social equality of the
sexes."[5] Along with de Beauvoir, Russell, Daly, and Collins analyze the male-female, subject-object split in human society as a division of human consciousness. However,
in contrast with de Beauvoir and more in line with the
nineteenth-century figures to be considered, they see the
resolution of this split as intrinsically linked to an
understanding of the true nature of religion.

My initial motivation in undertaking this comparative
study was to show the seriousness of contemporary feminist
religious thought. I think it has its own impetus which
raises as profound a challenge to Christian faith as did
the nineteenth-century movement. But, further, it is my
hope that this comparison will show that the feminists

have taken an important step beyond the nineteenth-century
thinkers in identifying a major obstacle to human freedom
and fulfillment. In my opinion, despite their own differences in evaluating the Christian tradition, all the feminist religious thinkers, by means of their definition of
the divisions in human consciousness and society, move to
uncover the roots of the epistemological and ethical problems with which the nineteenth-century thinkers struggled.

Friedrich Schleiermacher and Letty Russell

Friedrich Schleiermacher (1768-1834) believed that he
could affirm the "rights" of scientific consciousness and
still remain within the boundaries of the revealed tradition, still remain a theologian and a churchman. In *The
Christian Faith* (1821-1822), he described the splits between the claims of scientific reason and the claims of
biblical faith as false dichotomies that resulted from a
misunderstanding of the nature of religion. The rise of
reason had brought an increased, yet not final, knowledge
of the nature of physical and human phenomena, so that the
modern person correctly views the world as an uninterrupted
network of causal relationships. Within this network, the
knowing and acting person experiences himself/herself partly as free, as subject acting upon other beings, partly as
dependent, as object being acted upon by others. However,
in every human there exists a consciousness of the unity
of the self, a self-consciousness that is given immediately
together with the consciousness of partial freedom and partial dependency but that underlies both of these. This
self-consciousness, as an awareness of "whole, undivided
personal existence" that is anterior to any subject-object
distinction, is an awareness of one's existence as being
absolutely dependent, as being totally given, and as not
arising from one's own free agency or from the complex of
dependencies within the world. For Schleiermacher, just

this consciousness of the self and all other being as being posited by a force transcending both self and world is religion; religion is the consciousness of absolute dependence on a transcendent "whence."[6]

It might appear that this understanding of religion rendered the human self as nothing but an object, as totally posited. How did Schleiermacher reconcile this interpretation with the Enlightenment experience of the creative power of the human mind? He held that, to the extent that a person realizes clearly and consistently the absolute dependency of self and world on a transcendent source, he/she is liberated from confusion about the ultimacy of partial dependencies within the world and thus freed for purposeful, creative action. In this sense the religious awareness of total dependence is itself the ground of human freedom, and, as such, at the core of the true progress of modern civilization.[7]

Moreover, for Schleiermacher, this understanding of religion exempted dogmatic and biblical language from the criticisms of scientific reason, because it made clear that this language is an expression of immediate self-consciousness, not of objective existence or the constitution of the world. The *form* of religious utterances may include unscientific elements because these utterances were conditioned by language that was influenced by an individual's peculiar mode of expression or by a specific cultural situation. Rather than denying the truth of religious expressions, critical thought can actually play a role in freeing the true content from these unscientific elements for appropriation in modern times by producing a new form that is directly descriptive of the state of religious self-consciousness.[8]

Ultimately, however, it is not the advance of scientific thought, but response to the influence of the historical individual, Jesus Christ, that bears the possibility of the fulfillment of human religiosity, and thus of human perfection and freedom. The perfection of human religious

consciousness was given to humanity in Christ's own self-
consciousness. Schleiermacher did maintain the critical-
historical context of this assertion because he allowed
that Christ is open to historical investigation in those
gospels that contain his self-expression and that this expression was itself conditioned by the forms of speech of
the first-century culture. Yet, because Christ's self-
expression was *not* conditioned by the imperfection of the
religious consciousness of that age, historical relativity
pertains only to the *form* of Christ's self-expression, not
to the content of his self-consciousness.[9]

Letty Russell, in *Human Liberation in a Feminist
Perspective--A Theology*, maintains that the conflict between feminism and biblical faith stems from a misunderstanding of biblical religion. Rightly understood, biblical religion is the source for the realizable hopes of
feminism. Russell's method of arriving at this right understanding, like Schleiermacher's, is written out of experience but remains within the context of the hearing of
the biblical Word. For her, the experience is of female
oppression by male dominance. She interprets the domina-
tion-subjugation relationship between men and women to be
one instance of many situations of oppression in which a
dominating group denies to another group the freedom to be
subjects, thereby constituting the oppressed group as mere
objects. Thus, Russell's feminist experiences the fundamental human condition as the distortion of human relationships, the subject-object split throughout society.[10]

Although Russell's theology begins with an analysis
of the dynamics of social groups and, like other liberation
theologies, maintains throughout its link to *praxis*, her
conceptions of human deficiency and human freedom are similar to those that Schleiermacher derived from his analysis
of individual self-consciousness. Lack of human fulfillment is defined as lack of freedom due to a distortion of
human agency and dependency within the world; or, the root

of social ills is the distortion of human subjectivity.
And for her, as for Schleiermacher, true human subjectivity,
true human freedom, is to be found in the relationship to
a transcendent God. Authentic, free human existence comes
from understanding the self as "a *subject* of God's love
and concern, and therefore as a subject of his/her own individual and collective actions."[11] Thus, this human freedom, rather than being hindered by biblical faith, has its
source in it. It is by being children of God, by *receiving* God's promise through God's actions in history, that
humans understand what it is to be free.[12] In my opinion,
Russell locates this agency of God in the process of history more consistently and thoroughly than Schleiermacher;
her Christological focal point is understood within the
context of the history of revelation to Israel. Yet the
fundamental dynamic of biblical faith remains the same;
one is made a free human subject by receiving the creative
agency of a transcendent God, which agency is given fully
to humanity only in Christ. For Russell, as for Schleiermacher, Christ is the second, true Adam, who embodies "what
a truly human being (*anthrōpos*) might be like," and who
puts into human history the possibility of human fulfillment.[13]

But how can a biblical promise that is expressed in
predominantly masculine symbols and is perfectly realized
in a male redeemer be understood in a way that does not
further confirm the feminist experience of oppression?
Russell says that, although the central biblical motif of
God's promise of liberation was addressed initially to a
patriarchal society, the Jews, this message must be understood as "situation-variable," i. e., as addressed in different forms to different situations of oppression throughout history. With an interpretative method fully within
the tradition of Schleiermacher, she finds that, although
the *form* of the promise, e. g., its patriarchal imagery,
is relative to a particular culture, this relativity of

expression does not determine the content, the inner history, of the promise.[14] Even Christ's maleness is not determinative of his work. It is Christ's personhood, his subjectivity, that allows him to be "the ideal of the first human," opening up the possibility of authentic freedom for women as well as men.[15]

Both Schleiermacher and Russell find the essential capacities of the human person and their own cultural (or in Russell's case, counter-cultural) experiences lacking in the power to bring about human freedom. For both, freedom is to be realized only in a relationship of receptivity to a transcendent God. Moreover, it is just this understanding of true subjectivity as receptivity that leaves room in their theologies both for the determination of the present and future fulfillment of humanity by an event of the past as well as for the distinction between the content of the event and its culturally determined form. It is because they both find it necessary to retain one subject-object split, the distinction between a transcendent God and the creature, that they find the biblical Word speaking humanization.

David Friedrich Strauss and Mary Daly

Although David Strauss's most well-known statement on biblical religion was his *Life of Jesus* (1835), in which he denied the historical nature of most of the New Testament narratives and thus of the self-expressions of Jesus, in a later work, *The Christian Faith in its Doctrinal Development and in Conflict with Modern Science* (1840-1841), he concluded that historical study, by demonstrating the unscientific character of any claims for the absoluteness and uniqueness of Jesus, definitively breaks the link between the human Jesus and the Christ of Christian faith. Thus it was time for the modern age to liberate itself from such claims and with them from the biblical religion itself.

It was Strauss's interpretation of the religious experience of modernity that led him to this position. To
him, the true content of religious self-consciousness is
the realization of the *unity* of the infinite and the finite, a realization that develops in humanity while the
consciousness of the entire species develops. The principal experience of modern science, the philosophical experience of discovering the laws of the inner relationships
of the historical and natural world, is itself a stage, a
nearly final stage, in attaining this realization; it is
an experience that is essential to the completion of "revelation." Therefore, any particular historical event or
any individual of past history could only be a partial and
imperfect step in this development. The search for a complete realization of this truth in the symbols of biblical
religion, especially in one figure of the past, Jesus, is
merely an obsolete holdover from a pre-scientific age.
For if it is impossible to establish scientifically the
absoluteness or uniqueness of Jesus, then this search re-
introduces the ideal of salvation or of human fulfillment
as originating from beyond human development and compre-
hension. In fact, although the concept of Christ throughout its history has been considered to be the locus of the
unity of the infinite and the finite, it has functioned in
the opposite way because it contains its own dichotomies,
i. e., the separation of the activites of the two natures
of Christ and the distinction between Christ and all other
humans. Thus biblical religion, even in its central symbol, has retarded the progress of human religious consciousness by enslaving humanity to dependence on the infinite perceived as Other.[16]

For Strauss, the content of biblical symbols is inseparable from its form. The true content of religion,
the unity of the infinite and the finite, is present to
consciousness in an immediately intuited, pre-conceptual
feeling that contains both the subjective and objective

functions of human consciousness. While the religious symbols of past ages have attempted to express this perceived
unity, they were confined to being projections of merely
the "sensible, finite, purely subjective wishes and needs
of humans."[17] Because these symbols originated in a stage
of consciousness that was not aware of its unity with all
of reality, with the infinite itself, they projected the
infinite as particular and "other," as distanced from humanity. The present task was thus to expose the inadequacy
of these projections, to "tear the last veil" and bring
humanity to "pure, colorless self-awareness" of the univer-
sality and immanence of the infinite, a task that Strauss
thought could be accomplished only by the speculative
philosophy of Hegel, the philosophy that expressed the
culmination of the process of the Absolute.[18]

Like Strauss, Mary Daly finds that present experience,
in her case the feminist experience, contains a spiritual
potential that cannot be expressed by Christian symbols,
or, indeed, by Christianity's "entire conceptual system;"
rather these have served to frustrate the spiritual potential of the feminist experience. What is at issue between
Daly and Russell, as between Strauss and Schleiermacher,
is differing evaluations of the import of their experiences.
For Daly, the feminist experience does not merely raise new
questions calling forth new, more authentic formulations of
the content of biblical faith. Rather, the biblical symbols should be exposed as obsolete because the women's
movement, "in so far as it is true to its own essential dynamics," is an *ontological* spiritual revolution. It is
not even "just" a social revolution, but a "real leap in
human evolution" that points towards a new, never before
realized, never before conceived humanity.[19]

Daly disagrees with Russell's contention that masculine dominance is merely one instance of universal social
distortion; for her, it is the source of all other oppres-
sions. The roots of masculine dominance lie within the

human psyche itself, in its failure to appropriate the totality of the human self. For both Daly and Strauss, then, it is psychic alienation itself that accounts for "evil;" evil comes from the failure to affirm the true capabilities of the self and the resulting projection onto the other of these unrealized capabilities. In Daly's view, the most basic projection of the Other is against women, with the consequent social situation of patriarchy in all its forms of oppression.[20] In this sense, psychic alienation *is* patriarchal consciousness, the "dishotomiz-ing-reifying-projecting syndrome."[21] Accordingly, it is not merely the symbol of God the Father, an obvious pro-jection of social patriarchy, but it is the very objecti-fication of "God" as a being distinct from this world that is a product of alienated consciousness.

Although she explicitly rejects any conceptual system that does not grow out of, and seek to change, the con-crete situation of the social oppression of women, Daly's description of the spiritual potential implied in the fem-inist experience is similar to that of Strauss's descrip-tion of the experience of the unity of the infinite and the finite. She states, "The unfolding of woman-conscious-ness is an intuition of the endless unfolding of God."[22] The feminist spiritual experience is of participation in the creative power of the infinite, named as the Verb who is Be-ing. Thus, for her as well as for Strauss, contem-porary experience is itself revelatory of unity, or parti-cipation in the infinite as the ground of *self*-transcen-dence. Moreover, although she certainly would reject Strauss's Hegelian philosophy of Absolute Spirit as being incapable of adequately expressing her experience, she does turn to philosophy for her terms. Again, in contrast to Strauss, hers is not a philosophy that sees itself at the culmination of the process of the becoming of God; philosophy itself becomes, is immersed in process. Yet, because their philosophies share the theme of present par-ticipation in the infinite, they both find it problematic to assume "(at least implicitly) that past history (that is, some peak moments of the past) have some sort of prior claim over present experience."[23] Finally, for her, as for Strauss, it is impossible to separate the content from the form of biblical symbols. She takes a hard look at the history of the use of these symbols and finds no basis for extracting any pure, non-oppressive content, because, throughout history, they have been used to oppress women.[24]

Ludwig Feuerbach and Sheila Collins

Ludwig Feuerbach (1804-1872) agreed with Strauss concerning the projective nature of biblical faith. In *The Essence of Christianity* (1841), Feuerbach argued that traditional religious symbols and beliefs are fantastical projections of humanity's highest needs and ideals into a supernatural realm, an other-worldly "God." These projections then rule humans as the subject for which they are objects. But, most clearly in *Principles of the Philosophy of the Future* (1843), Feuerbach differed from Strauss in his program for describing the content and form of genuine human "religious" consciousness. First, more interested than Strauss in the genesis of religious beliefs, he outlined a religious anthropology. Moreover, not only did he contribute his own criticism of dogmatic theology, he took the step beyond Strauss of questioning the adequacy of his contemporary philosophical categories in any way to express human religiosity. This step was possible for Feuerbach because he also criticized the claims of speculative reason itself. It had succeeded in "negating the divine who is separated and distinguished from sensation, the world, and humans." But this negation had been accomplished "only in thought, in reason, and indeed in that reason that is also separated and distinguished from sensation, the world, and humans."[25]

Feuerbach thus denied not only the reality of the hypostatized God of biblical religion along with the dogmatic justifications of that God, but he also denied the

reality of the Absolute of the idealist philosophical tradition and of abstract thought itself, in favor of the opposite of philosophy, humanity in its concrete, sensible
existence. Even a philosophy of the identity of the divine
and the human, whether that identity is grasped by speculative reason or by intuition, could not express the truth
of human consciousness, for such a philosophy still con-
fines humans to subjectivity, isolates them within thought
or intuition from the concrete conditions of life. Since
Feuerbach believed that, on the contrary, reality can be
known only in immediate response to concrete, sensuous existence, he could say, "The identity of subject and object,
which in self-consciousness is only an abstract idea, is
truth and reality only in humans' sensuous perception of
humans."[26] The roots of truth are in the life, heart, and
blood of humans.

The motto of Feuerbach's intended philosophy of the
future, which he also called religion, was that the genuine
human is the human who excludes from himself/herself nothing that is essentially human. It was to be an open-heart-
ed, sensuous philosophy, including even physiology as an
adequate expression of human reality. Thus, the content
of this new "religion" would not be given in contemplation
or the mystification of thought, but in "practical-sensuous
activity." The content is all that pertains to humans in
their concrete existence, especially in their communality.
The proper form of expression of this content is love. As
Feuerbach states, "The human alone is human (in the ordinary sense); humanity with humanity--the unity of I and
Thou--is God."[27]

Sheila Collins, in *A Different Heaven and Earth*,
shifts the framework of the feminist discussion of religion
in a way that is strikingly similar to Feuerbach's nineteenth-century rejection of idealist philosophy. Just as
Feuerbach and Strauss held in common the theory of the
projective nature of biblical religious symbols, Collins

and Daly hold in common a criticism of Jewish and Christian religions as expressions of alienated, patriarchal consciousness. But Collins and Feuerbach differ with Daly and Strauss in their proposals for alternative religious expressions; while Daly and Strauss use philosophy to provide more adequate categories of expression, for both Collins and Feuerbach the modern religious experience carries within it a definitive critique of the claims and categories of philosophy. Collins makes it clear that she does not agree with the followers of Feuerbach that God is *merely* a projection of the human imagination. Yet she agrees with Feuerbach that "religious experience is real and pervasive" and, as he did, turns not to theology or philosophy, but to anthropology in order to explain its content.[28] She sets for herself the task of developing "a comprehensive anthropology of *homo religiosus*," for which she uses disciplines other than philosophy, such as archaeology, history, depth psychology, and, with Feuerbach, physiology.

Collins develops the intriguing hypothesis that the subject-object, male-female split in society has its basis in the binary structure of the human brain. Western, Judeao-Christian culture has stressed the left hemisphere of the brain (that area controlling language, logic, etc.) over the right hemisphere (that area controlling emotions and body responses). She further speculates that Western monotheism and patriarchy may have arisen as a reaction against an earlier agricultural society with a Mother Goddess religion in which the activities of the right side of the brain were predominant. In reaction, males developed the left side of the brain and projected onto woman the kinds of knowledge and activities controlled by the right side.[29]

For Collins, the religious experience for the feminist is the consciousness-raising experience in which women are coming together to discover themselves. The *content* of women's religion is thus "personal life history, the concrete daily experiences, dreams, frustrations, hopes, fears and feelings of women who live in a culture in which these experiences are devalued and in which women's person-hood is that of a subordinate 'Other'."[30] Moreover, in this consciousness-raising experience, "women get in touch with something that is so deep in them that words alone—conceptual language cannot express it."[31] Thus, the subject-object structure of conceptual thought and language cannot express the feminist religious consciousness. Rather than a "pre-conceptual grasp of a 'whence' of personal existence," or a "consciousness of participation in the infinite," the feminist religious experience is a getting in touch with the body and with deeply buried feelings and emotions. Its expressive forms are varied, ranging from "elemental sounds and gestures," through manifold sensuous and imaginative expressions, to collections of "images, concepts, and symbols."[32] The feminist need not search for alternative names of God, for she is generating a "new *way of naming*," and doing so in dialogue with others who are relearning their unity with their bodies and bodily modes of communication.[33] One could say that, for Collins as for Feuerbach, the form of religious expression is love, not as a generalized human ideal, but as embodied in the "life, heart, and blood" of humans being together.

Conclusion

I have attempted to point out structural similarities between two sets of persons in two different cultural situations as they grapple with the subject-object split in relation to Western religious tradition and experiences constitutive of the present shape of Western society. Divisions impairing human fulfillment are understood to be apparent not only in religion, but in intellectual thought, language, the human psyche and human society, and even in human physiology. This paper merely suggests the possible fruitfulness to contemporary feminist thought of further exploration of these structures. This is in fact a work

already begun by de Beauvoir; she herself relates the categories of Hegel to the anthropological studies of Claude
Lévi-Strauss.[34]

However, by undertaking the comparisons in this paper,
I do not mean to suggest that feminist thought will eventually be exposed to be the nineteenth-century revisited.
To understand the chasm between these two groups of thinkers, one would only have had to have been present in the
congregation when Schleiermacher, preaching to the Prus-
sian soldiers on their way to battle Napoleon, turned to
the women and said, "Blessed be your bodies which bore
such sons."[35] From the feminist's point of view, the new
religious consciousness of which the nineteenth-century
men spoke was incapable of resolving the dualisms with
which these men were concerned for it was by no means
"raised" to see women as full co-humans. On the contrary,
the parallel manner in which both groups become progres-
sively radical in their criticisms of the belief in the
biblical God as transcendent Other and their increasing
interest in anthropology can serve to point out that the
present feminist experience threatens to tear off the
"sacred canopy," not only by a force from the same direction as that of the nineteenth century, but also, as Mary
Daly suggests, with much more strength.[36] Feminism possesses this strength because it is confident that it has truly
identified the alienation between self and Other that these
men sought to overcome in their search for humanization.

NOTES

[1]Simone de Beauvoir, *The Second Sex*, trans. by H. M. Parshley (New York: Knopf, 1968) xvi.

[2]Ibid., p. xvii.

[3]David Friedrich Strauss, *Die christliche Glaubens-lehre in ihrer geschichtliche Entwicklung und in Kampfe mit der modernen Wissenschaft* (2 vols.; Tubingen: Osiander, 1840-1841) 1.10-11.

[4]Rosemary Radford Reuther, *Liberation Theology* (New York: Paulist Press, 1972) 17.

[5]Letty M. Russell, *Human Liberation in a Feminist Perspective--A Theology* (Philadelphia: Westminster, 1975) 19.

[6]F. D. Schleiermacher, *The Christian Faith*, ed. and trans. by H. R. Macintosh and J. S. Stewart (2 vols.; New York: Harper and Row, 1963) 1, §§ 1-6, 1-31.

[7]Ibid., §§32, 131-2.

[8]Ibid., §§16-17, 78-84, and 28, 122.

[9]Ibid., II, §§93-99, 377-424. See also Schleiermacher, *Das Leben Jesu* (Berlin: Reimer, 1864).

[10]Russell, *Human Liberation*, p. 145.

[11]Ibid., pp. 64-65.

[12]Ibid., pp. 41-49, 75.

[13]Ibid., p. 34.

[14]Ibid., chaps. 2 and 3.

[15]Ibid., pp. 138-39.

[16]Strauss, *Glaubenslehre*, 1.26-68.

[17]Ibid., p. 19.

[18]Ibid., p. 23.

[19]Mary Daly, *Beyond God the Father: Toward a Philosophy of Women's Liberation* (Boston: Beacon, 1973) 6.

[20]Ibid., pp. 10, 46.

[21]Ibid., p. 33.

[22]Ibid., p. 36.

[23]Ibid., pp. 73-74.

[24]Ibid., p. 72.

[25]Ludwig Feuerbach, *Principles of the Philosophy of the Future*, trans. by Manfred H. Vogel (New York: Bobbs-Merrill, 1966) 30. I have substituted "human" for "man" in Vogel's translation of "der Mensch."

[26]Ibid., p. 58.

[27]Ibid., p. 71.

[28]Sheila Collins, *A Different Heaven and Earth* (Valley Forge: Judson, 1974) 34.

[29]Ibid., pp. 101, 169-70.

[30]Ibid., p. 207.

[31]Ibid., p. 201.

[32]Ibid., pp. 208-227.

[33]Ibid., p. 217.

[34]de Beauvoir, *The Second Sex*, p. xvii.

[35]This incident is cited in Koppel S. Pinson, *Pietism as a Factor in the Rise of German Nationalism* (New York: Octagon Books, 1968) 1.

[36]Daly, *Beyond God the Father*, p. 23.

V. FEMININE LANGUAGE AND IMAGERY
IN CONSTRUCTS OF ULTIMACY:

Cross-Cultural Examples and Theological Proposals

DENIAL OF THE FEMALE - AFFIRMATION OF THE FEMININE
The Father-Mother God of Mary Baker Eddy

Susan M. Setta
The Pennsylvania State University

The value of incorporating the qualities most frequently associated with the feminine as well as those
qualities attributed to the masculine into one's life has
become an important theme in recent psychological and
theological studies. Mary Baker Eddy's thought can be
understood as an early attempt to achieve this goal by
integrating the masculine and the feminine in her image of
God and in her theology of Mind Heal. Any such integration of the masculine and feminine has important implications not only for the ideational structure but for the
resulting action or conduct of the individual in the world.
Thus, any theology has a direct bearing upon the way in
which the world is perceived and that includes the way the
individual perceives her- or him-self as a part of that
world. The relationship existing between theology and
social conduct is a dialectic one--theology affects conduct and conduct in turn affects theology. It is in the
light of this type of dialectic understanding that the
significance of Mary Baker Eddy's masculine-feminine image
of God can be appreciated. The Father-Mother God is both
a reaction against and a constructive step beyond the predominantly masculine oriented cultural and theological
milieu.

The interrelationship between the theology of nineteenth century American Calvinism and the societal roles
which resulted from and fed into that theology is important in understanding Eddy's theology of Mind Heal. Central to this theology is her image of the Father-Mother
God which can be seen as an early attempt to incorporate
the feminine into religion as well as a way to offer a

form of societal transcendence to women. However, in order
to incorporate the feminine into her image of God, Eddy
first found it necessary to negate her womanhood, as the
nineteenth century defined it, through the negation of her
body. Eddy was unable to see herself as flesh, passive,
or useless--qualities appropriate to the 'lady' of this
era; she had to transcend these qualities before she could
again become a human being and before she could include
the feminine in her image of God.

This study will illustrate the way in which Eddy's
theology developed as an alternative both to the role of
nineteenth century womanhood and to the masculine God of
that culture. The theology she developed served to help
the world make some sense to her, thus ridding her of the
feeling that she was a "slave of impeccable forces and
allowing her to control natural forces."[1] She made her
religion work for her by using Christian Science to sanction her beliefs about the body and the role into which
one was placed because of the body. Society could not and
would not sanction either the equality of woman and man
nor the inclusion of the feminine principle within the
diety, but her religion could.

Eddy felt very strongly that the whole of humanity
could be liberated through her discovery of Christian Science. The cure of ailments was more than a simple cure
for the symptoms of the age. It was a form of transcendence which allowed her to become neither female nor male.
Her newfound religion rescued her from the role of woman
and offered a conversion from the sinful state of the
flesh to the righteous state, childhood innocence. It
gave her a path by which she could return to an earlier,
or what she considered perfect, state of mind. Her religion proferred healing gifts which attempted to exorcise
maladies as well as to restore and reorient people suffering from the neuroses of nineteenth century American life.
For a woman of the nineteenth century it was difficult, if

not impossible, to lead an integrated life when she was caught up in the tension between a society which dictated passivity and a personality capable of action. To be healthy and productive, according to prevailing standards, Mary Baker Eddy would have had to become passive, protected and dependent. But those options offered her little. Nor did the religion of the nineteenth century Calvinists aid her. Its masculine nature and its refusal to incorporate positive feminine virtues into its system made it singularly unhelpful to women seeking transcendence. She tried illness, the other major option open to her, but found that being sick was to deny one's self any independence and to submit to nineteenth century demands upon women.

So, she engaged in a search: a search aimed at finding the core of her own humanity. She found that through Divine Mind, through the Father-Mother God, and through denial of the negative, she could become an emotionally mature individual who was no longer simply an object. She arrived at a concept of the spiritual unity of Divine Mind which united the masculine and the feminine into the Father-Mother God. By means of this concept she could become active by incorporating both the masculine and feminine into herself. Not only could she be loving and tender; she could be pure and strong, because the God she now worshipped also possessed all these qualities.

To understand the nineteenth century society into which Mary Baker Eddy was born it is crucial to realize that this period can be characterized as a great age for men. Needless to say it was not a great age for women. Men came to represent potency, power and success more than they ever had before. Women came to signify as stated previously, the flesh, passivity, uselessness. The utilization of manpower had proceeded to a point far exceeding that of previous generations; the utilization of womanpower declined to its lowest point. The more man succeeded, the more woman's position was undercut.[2] Mary Baker

Eddy as a nineteenth century individual was placed in the
unfortunate position of being intelligent, sensitive and
independent in a society concerned primarily with the fact
that she was female and as such should fill the clearly
delineated roles of wife and mother. The theology Eddy
develops is a direct result of societal designs for her
life and her inability to accept this as a given.

It was the age of the self-made man--a man who did
not need the formerly all important mother figure to shape
his life. The qualities of the self-made man were positively re-enforced by the Calvinist view of diety common
in the nineteenth century. Donald Meyer contends that the
nineteenth century Calvinists had uniquely American notions, more patriarchal and severe than those of Calvin.
The attributes of love, understanding, and compassion--so-
called feminine qualities--which even Calvin had stressed,
were pushed into the background in society and also in the
male's self-image. Both God and the male were called upon
to repress their emotions in an unrelenting drive towards
self-fulfillment, which meant success.

This age of the self-made man forced woman to compensate for her diminishing position and the resulting lack
of work, hence woman clung to the maxim, 'cleanliness is
next to godliness.' Woman created work by maintaining a
sterile home and by engaging in countless menial tasks,
which were for the most part, unnecessary. Eddy refused
to follow this maxim. She was not interested in menial
tasks, nor was she interested in maintaining a home. Instead she set out into the world to tackle not only societal problems but the problems of religion as well.

The position of woman in the church which developed
in Americanized Calvinism was little better, if not worse,
than her position at home. Because nineteenth century
American Calvinism was by, of, and for the male, it offered no escape nor any form of transcendence to woman.
Woman were not allowed to speak in church, to read the

scriptures at services or to offer prayers; the ordination of women was specifically forbidden. Consequently, woman could not bring to the church any creativity for she was assigned in the church, as in her home, to a role of passivity and submission.

When we look at the biography of Mary Baker Eddy we see a life in which the problems of the age were intensified. She was born to Abigail and Mark Baker in 1821. The interaction of Mary and her family in her childhood and adolescence played an important part in the later development of her philosophy of Mind Heal. Mary's father, Mark, was the epitome of the self-made man and his rigid adherence to Calvinist dogma was typical of his family and his culture. His rigidity and sternness of conviction were his most isgnificant contributions to his daughter's development. The dogma which he presented to his family was extremely male-oriented and patriarchal, as was most New England religion; it is against this kind of patriarchal dogma that Mary Baker Eddy later reacted in her theology. Mary's father worshipped a God who was a father and his religion caused him and his family to be devoted, for the most part, to this omnipotent male figure. Even at a tender age Mary Baker rebelled against her exclusion from the religion of her father. She suffered from many varieties of nervous spells, throughout her childhood, until finally she was forced to remain at home and not attend the local school. These spells often came after she and her father had engaged in theological disputes.[3] Mark Baker attributed his daughter's nervous condition and the resulting spells to the fact that "her mind was too big for her body."[4] Mary's father believed as did other men of his society, that women in general were frivolous, that they should not become involved in matters pertaining to the church, and that they should remain at home and keep silent. Because of Mark Baker's determination to exclude his daughter from the church and from education, she resorted, even as an adolescent, to sham emotions. This particular type of emotion had come to be a characteristic of the nineteenth century female existence. In the opinion of Simone de Beauvoir this type of response to a situation develops because the 'lady' of this era "...is always busy, but she does nothing, she has nothing, she is nothing."[5] The passivity and weakness of woman fostered by the coming of the self-made man resulted in the inability of woman to maintain herself; therefore, she was required to depend solely upon the male.[6] In order to fill this void which resulted from her relatively meaningless position, the woman indulged in play-acting and falsification.[7] A primary means of escape from the tedium of this society was illness. For the pure but weak the project of getting well as an escape from dependence because it was something that could be pursued entirely within one's self.[8] Therefore, in nineteenth century America, a variety of new diseases emerged which included such symptoms as insomnia, cerebrel irritation, and other ailments not present in European society. It is evident that the quest for success, on the one hand, left woman to her 'sham emotions' while on the other hand, it caused the repression of emotions and nervous exhaustion in the male. Reflecting this situation, Dr. George Beard, a noted nineteenth century New York City neurologist, argued that a new individual had appeared on the scene, the "nervous American."[9]

Mary Baker Eddy not only exhibited sham emotions during adolescence but she also fell prey to many of the new illnesses of this century. This problem continued to plague her until her discovery of Christian Science. Her biography is a chronology of extreme illness sometimes to the extent that she had to be continually rocked in an adult sized cradle. It is not surprising that her illnesses coincided with those situations in her life in which her 'femaleness' was most pronounced. On the occasion of her first marriage, following the birth of her son, George Washington Glover, Jr., during her engagement and marriage

to Dr. Daniel Patterson and in other similar situations
she became sick. In all these situations Eddy considered
herself female and for the individual of the nineteenth
century being female did not necessarily imply that one
was human. To be sick had been for Eddy and other nineteenth century women, to engage actively in something;
illness was the only way in which Eddy and other women like
her could assert themselves as human beings.

Eddy was but one of a number of individuals attempting
to cure the societally induced illnesses. She was, however, more successful than any of her contemporaries for
two reasons: by teaching denial of the body, she allowed
people to escape the societal roles that had become far
more rigid than at any other period in American history.
She also replaced the discriminatory separation of male
and female with the liberating union of masculine and feminine.

The way in which Mary Baker Eddy was taught to take
on the woman's role had followed the established pattern
of New England family life. The use of these tactics was
her initiation into the mold of the nineteenth century
American woman. In myth and in most historical periods
woman's body has been considered the possessor of evil.
While Prometheus steals fire from the sky, Pandora is opening her box of evils to the world and Tertullian is crying:

> Woman, you are the devil's doorway. You have led
> astray one whom the devil would not dare attack
> directly. It is your fault that the Son of Man
> had to die. You should always find yourself in
> mourning.[10]

Countless others saw woman as evil or as the instigator of
evil. "It was contended that there was a good principle
which had created all order, light, and man: and a bad...
which had created woman."[11] By man's associations with
woman he has opened himself to the forces of evil which
emanate and work through her.[12] Woman must, therefore,
conceal this feminine body, find shame in the natural body
functions, and must conceive of her body as sinful because

"she is the 'sex' which is the flesh, its delights, its
dangers."[13] The shame and embarrassment over the female
body was instrumental in Eddy's formulation of Mind Heal.
Her conviction that all matter is an illusion grows out of
her difficulties with womanhood. The devastatingly simple
statement that the body is illusion is a statement made
after countless instances when the female body brought
Mary Baker Eddy pain and suffering. Because she was female
whe was expected to be passive. Because she was female she
was somehow evil--the cause of man's sin. Because she was
female she had no socially important position. When Mary
Baker Eddy pronounces that the body is illusory and an error of the mortal sense it is after many years of suffering, suffering which came about to a great extent because
of her female body. The body, which in Mind Heal becomes
illusion and error is cast aside by Eddy and she becomes
free to enter society as the equal of men.

In an article which appeared in the Boston Herald,
Eddy foretold the coming elimination of gender and the end
of the division of roles by sex as well.

> Look long enough and you see male and female one--
> sex or gender eliminated: you see the designation
> man meaning woman as well, and you will see the
> whole universe included in one infinite Mind and
> reflected in the intelligent and compound idea,
> image, or likeness called man...[14]

Before Eddy could assert the spiritual equality of man and
woman she had to deny the body because it was this female
body that, in her view, caused all of society's problems.

Throughout her writings, illusion is the cause of sin,
sickness, and evil of mankind. For her, evil has no reality. It is neither person, place, nor thing. It is instead a belief, i. e., an illusion of the material sense.[15]
Evil has no reality because her body had no reality in her
life. She was forced to hide it and conceal its functions.
She was called upon to recognize that woman is flesh and
is therefore contaminated. In order to cope with society

she was instructed in the methods of repressing bodily desires and masking her appearance. When she comes to the
full realization that her body is illusion, it is after
years of careful shrouding.

> The Science of Being unveils the errors of sense,
> and spiritual perception, aided by Science,
> reaches truth. Then error disappears. Sin and
> sickness will abate and seem less real as we
> approach the scientific period in which mortal
> sense is subdued and all that is unlike the true
> likeness soon disappears.[16]

"If mankind," she writes, "can become conscious that life
and intelligence are purely spiritual, then the body will
utter no complaints."[17] Thus for Eddy, existing as purely
spiritual being means freedom from the lie of the female
body and freedom from the pain that accompanies fleshly
pleasure.[18] Before she could assert the spiritual equality
of men and women she had to deny the body because it was
this body that, in her view, caused all of society's problems. The denial of the body, however was not sufficient
to assure the spirituality of women so Eddy strongly affirmed the feminine by including in her system a God which
was mother as well as father. The union of these qualities
in the diety had, in her opinion, profound implications for
society as well. By acknowledging that God was both masculine and feminine she could then acknowledge that masculine
and feminine, or male and female were equally important
within society.

While in the nineteenth century God was male, the father served as the most important member of the family, and
the woman was relegated to a subordinate position in the
home and in society in general, this was not the case in
earlier American civilization. In the society of the New
England Puritans it was the mother who was central to the
family unit. Not only was the female important to society
but the quality of the feminine was also of utmost importance to their religion. For example, Christ was frequently depicted as a nurturing figure. In the nineteenth

century, however, the mother had become little more than a
domestic servant, bound to her home and family by the un-
rewarding and often unnecessary work she had created in
order to fill the gaps caused by the appearance of the
self-made man. In addition, and not surprisingly, the
feminine was sharply separated from religion in this male
monopolized century.

It is not atypical that little is known about the life
of Mary's mother Abigail; neither is it unusual that not
much is written concerning her personal convictions, since
it was assumed that a wife adhered to the religious beliefs of her husband. It is clear, however, that Abigail
represented that strain of New England womanhood that rebelled against the stark absolutes of nineteenth century
Calvinism.[19] It is discernible from the correspondence
between Abigail and her daughter that the inclusion of
love and understanding in Abigail's religion helped to
compensate for the lack of such qualities in the primarily
masculine religion of the time. Abigail, along with many
of her female contemporaries not only saw the masculiniz-
ing of religion take place but also saw their roles being
stripped of social and economic importance.

Later in her life, through her association with the
Shaker Community at Canterbury, Mary Baker Eddy became
more aware of the injustice of a situation in which so few
roles were left to woman by her society and her religion.
Through the Shakers' teaching, she could readily see that
there was a way to view woman as important to society.
Moreover, it was Ann Lee who first illustrated and challenged the patriarchal God in America by setting forth the
image that God was both male and female, an idea which became central for Eddy. In Eddy's idea of the Father-Mother God, an explicit challenge to the patriarchal religion
of her father and society is found.

Beauvoir has argued that men create gods and women
worship them. However, Eddy was unable to associate herself with, or worship the god that had been created for her.

She could not comprehend the stern and seemingly unloving,
uncreative qualities which were established by her father
and her culture, but felt and wrote instead: "God could
not be less loving than my mother."[20] It is not surprising
that she developed a conviction of a loving God or that
she sided with her mother and created a conception of a God
who possessed not only the masculine qualities of the age,
but also the feminine virtues of love, compassion, and
creativity. Much later in her life this idea became solid-
ified and she wrote:

> These three: God, the Father-Mother; Christ, the
> spiritual idea of Sonship; Divine Science or the
> Holy Comforter; represent a Trinity in Unity.
> Father-Mother is the name for the Deity.[21]

This perception of God was a refusal on her part to accept
the terrifying God of her father and his peers.

It is the masculine religion of men like Mark Baker
that Beauvoir calls: "...a justification, a supreme com-
pensation, which society is ever wont to bestow upon wom-
en."[22] Beauvoir strongly states that there must be a religion for women as there must be for the common people,
and for exactly the same reasons. When a class or sex is
condemned to immanence, it is necessary to offer it some
form of transcendence.[23] Through the use of the terminol-
ogy "Father-Mother God," Mary Baker Eddy begins to cast off
the exclusive maleness of nineteenth century American religion. For her it is the beginning of many theories
aimed towards transcendence as well as being the first step
in the creation of a religious system in which both men
and women could gain freedom from oppressive sex roles formerly placed upon them by both religion and culture. The
triumph of her womanhood over her female body allowed her
to include within her doctrines those features which were
missing from the conceptions of God common to age.

> The eternal intelligence, was a Principal, Love
> (feminine) and Wisdom (masculine). Love was a
> solution of intelligence before ideas were
> formed by Wisdom. The earth was simply an idea

> or shadow of the Principle. It was dark and
> void and had not intelligence of its own and
> was solely the identity Wisdom gave to it.[24]

Thus we see that the re-introduction of the feminine principle into the concept of God is, for Eddy, the re-inclu-
sion of the creative powers of God.

By returning the creative powers to God, Mary Baker
Eddy returned creative ability to woman as well. In order
to accomplish this she not only had to reject societal
ideas concerning the role of woman but she also had to reject the contemporary ideas regarding motherhood. Society
had imposed upon motherhood sacred duties and virtues.
Eddy, however, was unable to associate herself with these
ideas; consequently she developed her own concepts concerning the importance of motherhood.[25]

> As Elias presented the idea of the fatherhood of
> God, which Jesus afterwords manifested, so the
> revelator completed this figure with woman typ-
> ifying the spiritual Ideas of God's Motherhood.[26]

In her thought we see God and not society delineating the
qualities of spiritual motherhood. Woman, as well as man,
becomes a spiritual being and not only is she spiritual
but she also becomes active rather than passive. This new
concept of Motherhood and its link with the divine represents a denial of the self-made man and an affirmation of
the importance of womanhood in the development of ideas.
Mary Baker Eddy justifies her reproductive role with which
she had formerly been unable to contend. She sees the
statement in Revelation, "And she brought forth a manchild,
who was to reason and was to rule with a rod of iron, and
her child was caught up unto God and to his Throne" (Rev
12:5), as a reference to the fact that she had conceived
and delivered the idea that was Christian Science. Thus,
her creativity was not based upon her biological role, but
was instead a creativity of the mind. Eddy had discovered
a way in which she could destroy man, woman, and the idols
created by her father and her culture without leaving

herself open to punishment. Through Christian Science she could become a woman not subject to the 'womanness' of the nineteenth century standards; she was now so spiritually perfect that neither God nor man could pose a threat.

NOTES

[1] Louis Rose, *Faith Healing* (New York: Victor Gollanz, 1968) 23.

[2] Donald Meyer, *The Positive Thinkers*, (Garden City, NY: Doubleday, 1865) 48.

[3] Robert Peel, *Mary Baker Eddy* (New York: Hold, Rinehart and Winston, 1966) 46.

[4] Ibid.

[5] Simone de Beauvoir, *The Second Sex*, trans. and ed. by H. M. Parshley (New York: Alfred A. Knopf, 1953) 334.

[6] Meyer, *Positive Thinkers*, p. 58

[7] Beauvoir, *Second Sex*, p. 334.

[8] Meyer, *Positive Thinkers*, p. 59.

[9] George Beard, *American Nervousness* (New York: G. P. Putnam's Sons, 1881) iv.

[10] Beauvoir, *Second Sex*, p. 90.

[11] Ibid.

[12] Ibid.

[13] Ibid.

[14] This letter reprinted by Gail Parker, "Mary Baker Eddy and Sentimental Motherhood," *The New England Quarterly* 43 (March, 1970) 3, written by Mary Baker Eddy to the *Boston Herald*, appeared in that newspaper on March 5, 1905; further publication information is not available.

[15] Mary Baker Eddy, *Science and Health with Key to the Scriptures* (Boston: Trustees Under the Will of Mary Baker G. Eddy, 1875) 71.

[16] Ibid., p. 406.

[17] Ibid., p. 14.

[18] Ibid., p. 6.

[19] Peel, *Mary Baker Eddy*, p. 3.

[20] Ibid., p. 23.

304

[21] Eddy, *Science and Health,* pp. 331-32.

[22] Beauvoir, *Second Sex*, p. 621.

[23] Ibid.

[24] Peel, *Mary Baker Eddy*, p. 207.

[25] Mary Baker Glover gave birth to a son George, Jr., in 1884. However, the amount of time she spent with him throughout her life was negligible. Christian Scientists normally defend this by commenting on her weak physical condition, and in fact she was quite ill much of the time. Non-Christian Scientists however, who have a particular axe to grind with either Eddy herself or her philosophy, assert that she wasn't ill at all but merely neglected her maternal duties. This debate has gone on endlessly and serves little purpose. Suffice it to say here that she did not spend time with her son, George, but did develop some interesting theories concerning motherhood.

[26] Eddy, *Science and Health*, p. 250.

SEDNA:
Images of the Transcendent in an Eskimo Goddess

Gael Hodgkins

The Central Eskimo of the Canadian Arctic consider
Sedna, also known as Nuliajuk, their supreme or most important and powerful deity. She represents an aspect of
the transcendent in Eskimo culture, a dimension defined
here as that which is beyond and greater than the purely
human. Two of the important images of this transcendence
are depth and creativity, and it is these which I would
like to consider, giving special attention to the latter.

First, however, a generalized picture of this marvelous creature is in order, and I think one of the best descriptions comes from the journal of an Englishman who
sailed into the Central Eskimo region in 1821. One of his
Eskimo informants described her in this way:

> She is very tall, and has but one eye, which is
> the left, the place of the other being covered
> by a profusion of black hair. She has one pig-
> tail only, contrary to the established fashion
> in the upper Eskimaux world...and this is of
> such immense magnitude, that a man can scarcely
> grasp it with both hands. Its length is exactly
> twice that of her arm, and it descends to her
> knee. The hood of her jacket is always worn up.[1]

This informant also said that:

> In addition to her power over animals, Aywilliayoo
> [another name for Sedna] has a boundless command
> over the lives and destinies of mankind. Bad men
> and women are punished by her...and her own sex
> are afflicted with many disorders, and sometimes
> killed, in consequence of their being careless
> in the regulation of their diet at certain periods,
> and otherwise neglecting the established customs:
> all women therefore profess the utmost dread of
> this female avenger, but at the same time acknow-
> ledge that she is very good. Her house [at the
> bottom of the ocean] is exceedingly fine, and...
> it contains plenty of food. Immediately within
> the door of her dwelling, which has a long passage

of entrance, is stationed a very large and fierce
dog, which has no tail, and whose hinder quarters
are black. This animal is by some called the
husband, and by others merely the dog of
Aywilliayoo.[2]

There are two myths (sometimes appearing separately,
sometimes combined) generally associated with her, and
these, too, will help convey an overall portrait of her.
I will summarize them. In one, which I refer to as the
Sedna-fulmar myth, she marries a fulmar, a seagull-like
bird, and taking her sewing bag with her, goes off to live
with him. However, she is quite miserable there because
he lives on different kinds of food that she is used to.
Her father goes to visit her, and when he finds how unhappy
she is, he takes her into his boat, and the two of them
start home. The bird-husband pursues and when he causes a
terrible storm to rise on the sea, Sedna's father throws
her into the water. She clings to the side of the boat,
but he chops off her first finger-joints which fall into
the water and bob up as seals. Again she tries to save
herself, clinging to the side of the boat with her second
joints. The father chops these off which, falling into
the water, are transformed into a larger kind of seal.
Yet a third time the poor girl clings to the side of her
father's boat, but he hacks off the third joints which fall
into the water and become walrus (or sometimes whales).
When again Sedna approaches the boat, her father knocks
out one eye, thus accounting for her one-eyed appearance.
Finally she sinks down to the bottom of the sea where she
now lives, usually with her father and with the animals
created from her fingers.[3] In this myth, images of both
depth and creativity appear: Sedna sinks to the bottom of
the sea, and the sea mammals are created from her severed
finger joints. Before reflecting on these, however, I will
summarize the other myth associated with her.

In this second story, Sedna refuses to marry so that
her father becomes angry with her and says, "May you have

a dog for a husband then." Indeed, that night a dog, disguised as a human being, comes in, "lies" with her (as the myths usually put it, although I'm sure the Eskimos were not so straight-laced), and the two are considered married. The father, however, not wanting to be bothered with his dog-human grandchildren, takes his daughter, son-in-law and their children to an island and leaves them there. Ultimately Sedna's father causes her dog-husband to drown; Sedna revenges this act by ordering her children to kill or maim their grandfather, and she is left alone to provide for them on this isolated island. Clever girl that she is, however, she transforms the soles of her boots into ships and sends her children off in them, some to become the ancestors of white people, some to become ancestors of the Indians, and some to become ancestors of certain spirits-- none, however, to become ancestors of the Eskimos, who, like all peoples, consider themselves to be the true human beings.[4]

In this myth, then, the image of Sedna as a creatrix appears again: she creates children in a purely natural, that is biological, way, but she also creates in a willed or volitional way when she transforms her shoe soles into boats. I want to pursue these two images--depth and creativity--images which point to this deity's transcendence. I will first take up the image of depth and then move to some reflections on the different images of creativity presented in the myths and elsewhere.

In the Sedna-fulmar myth, several versions make it very clear that she sinks to the bottom of the sea, not just into the sea, and this descent, of course, is strikingly similar to the ascent of the High God after his useful work has been done here on earth. Elsewhere in Eskimo literature, Sedna is portrayed as living on a small strip of land surrounded by water so that she becomes, almost literally the ground of being, or as Eliade writes of her in *Shamanism*, the "source and matrix of all life."[5] And here

in the depths she sits "and broods over the fate of man"
as one Eskimo informant put it.[6]

It is about the dimension of depth that I wish to say
more. Inasmuch as Sedna lives not just in the water, but
in the depths of the water, she participates in or "represents" (with Eliade)[7] not only water but depth as well.
In fact, the word "Sedna" itself may mean something like
"'she down there in the sea.'"[8] Even though depth is a
very powerful image, little attention has been paid to it
by historians of religion. There are two reasons for this.
One is that we have been preoccupied with the High God
whose transcendence is ostensibly due to his association
with height, and the other is that depth has apparently
been subsumed under the categories of water and earth;
that is to say, the meaning of water and earth rather than
the *depth* of these has been the focus of attention. However, Eliade, without lifting it out for special attention,
confirms its importance, maintaining that water animals
derive their meaning from the fact that they live at the
bottom of the water: "Hidden in the *depths* of the ocean,
they are infused with the sacred power of the abyss"
(Italics mine). Sea-spirits too derive their "sovereignty
and sanctity" from the depths of water since, according to
Eliade, "magico-religious power lies *at the bottom* of the
sea."[9] (Italics mine). Depth suggests infinite darkness
and infinite mystery; it is the unfathomable, the immeas-
ureable. Far more than height, it seems to me, it expresses that which is mysterious, unknowable, and within
Eskimo culture, dangerous. Therefore, depth is at least
as powerful a symbol of transcendence as is height, and it
is precisely this dimension which accounts for much of
Sedna's transcendence.

The question arises, of course, as to whether the
dimension of depth can be claimed for the feminine as
height has been preempted for the masculine.[10] Among the
Eskimo, I believe that equation--depth equals the

feminine--can be made. It is also possible that this is
the case for some other Paleo-Siberian cultures.[11] One or
two swallows, however, do not make a summer. On the other
hand, I think that wherever female deities are found living in the water or in the earth, the images associated
with them should be examined to see if the dimension of
depth accounts in part for their transcendence. Depth has
received far too little attention, and only after the data
have been examined will it be possible to determine whether
femininity is associated with depth as frequently as masculinity is associated with height.

The second image I wish to reflect on is that of creativity since it is clear from the stories about Sedna that
she is endowed with generative powers. In the Sedna-fulmar
myth, the sea mammals originate from her fingers; in the
dog-husband myth, she gives birth to offspring who become
the ancestors of the non-Eskimo people; and at the end of
the same myth she transforms her boot soles into ships so
that her children can escape the island. In other words,
different images are used in representing her creative
powers, and I believe these images represent different
types of creativity, one which is purely biological, i. e.,
natural, one which I designate catalytic since it takes
place with the aid of another substance, and one which is
willed or volitional since Sedna herself decides what it
is she will create.

The Sedna-fulmar myth depicts the catalytic type of
creativity since Sedna's fingers are transformed into sea
mammals through the agent of water. It is my contention
that it is her fingers which are so transformed because in
Eskimo culture, women are seamstresses *par excellence*;
their fingers transform animal skins into useful goods. I
believe it is not accidental that three versions of the
Sedna-fulmar myth picture her going off with her bird-husband only after she has made certain that she has her sewing bag with her.

In the dog-husband myth, she appears as biologically creative inasmuch as she gives birth to numerous offspring. But in this same myth she is portrayed as possessing another type of creativity which I call volitional. To quote directly from one version of the myth, "She took the sole of one of her boots, made masts of whalebone, and transformed it into a ship." She is able, through extraordinary means, to produce the non-existent. Here, in contrast to the above two types of creativity, she emerges not as a somewhat passive instrument of creative power but as an active agent of generation.

Not only is she portrayed this way in the dog-husband myth, but there is a story about her which tends to support this interpretation. In the story, Anarte, whose brother has been drowned by Sedna, dives down to the bottom of the sea (the depths again) to try to secure his release, and Sedna is cajoled into literally putting the dead man back together again. Amarte entered Sedna's house with a spiked stick hidden in his clothes and asked:

> "Where has my brother gone?" But Nuliajuk [Sedna] did not know. Anarte questioned her eagerly, but kept his horn staff with the sharp spikes still hidden. Now her father Isarrataitsoq began to take part in the talk, and mentioned various breaches of taboo which Anarte's little brother had committed. Then Nuliajuk lifted up the skin hangings and took out a lot of human bones, and putting the bones together, tried to make the skeleton stand up, but the skeleton fell down. Some of the bones were missing, and these she looked for, and setting them into the skeleton with the rest, tried again to make it stand up, but again it fell down. She could not find the missing bones, she said, but now Anarte brought out his stick, and Nuliajuk at once went very red in the face and found some more bones, and now the skeleton could stand up: it was Anarte's brother.[12]

In this story, Sedna is again portrayed as having the power to create according to her own volition and this time she creates or re-creates human life.

Her powers of creativity represent the transcendent inasmuch as human beings cannot create animals or produce creatures who become the ancestors of certain races of people, nor can we make boats from shoe soles or give life to the dead. Sedna exceeds the limited human power to create.

What follows is somewhat of a digression from the topic of symbols of transcendence. However, my effort to explain the meaning of certain images associated with Sedna--her sewing bag, her fingers, the transformation of her boots--led me to certain aspects of women's role within society, and it is to this role which I would like to turn now. If a volitional type of creativity is sought for in the social order, it gradually becomes apparent that women are seamstresses *par excellence* in Eskimo culture. I say "gradually becomes apparent" because anthropologists have given sewing very short shrift indeed in comparison to the lavish attention they have devoted to the male activity of hunting. Not only do women make all the clothes of the Eskimos, clothes which are both utilitarian and of handsome design, but they make all the skin tents, boat covers, sleeping rugs, etc., as well. In other words they are totally responsible for turning animal skins into useful and handsome articles--they transform nature into culture. In addition, because of the numerous taboos related to working on animal skins, women must complete their sewing within a relatively short period of time; therefore, it is possible that their creative powers might be viewed as having a superhuman quality. I am not suggesting here that because women are the sewers in the social order, they are perceived as creators in myth. What I am asserting is that there is an isomorphism between one activity of women in Eskimo society and one of the ways the Eskimo perceive one of their super-human beings.

Since this is not a paper devoted to the role of Eskimo women, it would not be relevant to my chosen topic to further pursue the question of the extent to which women are

associated with culture rather than with nature in this
particular society. However, my effort to interpret the
Sedna materials has led me to conclude that two of the
traditional ideas about women which need re-examination
are: (1) women are associated with nature while men are
associated with culture, and (2) women's creativity is
homologous with biological creativity. Our revered Mircea
Eliade espouses both these ideas. See for instance his
interpretation of men's and women's initiations where the
male-is-to-culture as female-is-to-nature dichotomy is
used.[13] In *Patterns*, it is in his section on "Cosmo-Biol-
ogy and Mystical Physiology" that weaving is discussed although Eliade also acknowledges that one who weaves really
creates.[14] Erich Neumann in *The Great Mother*, following
Bachofen has perpetuated the second idea claiming that
weaving, even on a cosmological plane, is simply an extension of the biological function of weaving life in the
uterus.[15] More recently in a collection of essays by
women anthropologists, these same two ideas appear again.[16]

In closing I want to reiterate the way in which the
images of depth and creativity may be significant for us
today. We should examine images of depth whether these be
related to the sea, the earth or the human psyche, and to
the extent that this dimension is related to the feminine
we should claim and magnify it as our own. Similarly,
images of creativity and generation should be scrutinized,
and, where warranted, the old concept--woman is to nature/
male is to culture/dichotomy--should be discarded. We
must claim as our inheritance not only the power to gener-
ate biologically but the power to create the culturally
new and significant as well.

NOTES

[1] George Francis Lyon, *The Private Journal of Captain G. F. Lyon of H. M. S. Hecla During the Recent Voyage of Discovery Under Captain Parry, 1821-23;* Introduction and illustrations by James A. Houston (Barre, MA: Imprint Society, 1970) 231. It is interesting to note that in this description Sedna transcends the purely human simply by being larger in size than a normal person.

[2] Ibid.

[3] Two versions of this myth will be found in: Franz Boas, *The Central Eskimo* (Lincoln, NE: University of Nebraska, 1964) 175-77 and Knud Rasmussen, "Intellectual Culture of the Iglulik Eskimos," in *Report of the Fifth Thule Expedition, 1921-24,* Nos. 1-2 (1931) 63-66.

[4] Two versions of this myth will be found in: Franz Boas, *The Central Eskimo*, p. 229 and Frank Boas, "The Eskimo of Baffin Land and Hudson Bay," *Bulletin of the American Museum of Natural History* 15, Part 1 (1901) 165-67.

[5] Mircea Eliade, *Shamanism*, trans. Willard R. Trask (New York: Routledge and Kegan Paul, 1964) 294.

[6] Rasmussen, "Iglulik Eskimos," facing p. 145.

[7] Mircea Eliade, *Patterns in Comparative Religion*, trans. Rosemary Sheed (Cleveland: World Publishing, 1958) 204.

[8] William Thalbitzer, "The Cultic Deities of the Inuit (Eskimo)," in *Proceedings of the 22nd Annual Meeting of International Congress of the Americanists* (1928) 378.

[9] Eliade, *Patterns*, pp. 207, 210.

[10] The question of whether the data support the notion that height is almost invariable associated with the masculine is beyond the scope of this essay. However, it should be pointed out that in some cases, the male High God does not dwell by himself but has a wife and children. Similarly Sedna lives with her father and/or dog-husband although she is always the most powerful of the three figures.

[11] Thalbitzer, pp. 382-83.

[12] Rasmussen, "Iglulik Eskimos," p. 101.

[13] Mircea Eliade, *Rites and Symbols of Initiation*, trans. Willard R. Trask (New York: Harper & Row, 1958) 47.

314

[14]Eliade, *Patterns*, pp. 178-81.

[15]Erich Neumann, *The Great Mother*, trans. Ralph Manheim (New York: Bollingen Foundation, 1963) 227.

[16]Michelle Zimbalist Rosaldo, "Woman, Culture, and Society: A Theoretical Overview," and Sherry B. Ortner, "Is Female To Male as Nature is to Culture?" in *Woman, Culture and Society*, Michelle Zimbalist Rosaldo and Louise Lamphere eds. (Stanford, CA: Stanford University, 1974) 31, 87.

PERFECTION OF WISDOM:
Mother of all Buddhas*

Joanna Rogers Macy
Syracuse University

The texts which mark the emergence of Mahāyāna Buddhism, in the Second Turning of the Wheel of the Law,
honor her whose name they share: Prajñāpāramitā, the Perfection of Wisdom. They do not present her as a divine
being or an immortal essence, for the Dharma, apprehending
reality as process, posits no eternal entity. She persona-
fies rather than very insight which perceives the dynamic
and interdependent character of reality. She is, consequently, the ultimate saving wisdom. As such, she is
called the mother of all the Buddhas, their nourisher and
teacher.

This paper is drawn from a study of the first of these
texts that we have, the *Astasāhasrikā Prajñāpāramitā* or
Perfection of Wisdom in Eight Thousand Lines, with its preliminary verse form, the *Ratnagunasamcayagatha* (Storehouse
of Precious Jewels), which embody all the concepts central
to subsequent Prajñāpāramitā literature.[1] While the date
of this sūtra and its place of origin are still a matter
of debate (evidence suggests South India, Andhra, of the
late second and first centuries B.C.[2]), scholars agree that
it represents the advent of Mahāyāna Buddhism, and that,
furthermore, its teachings are fundamental to subsequent
developments of the Dharma from Madhyamika to Vajrayāna to
Zen.[3]

Many works have been devoted to the study of this perfect wisdom, as presented in the treatises of Madhyamika
philosophers, the art and ritual of Tibetan Vajrayāna, or
the koans of Zen masters. Little attention, however, has
been paid to the feminine form in which it first appeared.
Yet, by looking at her as she then emerged, as Mother of

315

the Buddhas, we can acquire a fresh perspective. We can
gain, by considering the attributes accorded her, images
of ultimacy which enrich our understanding of *prajñā* (wisdom). These attributes also can enrich our notions of the
female principle, for they point to an archetypal structure
in which the feminine is no longer bound to the chthonic,
and thereby released to display other characteristics.

To appreciate her novelty, let us first recall how
wisdom was understood in previous Buddhist thought. Turning then to Prajñāpāramitā and her message, we will consider her symbolic attributes. These, then, we will contrast
with the prevailing Hindu concept of the female principle.
In conclusion, we will offer a hypothesis to account phil-
osophically for this contrast--to show what in the Buddhist
vision permits a transcendence of the metaphysical sexual
typing that allies the feminine with the arbitrary and devouring forces of nature.

> As Buddhas, world teachers
> Compassionate, are your sons,
> So you, O blessed one, are
> Grandmother of all beings.
>
> ...He who sees you is liberated,
> And he who does not see you is liberated, too.[4]

How is she different from earlier Buddhist views of
wisdom?

In the early canon (the Nikayas and the Vinaya),
paññā (the Pali term for wisdom) has been seen as the knowledge of dependent co-origination as taught by the Buddha,
the conceptual content, so to speak, of his enlightenment.
Wisdom is featured as one of the three essential aspects
of the Path, along with moral conduct (*śīla*) and meditation
(*dhyāna*). Central to it was a nonsubstantial view of the
self--self perceived as a congruence of aggregates (*skandhas*), the *skandhas*, in turn, but a series of *dharmas* or
units of experience.

In following centuries, with the development of
scholastic Buddhism, the nature of these *dharmas* themselves

became a focus of concern—both as an aid to meditation (to dissolve the conventional view of experience) and as a philosophical inquiry relative to causation (to explain the appearance and sensation of continuity). If, as the Dharma proclaimed, there was no permanent self, it was a matter of importance, and some fascination, to understand the flux of *dharmas* from which the illusion of self arose. They were listed, typed, and classified. There were conditioned *dharmas*, like feeling and sensation, and unconditioned *dharmas*, like space and nirvāna. Differing views, as to how these *dharmas* should be classified and especially how they relate to each other in a causal pattern, engendered differing schools of thought. The Sautrāntikas posited *dharmas* as self-destructing instantaneous flashes, related, however, to a seed-bearing substratum, while the Sarvāsti-vādins posited a noumenal essence of all *dharmas*, to which continuity and reality can be assigned. Wisdom became, in short, a rational and analytic exercise, comprising enumer-ation, categorization and speculative theory. The debates engendered threatened to go on endlessly, when from the wings, so to speak, a new wisdom moved onto the scene.

Because the writing was now in Sanskrit, she was termed not *paññā*, but *prajñā*; because she pointed to a reality that eludes our classifications, she was termed *pāramitā*, which means "gone beyond" or to the "other side" as well as "perfection." To those who were dryly and dog-gedly reviewing the *dharmas*, enmeshed in their own intel-lectuality like flies in fly-paper, she offered not theo-ries, but paradoxes. The sūtras abound in them. "All is based in the Dharma, there is no basis in the Dharma," or "The Buddha has led many beings to nirvāna and none have been led." "The bodhisattva will go forth, but he will not go forth to anywhere."

No formula captured her insight, but through the para-doxes shone a light offering release from the self-adhesive

nature of human logic. It was an insight that went beyond
the nonsubstantiality (*asvabhāva*) of the person and beyond
its atomization into *dharmas*, to perceive that the *dharmas*
themselves and our very notions of them, indeed all our
concepts, are *asvabhāva*, nonsubstantial, empty. That is,
she returned to the Buddha's central notion of dependent
co-origination to free us from absolutizing concepts.

In the Prajñāpāramitā sūtras it is Śāriputra, traditionally revered as the Buddha's most learned disciple,
who represents the scholastic mentality. He asks the
questions that are answered by the Buddha and by Subhūti,
a follower who is now raised up as an example of one who
really sees into the co-dependently arising nature of
things. Śāriputra, weighted with logic and literalness,
struggles with the paradoxes of the new wisdom, spurs
their reiteration.

Through them Prajñāpāramitā emerges as the Third
Noble Truth. Given the emptiness of *dharmas*, there is, if
one can grasp this emptiness, nothing to desire, nothing
to grasp; seeing this is liberation. From this two cor-
relaries: 1) one cannot think one's way into this *prajñā*,
it is a way of seeing. And 2) wisdom is now raised from a
means to an end. As transforming insight, it is both the
ground of all the virtues and their goal. Without it,
śīla, *dhyāna*, even the Dharma itself, are subject to ob-
jectification and attachment; with it, this world, *saṃsāra*,
is altered--not suppressed or dispelled, but transfigured.

Now let us look at the symbols that are used to convey and characterize this wisdom. To begin with, it is,
as already noted, feminine.

> The Buddhas in the world-systems in the ten directions
> Bring to mind this perfection of wisdom as their mother.
> The Saviours of the world who were in the past, and also
>   are now in the ten directions,
> Have issued from her, and so will the future ones be.
> She is the one who shows this world (for what it is),
>   she is the genetrix, the mother of the Buddhas.[5]

The mother, like the wisdom she offers, is elusive,
"signless." She is barely personalized in the sutra; no
stories attach to her, no direct speech is accorded her,
no physical descriptions of her are offered--none of the
gestures, colors, adornments that will figure in the images made of her centuries later, although these will
emerge from and portray the qualities of her that are presented here. The dozen or so anthropomorphic references
to her in our sutra most frequently appear in passing, as
if self-understood--"Prajñaparamita, the mother," "Mother
of the Tathagatas," "Mother of the Sugatas," "Mother of
the bodhisattvas," "instructress of the Tathagatas in this
world," "genetrix and nurse of the six perfections."[6] One
is urged not to be frightened on hearing the "Mother's
deep tenets" and to "have faith in this Mother of all the
Jinas, if you wish to experience the utmost Buddha cogni-
tion."[7]

As children revere in gratitude, and cherish and care
for their mother, who brought them forth, so:

> fond are the Buddhas of this Perfection of Wis-
> dom, so much do they cherish and protect it.
> For she is their mother and begetter, she
> showed them this all-knowledge, she instructed
> them in the ways of the world....All the Tat-
> hagatas, past, future and present, win full
> enlightenment, thanks to her.[8]

In addition to such direct references to her as mother, the sutra features analogies and similes which further
suggest a feminine mode. In his eagerness to hear the
wisdom and his sense that his time has come "to speedily
experience enightenment," the bodhisattva is likened to
"a pregnant woman, all astir with pains, whose time has
come for her to give birth."[9] He is "like a mother, min-
istering to her only child," in his devotion to the welfare of other beings.[10] "Just as a cow does not abandon
her young calf," so does the bodhisattva follow the reciter
of the Dharma until he knows this Perfection of Wisdom by
Heart.[11] In his constant pondering of this wisdom, he is
like a man who "had made a date with a handsome, attractive

and good-looking woman." "And if now that woman were held back by someone else and could not leave her house, what do you think, Subhūti," asks the Buddha, "with what would that man's preoccupations be connected?" "With the woman, of course," Subhūti answers, "he thinks about her coming, about the things they will do together, and about the joy, fun and delight he will have with her." Just as preoccupied as such a man, says the Lord, is the bodhisattva with thoughts of Prajñāpāramitā.[12]

As we turn now to consider the particular qualities that characterize this Prajñāpāramitā, we find: light, emptiness, space, and a *samsāra*-confronting gaze that is both clinical and compassionate.

"The Perfection of Wisdom gives light, O Lord. I pay homage to the Perfection of Wisdom!" cries Śariputra after listening to Subhūti and the Lord. "She is a source of light, and from everyone in the triple world she removes darkness, and she leads away from the blinding darkness caused by the defilements and by wrong views....She brings light to the blind, she brings light, so that all fear and distress may be forsaken. She has gained the five eyes, and she shows the path to all beings. She herself is an organ of vision."[13]

As light and insight, she reveals that "all dharmas are void, signless, and wishless, not produced, not stopped and non-existent."[14] Therefore, Perfect Wisdom herself is empty, *śunya*.[15] "One should know that the Perfection of Wisdom is without own-being just as beings are without own-being. Her very essence is the absence of own-being in beings."[16] The centrality of the *śunyatā* concept to any notion of her is manifest in later Tantric symbolism, where she appears frequently as Nirātmā and Nairātmyā.[17] The no-selfness, which both names mean, is repeatedly emphasized in our sūtra. She is "not a real thing," just as *dharmas*, Buddhas and bodhisattvas are "not real things" and "offer no basis for apprehension."[18] Now the text recognizes that this is fearful to contemplate. It acknowledges that this teaching from the other side (*pāramitā*) of reality is "alarming" and "terrifying." Those who are not distressed, "not firghtened on hearing the Mother's deep tenets," "not cowed, paralyzed or stupefied," those "who do not despair, turn away or become dejected," reveal their advancement on the Path, their potential for Buddhahood soon.[19]

While, on the one hand, Prajñāpāramitā reveals the awesomeness of *śūnyatā*, on the other she seems to recognize the terror it can initially induce, for she also offers comfort. The text speaks of the protection and power she provides. "In her we can find shelter....She makes us seek the safety of the wings of enlightenment." "She protects the unprotected, with the help of the four grounds of self-confidence." In her we find "defence and protection."[20] The reassurance she gives is symbolized in the *abhaya* mudra of her right hand, the fear-not gesture, that we encounter in later Tantric images of her.[21]

Her compassion, evident in this provision of help, is not seen as a cradling, cuddling or clasping to the bosom; rather it inheres in her very seeing, and in implicit in her clear-eyed vision of this world's suffering. The many eyes, to which Śāriputra referred above in connection with her light-bringing insight, becomes in later Tantric images symbolic of this compassion. When she will assume the form of Tārā, these eyes, set in her forehead, hands and sometimes feet, express her caring and the succor she offers.[22] It is not surprising that in our text metaphors of sheltering, housing, enclosing, are found relatively rarely for Prajñāpāramitā. Since, as the bodhisattva is repeatedly reminded, there is no basis, no place to settle, no ground to stand on, the predominant movement is to image her in space, in boundless immensity.

In *ākāśa*, the infinite expanse of space or ether, the notions of light and void conjoin. In our sūtra it is the metaphor *par excellence* for Prajñāpāramitā. Like space,

she is endless, *ananta*. Like space, she is immeasurable,
incalculable and insubstantial; like space she cannot be
increased, decreased, or confined in categories.[23] Like
sheer space, she can terrify, but the bodhisattva must
plunge right into it, unafraid and ready to delight.[24] If
he is not frightened and trusts her, he becomes "like a
bird who on its wings courses in the air. It neither falls
to the ground, nor does it stand anywhere on any support.
It dwells in space, just as in the air, without being
either supported or settled therein."[25]

  This space into which the bodhisattva dares is not the
old realm of the sky gods, traditionally accorded to the
male in the mythical dualities of sky father-earth mother.
Attributes of the sky father featured the sovereign heights
of his heavens, his astronomical regularity and law, the
power of his thunderous downpours.[26] No such references
are made to the Mother of the Buddhas, no allusions to the
majesty, order or power of heavenly phenomena. The one
attribute she shares with him is that of all-seeing. Furthermore, she is not set in opposition to the recumbent
earth; on the contrary, she is, on one or two occasions,
metaphorically equated with it as ground of being. "As
many trees, fruits, flowers as there are have all come out
of the earth and originate in it...(so have) the Buddha's
offspring, and the gods and the dharmas...issued from Wisdom"[27] This wisdom, as Wayman suggests, is also linked
with earth by the act ascribed to the Buddha during his
enlightenment vigil, in which he called her to witness.[28]
He reached down, touched her, to affirm his right to be
there and to destroy Māra's illusions.

  The measureless space of Prajñāpāramitā extends not
only outwards and up, but also inwards and down. It is
deep space. "Deep is the Perfection of Wisdom," says
Subhūti. And the Lord answers, "Yes, with a depth like
that of space."[29] "With the depth of space is this Perfection of Wisdom deep."[30]

A new dimension is added to our understanding of Prajñāpāramitā's space, when we learn how terms, used in the
sūtra to qualify it, played a role in the development of
mathematics in India, and particularly in the emergence of
the concept of zero.

As background, let us briefly recall that a place-
value system (on the base of sixty) had been developed
very early by the Babylonians. It had been hampered, however, by the lack of a symbol for zero. This made for in-
accuracies in transcribing large amounts, until a sign
(like an upended W) was devised to fill the empty position
in a number sequence.[31] This place system of the Babylonians was not adopted in the Mediterranean area, and "fell
on fertile soil only among the Hindus."[32] Indian mathematicians in the early centuries A.D. evolved the decimal
system, the numerical notations, and the crucially important concept of and symbol for zero. All of this, transmitted to the West by Arabs in the 9th century, became the
basis for European numbering and computation.

Now Ananda K. Coomaraswamy has pointed out that in
India, previous to numerical notations, verbal symbols
were used technically. For the concept of zero, in particular, a variety were employed, and these technical verbal
symbols for zero had, he maintains, roots in Indian metaphysics. These words are *kha, śūnya, ākāśa, ananta,* as
well as *purna, vyoma, antariksa* and *nabha.* Three of them
we recognize as chief attributes of Prajñāpāramitā.

Coomaraswamy's observations on these terms are helpful
to an understanding of the metaphysics of her "space."
Pointing to the use of both *śūnya* (empty) and *purna* (full)
for the referent in question, he states that this implies
that to the Indian mind "all numbers are virtually or potentially present in that which is without number...(or)
that zero is to number as possibility is to actuality."[33]
Coomaraswamy further reflects that the use of *ananta* (endless) implies an identification of zero with infinity;

"the beginning of all series being thus the same as their end."(*Ākāsa*) represents "primarily not a concept of physical space, but of a purely principal space without dimension...though the matrix of dimension."[34]

This zero space becomes the still center of the turning world. *Kha* and *nabha*, two other terms used technically by the mathematicians, originally meant "the hole in the nave of a wheel through which the axle runs." For the wheel to revolve the center must be empty. From it perhaps the sign for zero came. It is the circle in which end and beginning merge. That O can also be a sexual sign for the female, suggesting another link between the feminine and the void, like that which we see in the Prajñāpāramitā. Around the śūnyatā, which she represents, the Wheel of the Dharma turns. That void is, as D. T. Suzuki said, "not an abstraction but an experience, or a deed enacted where there is neither space nor time."[35]

The conjunction in Prajñāpāramitā of these symbols, which inform the zero concept, triggers recollection of a similar conjunction in the *Four Quarters* of T. S. Eliot.

> "Garlic and sapphires in the mud
> Clot the bedded axle-tree."

> "At the still point of the turning world
> ...there the dance is."

> "We must be still and still moving
> Into further intensity
> For a further union....
> In my end is my beginning."

The final aspect of Prajñāpāramitā which we would consider here is her attitude vis à vis this world. The liberation she offers is no turning away from *saṃsāra*. "Those who are certain that they have got safely out of this world are unfit for full enlightenment."[36] The light that she bestows does does not dazzle, eclipse, or blind one to mundane phenomena and the traffic of beings; rather, clear, cool, it illumines the world "as it is." Seeing *vathābū-tham* (as it is), which D. T. Suzuli elucidates as seeing things in their aspect of Suchness without denial of their multiplicities and particularities, [37] is repeatedly stressed as a gift of the Mother of the Buddhas. [38] It is relevant to note that, in subsequent sutras which elaborate the ten *bhūmis* or stages of development of the bodhisattva, the sixth--the one representing his attainment of *prajña*-- is called *Abhimukhi*, "facing." The name underscores the *yathābūtham* aspect of wisdom, its frontal gaze upon the world.

This facing of *samsāra* springs, I believe, from a knowledge that mind and matter are neither opposed nor ultimately separable and that, therefore, the material world presents in itself no inherent bondage to the spirit. The Buddha's original teachings of dependent co-origination are retrieved and reaffirmed in the Second Turning of the Law. Our sūtra reiterates that matter is as empty of own-being as concepts are, as any *dharma* is. [39] In physical form (*rupa*) is the depth of emptiness; "as deep as Suchness, so deep is form, Subhūti." [40] Consequently, while the world is presented in the text as dream, illusion and magic show, one does not shun it--for there is no *dharma* that is *more* real or for whose sake or in whose pursuit the bodhisattva would lift his gaze from things-as-they-are.

The Mother of the Buddhas, therefore, does not call the bodhisattva beyond this world, to final nirvana. She retains him on this side of reality, for the sake of all beings. [41] "In this dwelling of Perfect Wisdom...you shall become a saviour of the helpless, a defender of the defenceless...a light to the blind, and you shall guide to the path those who have lost it, and you shall become a support to those who are without support." [42] In our sūtra, in such passages as these, the bodhisattva path is, for the first time, fully expressed--and as a calling and challenge to all persons. It bears reflection and emphasis that this glory of the Mahāyāna way springs from a wisdom first envisaged as feminine--from this wisdom's refusal to hold

aloof from the mundane. In this first utterance of Perfection of Wisdom, such a response to the world is accorded irreducible value. The skill in means (*upāya*), by which
the bodhisattva responds and acts within the realm of con-
tingency and need, is seen as essential to faith and, indeed, his enlightenment.[43] *Upāya*, the readiness to reach
out and improvise, is the other face of wisdom. Together
they constitute both ground for ethical action and basis
of delight--revalorizing *saṃsāra* while assigning no fixed
reality to its separate manifestations.

Such is the wisdom of the Mother of all Buddhas, empty
of preconception, pregnant point of potential action, be-
holding the teeming world with a vision which transfigures.
Now let us turn briefly to a contrasting view of the feminine. Prajñāpāramitā appears dramatically different from
the feminine archetype prevailing in the surrounding Indian tradition. That she should be symbolized as wisdom,
light, space runs counter to Hindu views and uses of the
female principle.

Hindu culture presents a mytho-philosophical world-
view rooted in polarities posited between earth and sky,
nature and consciousness, matter and mind. The aboriginal
Dravidian culture would provide a basis for this, in its
worship of a goddess representative of fertility. Like
other neolithic societies dependent on agriculture, it worshipped the productivity of nature (seen as female because
of its birthing capacity), while recognizing its remorse-
less vegetative cycle of growth and death. The goddess of
the Dravidians was driven underground by the invading Ary-
ans and their chariot-driving, warrior sky-gods. Centuries
later, circa the eighth century B.C., she resurfaced,
clothed in respectability, in the Sāmkhyan philosophy.
Sāmkhya re-established her in the form of the eternally
evolving and fecund *prakṛti* (nature principle). She is
dynamic and unconscious as opposed to *puruṣa*, the conscious
spirit. He is luminous in opposition to her darkness,

male, passive and plural; only in his purity and isolation
from her, from all change and materiality, comes transcendence and release.

The ancient matriarchal element also reasserted itself
in the later development of the Devī and her cult. Represented variously as Dūrga, Kālī, Caṇḍī, etc., she is essentially one--Devī, the "goddess." Whether adorned with
peacock feathers or garlanded with skulls, she is the
ceaselessly active one, *prakṛti*, *māyā*, *śaktī*. She is the
restlessness of primal matter, the fecund and devouring
forces of nature, the doting and cruel mother. As the
creative power of the male gods, from whom she issues, she
is a complement to their pure, passive intelligence.

The goddess is both indulgent and terrible. The ambivalent feelings about the mother figure which she reflects can be related to the dual status of women in traditional Hindu society. As a sexual partner, the woman
tends to be seen as a dangerous and enfeebling seductress;
but as a mother, especially the mother of a son, she is
revered and accorded prerogatives denied her as a person.
Childbirth, then, can serve the cause of self-assertion.
Consequently, the indulgence that a mother lavishes on her
son is not unmixed; as Lannoy puts it, "with her feeling
of maternal love coexist feelings of envy and retalia-
tion."[44] Lannoy, studying this phenomenon, links it per-
suasively with the prevalence of the "terrible mother" in
Hindu myth, and its imagery expressive of both dependence
and aggression.

Be this as it may, there are philosophic grounds, I
suggest, for this image of the feminine in the Hindu tradition. It is my thesis that a differing apprehension of
reality is at the root of the contrasting feminine image
which the Perfection of Wisdom, Mother of all Buddhas, presents. A dichotomy on the metaphysical level between consciousness and nature leads to a vision of spirit as strug-
gling to be free from the toils of matter. In such polarization matter comes to be seen as polluting and binding,

her fertile nature as arbitrary, lavish, cruel. An ambivalence on the part of the spirit is inevitable. As creature one is dependent on that very element from which one
seeks release; that dependence breeds resentment and an
exaggerated sense of that element's power. Such a love-
hate relationship with matter is reflected in extremes of
asceticism, the yogic austerities from which Gautama
turned away. As James Hillman suggests in discussing the
Great Mother complex, that love-hate relationship is evident also today in science's fantasy of conquering matter,
reordering the world.[45] When the archetypal mother is
linked with the chthonic in opposition to the psyche, a
dual response is elicited from the son, the spirit. Either
the spirit rebels (in devalorization and eradication of
matter, be it by mortification or defoliation), or it
seeks to seduce and possess the mother (in accumulation
and consumption of goods). Either way, matter, mater, ex-
erts her power and fascination.

Even when *māyā* (or matter) is understood as derivative
of the transcendent One, as in Vedānta, it is perceived as
both binding and maternal. As Kṛṣṇa says in the Bhagavad Gitā (VII.14-5), "For all this (nature) is my creative
power (māyā)...hard to transcend. Whoso shall put his
trust in me alone shall pass *beyond* this (my) uncanny
power (māyā)" (Emphasis added). Zaehner, commenting on
this passage, reflects the dualistic assumption: "(The
spirit) is made flesh in the womb of nature...but matter
binds; and, *like any mother, is unwilling to let her son
go free*: hence she does all she can to deceive him: as
such she is māyā which, at this stage of the language,
means both 'creative power' and 'deceit'"[46] (emphasis
added).

I suggest that Prajñāpāramitā, the Perfection of Wisdom, escapes this role and presents a radically different
feminine archetype by reason of Buddhism's non-substantial
and non-dichotomous view of reality. The doctrine of

dependent co-origination permits no polarization of consciousness and nature. Matter, seen as co-emergent and co-dependent with mind, is neither temptress nor trap. From this follows that faith in this wisdom mother is very different from devotion accorded to the Devī. Prajñāparamitā is not a mother to be placated or cajoled. Faith in her is not a seeking of favors, but a letting go, a falling into emptiness. It is the release of one's clutching onto *dharmas* and concepts, a venturing outward, a leaning into space. Such a faith is a self-naughting, a passing through the zero point. Because such a zero experience is a kind of birth, generative of new worlds, it is fitting that she who leads us through it is seen as 'genetrix' and mother.

Centuries later, in profusion of graphic imagery, Prajñāparamitā plays a dominant role in Buddhist tantrism. She is, as Snellgrove maintains, the prototype and essence of all the female figures featured in tantric Buddhist interplay.[47] With serene aplomb she copulates with *upāya*; skill in means, her "other face," has become her male consort. Scholars and art lovers have wondered and debated why, in these Buddhist figures, the sexual roles are reversed from the Hindu brand of tantrism. There in connubial embrace it is Śiva who is the sublimely passive partner, and his consort Śaktī who represents synamism. Our discussion of Prajñāparamitā makes it clear that she cannot, without misrepresentation, be equated with Śaktī, and reveals, furthermore, that what we encounter here is no mere reversal of sex roles. Displayed in the Buddhist *yab-yum* (mother-father embrace) is a different vision altogether.

The fundamental difference is one of ontology: Prajñāparamitā as wisdom is empty, *asvabhāva*, not real, whereas Śiva as wisdom is the ultimate real essence with which, by aid of Śaktī, the adept would merge. In the Hindu pair, *mokṣa* (release) and *māyā* (material manifestation) are assigned separate poles; ultimate liberation is seen as a

merging of one less real and less valuable pole *into* the
other more real and more valuable pole. In contrast to
this, the tantric symbolism of Buddhism represents not a
cancelling of one pole, but the continual interplay of both.
These poles are not *mokṣa* and *māyā* or pure consciousness
over against energy/matter, but rather two kinds of con-
sciousness/energy. In the embrace of *prajñā* and *upāya*,
life's dialectical modes of vision and action are held in
balance, complementary and mutually essential.

Tantric Buddhism was adopted, as we know, in Tibet
and flourished there long centuries after the demise of
the Dharma in India. The ease with which its imagery took
root is probably related to that nomadic culture's traditional view of the female--to which it accorded a dignity
and freedom unknown in North Indian society.[48] Being essentially pastoral, its religious life had not centered
around the fertility cults that characterized agricultural
societies, and being highly mobile, rigid patterns of sex
segregation were not practical. It would not be so difficult under such circumstances to image wisdom as female,
and mother as, not possessively nurturing, but nurturingly
liberating. In such a society an a-chthonic female principle could flourish, and serve to express the Buddha's insight into the relationship of mind to matter.

That vision of reality, as dependently co-arising, was
central to the Buddha's enlightenment and his teachings.
In the Second Turning of the Law, that insight took on the
vitality of symbol, the power of rediscovery. In Prajñāpāramitā, Mother of all Buddhas, it emerged as the fundamental and saving wisdom. Imaged as light and space, pregnant zero and matrix of dimension, this clear-eyed, compassionate Mama was, at a key point in the Dharma's history, its channel and its symbol.

NOTES

[*]This essay has appeared in *Anima*, 3/1 (Fall Equinox, 1976) 75-80.

[1]*The Perfection of Wisdom in Eight Thousand Lines and Its Verse Summary*, trans. Edward Conze (Bolinas: Four Seasons Foundation, 1973); hereafter abbreviated as *A* (for the main prose text) and *AV* (for verse summary).

[2]Cf. Etienne Lamotte, *Histoire du Bouddhisme Indien* (Louvain: Museon, 1958); Edward Conze, *Thirty Years of Buddhist Studies* (Columbia, SC: University of South Carolina, 1968), and *Prajnaparamita Literature* (The Hague: Mouton, 1960).

[3]Cf. above and D. T. Suzuki, *Essays in Zen Buddhism, Third Series* (New York: Samual Weiser, 1971) Section VI.

[4]From a stotra written by Rahulabhadra, also known as Saraha, which served as preface to many Prajnaparamita sutras, cited by E. Lamotte, *Traite de la Grande Vertu de Sagesse*, p. 1061.

[5]*AV* XII. 1, 2.

[6]Cf. *A* 254, 257, 273, 276, 398, etc.

[7]*AV* I.15; VII.7.

[8]*A* 254.

[9]*AV* X.8.

[10]*AV* XXIX.14.

[11]*A* 284

[12]*A* 343; *AV* XVIII.3.

[13]*A* 170.

[14]*A* 482.

[15]*A* 405.

[16]*A* 175.

[17]David L. Snellgrove, *Hevajra Tantra* (Oxford: Oxford University, 1939) 24.

[18]*A* 408.

[19] *AV* II.6; *A* 5; *AV* I.10; *A* 280; *A* 5.

[20] *A* 170, 171, 197.

[21] N. K. Bhattasali, *Iconography of Buddhist and Brahmanical Sculptures in the Dacca Museum* (Dacca, 1929) 42.

[22] The idea that seeing is symbolic of compassion will be found also in the figures of Kwan-Yin and Avalokiteś-vara who "look down" from above in tender caring.

[23] *A* 278.

[24] *A* 302.

[25] *A* 374.

[26] Cf. Mircea Eliade, *Patterns in Comparative Religion* (New York: World Publishing, 1970) chap. II.

[27] *AV* XXVIII.3, 4.

[28] Alex Wayman, *The Buddhist Tantras* (New York: Samuel Weiser, 1973) 167-68.

[29] *A* 194.

[30] *A* 410.

[31] "Numbers: A Long Way From Zero," in *Mathematics* (New York: Life Science Library, 1969) 16-17.

[32] M. J. Babb in *Journal of the American Oriental Society*, Vol. 51, quoted by A. K. Coomaraswamy, "Kha and Other Words denoting Zero in Connection with the Metaphysics of Space," *Bulletin of the School of Oriental Studies*, Vol. VII, Part 3, (London Institution, 1934) 496.

[33] Coomaraswamy, op. cit., p. 487.

[34] Ibid., p. 493.

[35] D. T. Suzuki, *On Indian Mahayana Buddhism* (Harper Torchbook, 1968) 72 ff.

[36] *A* 34.

[37] Suzuki, *Essays in Zen Buddhism*, p. 238.

[38] *AV* XII.2, *A* 254.

[39] *A* 185, 315.

[40] *A* 342.

[41] *A* 444.

[42] *A* 449.

[43] *A* 377.

[44] Richard Lannoy, *The Speaking Tree*, (Oxford: Oxford University, 1971) 107.

[45] James Hillman, "Great Mother and Puer," in *Fathers and Mothers* (Spring Publications, 1973).

[46] R. C. Zaehner, *The Bhagavad Gita*, (Oxford: Oxford University, 1964) 14.

[47] David Snellgrove, *Buddhist Himalaya*, (New York: Philosophical Library, 1957).

[48] Robert B. Ekvall, *Fields on the Hoof* (New York: Holt, Rinehart & Winston, 1948) chap. 4, pp. 24ff.; R. A. Stein, *Tibetan Civilization* (Stanford, CA: Stanford University, 1972) 94ff.

A CROSS-CULTURAL APPROACH
TO WOMEN'S LIBERATION THEOLOGY

Paul K. K. Tong
Glassboro State College

I. Introduction

The International Women's Year Conference held in
Mexico City this past year demonstrated that even though
women all over the world suffer in varying degrees from
sexist oppression, their respective responses to it are
shaped and limited by their own cultural traditions. No
common understanding or program for women's liberation
could take shape at this gathering because every delegate
spoke in her own tongue and viewed the liberation movement
from her own limited perspective. Ironically, few women
at the International Women's Year Conference had anything
akin to an international consciousness or awareness and
fewer still realized the theoretical urgency to raise the
issue of internationalism in the liberation movement. I
feel strongly that if the most important aims of the wom-
en's liberation movement are to be achieved, it must become international in scope and purpose for the following
reasons:

1. The oppression of women is not limited to
    any one culture or society but universal on
    the planet-earth. Women have not been ac-
    corded equality in the written history of
    any nation. This universal nature of women's
    oppression gives the liberation movement an
    inherent international orientation. The
    failure to recognize this would render the
    movement inauthentic as well as shortsighted.

2. Solidarity is a necessary condition for the
    success of the women's liberation movement.
    If the solidarity of women is not interna-
    tional in scope, there will arise certain

contradictions and tensions among national
or ideological groups seriously jeopardiz-
ing the liberation movement both here and
abroad.

3. Each culture has developed its own institutions and rationalizations for male dominance. Certain myths, religious or social,
have reinforced this unfortunate state of
affairs. In some cultures these antifeminist myths are considered to be absolute
truths. There is no better weapon to com-
bat these cultural biases than a cross-
cultural analysis, since what is considered
absolute truth in one culture is often found
insignificant or even irrelevant in another.

4. In our badly divided world people seem incapable of thematizing a universal horizon
for human history. It may well be the historical mission of the women's liberation
movement to provide future generations with
just such a horizon thereby making diverse
cultures and conflicting ideologies compre-
hensible to each other.

For these same reasons the theological discussion of
women's liberation should be raised to the international
and cross-cultural planes. Religion, no less than any
other social institutions, has often been colored by particular cultural and even tribal accretions. This is especially true of western religions which are so closely
identified with the antifeminist stream of thought of the
Judaeo-Greek culture. Though we all concede that religion
is trans-cultural, nonetheless religionists seem to have a
myopic concern for their own traditions. The women's liberation movement can provide a platform for not only such
people, but all people, to speak in a cross-cultural and
trans-cultural way. It is within such a cross-cultural

context that I would here like to discuss some theological
issues in the hope of forging a universal religious horizon
for the women's liberation movement.

II. Critique of Religion

As dealt with by the Judaeo-Christian tradition, wom-
en's liberation literature on religion may be conveniently
divided as follows: that literature concerned with the
critique of religion, and that literature concerned with
the reconstruction of theology.

Karl Marx once remarked that the critique of religion
constitutes the critique of all critiques. Indeed, in any
revolutionary movement criticism is both an imperative and
an inevitability. Women liberationists have been atune to
this reality and have subjected western religious tradition
to a thorough-going and severe analysis; they have revealed
its sexist biases in theory as well as in praxis. Today we
are well aware that patriarchal prejudices were reflected
in biblical narratives and theological interpretations;
that the Church Fathers twisted the early Christian teachings to afford justifications of ecclesiastical practices
against women; and that Christian spirituality became an
ideology pitted against the flesh and sexuality, i. e.,
against women. Moreover, it is by now obvious that the
Judaic and Christian churches have sacralized, internalized
and transformed cultural prejudices against women into
dogmas and articles of faith. A recent example of this is
given by Archbishop Bernardin, the president of the National Conference of Catholic Bishops. With respect to the
official teaching of the Roman Church on the ordination of
women to the priesthood, the Archbishop stated:

> It is not correct to say that no serious theolo-
> gical obstacle stands in the way of ordaining
> women to the priesthood, and that the fact that
> women have not been ordained up to now can be
> explained simply by culturally conditioned no-
> tions of male superiority. There is a serious

theological issue. Throughout its history the
Catholic Church has not called women to the
priesthood. Although many of the arguments presented in times gone by on this subject may not
be defensible today, there are compelling reasons
for this practice.

Quoting from a report from the NCCB Committee on Pastoral
Research and Practices, the Archbishop continued:

The constant tradition and practice of the Catholic
Church against the ordination of women, interpreted (whenever interpreted) as of divine law,
is of such a nature as to constitute a clear
teaching of the ordinary *magisterium* of the
Church....The well founded present discipline
will continue to have and to hold the entire
field unless and until a contrary theological
development takes place, leading to a clarifying
statement from the *magisterium*.[1]

Shocking as this ecclesiastical logic may seem, it is
not surprising. In the not too distant past Christian
theologians used similar arguments to justify slavery and
western colonialism. I wholly endorse a continuing critique of the sexist biases manifested in western religious
beliefs and practices, with the cautionary remark that such
a culturally limited and relatively valid critique cannot
apply equally to eastern religious traditions. After all,
eastern women have played a different role in religion
than their western counterparts. For example, some Hindu
female deities enjoy considerable homage. In Shakti tradition, Shiva's consort, Kali is praised thus:

When you lie down,
Think you are doing obeisance to Her;
When you sleep, meditate on the Mother.
When you eat,
Think you are offering oblations to the Mother;
Whatever you hear with the ear is Her sacred incan-
    tations;
Each one of the fifty letters of the alphabet rep-
    resents Her alone.
Rāmaprasād declares in joy:
The Mother persuades everything;
When you move about in the city, you are walking
    around the Mother.[2]

Similarly, Orthodox Chinese religious tradition praises woman, making no derogatory references to her. In Chinese mythology, there is no female figure like Eve; so no evil, cosmic or human, is attributed to woman. In the Yin-Yang school, male and female play equal roles in the evolution of the universe, alternatively complementing and completing each other.

Nonetheless, in these societies women have been discriminated against just as much if not more than in western cultures. This may indicate that religion plays not a determining but a participatory role in the socialization of the sexes. The reactionary stance of some churches today toward women's liberation is no proof of their original evil genius, or of their influence on the way society perceives women. Society has shaped religion much more than religion has shaped society. As soon as a religion adapts to its social *environ*, its critical or counter-cultural impact is weakened. Gradually it loses any ability it may have had to transform society; and ultimately it becomes a mirror for the culture which has overpowered it.

III. The Reconstruction of Theology

A number of writers in theology have attempted to reconstruct a liberation theology. Few have equalled the philosophical sophistication of Dr. Mary Daly. In several articles and books she has developed a transcendental methodology aimed at extricating God from Christian anthropomorphism and restoring the Ultimate as an ontological ground of Being. According to Ms. Daly:

> It has sometimes been argued that anthropomorphic symbols for 'God' are important and even necessary because the fundamental powers of the cosmos otherwise are seen as impersonal. One of the insights characteristic of the rising women consciousness is that this kind of dichotomizing between cosmic power and the personal power need not be. That is, it is not necessary to anthropomorphize or to reify transcendence in order to

> relate to it personally....The dichotomizing-
> reifying-projecting syndrome is characteristic
> of patriarchal consciousness, making the 'other'
> the repository of the contents of the lost self.[3]

Without belaboring Ms. Daly's transcendental theology, I
would like to point out some weaknesses in her system due
principally to her lack of cross-cultural understanding.

First, Ms. Daly seems to imply that personality and
sexuality are not only separable in principle, but that
they are also inamicable. The liberation of God from human
genderization is the prototype for women's liberation from
her own sexuality. The inescapable implication of this is
that women are oppressed because they are sexed. This reflects the vague but nagging belief in the West that women's
liberation is identical with sexual negation. Women of
eastern cultures do not share this belief. For them sexuality is not something to be transcended or overcome or
even understood, but something to be lived, experienced,
and internalized. Sexuality is not viewed as woman's, or
as man's, adversary, but as that through which a person
achieves authentic relations.

Secondly, transcendence is now and has always meant
the rejection and negation of sexuality, the immanent
reality *par excellence*. Transcendence has been the tool
that patriarchal religions have used to keep women in their
place. As Altizer observed: "God is the transcendental
ground of oppression." Indeed, transcendence without immanence is not liberation, but a way to madness. In the
name of the transcendent God we have raped the earth; we
have trampled upon its values and meanings. For the sake
of the ultimate concern we have righteously neglected and
illegitimated our proximate concerns. With the banner of
the *Geist* we have relentlessly dehumanized history. In
the wake of *Übermensch* we have remorselessly sacrificed
millions of lives at the altar of transcendence. In our
quest for Utopia we have painted the face of the earth red
with blood. A cursory knowledge of eastern religions, and

their emphasis on the immanence of the Ultimate, would
have helped Ms. Daly avoid the pitfall of an overly-trans-
cendent and triumphal conception of religion. In the East,
God does not scorn or disdain human sexuality; rather God
is manifested in and through it. This makes for a more
sane and realistic approach to one of the fundamental dimensions of human existence.

IV. Cross-cultural Methodologies

I would suggest the following methods in developing a
cross-cultural appraoch to women's liberation theology:

1. The *Jungian archetypal method*. According to Carl
Jung religious archetypes are cross-cultural and trans-
cultural. Using archetypal myths, stories, and even dreams
a cross-cultural theology could be constructed.

2. *Dialogical method*. A dialogical theology could be
developed by comparing and synthesizing the western theology of transcendence with the eastern theology of immi-
nence. Cross-cultural predications of God's androgeneity
could and indeed would result from such a hermeneutics.

3. *Ontological method*. Theology need not begin with
God but with people in their concrete existential modes as
males and females. I would like to expand briefly this
last approach as a meta-theology in a cross-cultural context.

Correctly or incorrectly, male and female have been
used as the paradigm of all other dualities, be they cosmological, sociological, biological or whatever. An ontological analysis of duality could provide a basis for a
truly humanistic and cross-cultural theology. This analysis is much needed, since duality has been misrepresented
in the West. What has passed for dualistic thinking is
nothing other than a one-sided monism in disguise. For
example, the chauvinist is said to espouse a dualistic
framework, in so far as he conceives of reality as composed
of two terms--male and female.[4] But by asserting male

superiority, he betrays his secret monism: reality is to
be explained in terms of its masculine elements; femininity is an aberration, that which is to be vanquished and
overcome. Other supposed dualities--such as spirit/flesh,
mind/body, man/nature, good/evil--are also disguised versions of monism. Spirit, mind, man, and the good are real
and true; flesh, body, nature, and evil are somehow inauthentic and dispensable. In what, then, does genuine
dualism consist? In the main, if dualism is not to give
way to the unidimensionality of monism, both terms of the
putative duality must be seen as real, as true, as existing in a constant tension which can nonetheless result in
a higher form of union. Genuine duality or multiplicity,
then, is the given, the immanent reality, of human existence; and unity--which I oppose to mere monism--is the
transcendent ideal of existence.

Given this understanding of inauthentic dualism and
monism, of genuine dualism and encompassing unity, I would
like to re-define the male/female bipolarity. Since com-
pleteness requires two terms for a full relation, the duality of man and woman embraces what I consider the fundamental interpretative categories of existence, transcendence and immanence. Any "double relationship" consists
of a *transcendental* commonality or symmetric relation and
an *immanent* difference or asymmetric relation. In the
case of man and woman, personhood is their symmetric or
transcendental relation and maleness and femaleness is
their asymmetric or immanent relation.

Using traditional philosophical categories we could
term the symmetric relation "essential" and the asymmetric
relation "existential." The symmetric relation is static;
the asymmetric, dynamic. The former relation is the ideal
principle, the latter the acting principle. Our concept
of equality is rooted in the nature of the symmetric principle, and inequality results from one-sided application
of the asymmetrical principle. Since the asymmetric relation is non-equilibrant, it begets dynamic action through

alternating roles described as acting-reacting, moving-resisting, giving-receiving, etc. In the case of people, whether between males and females or between persons of the same gender, all relations have an asymmetric form: one speaks and the other listens; one advances and the other waits; one gives and the other receives. At any given moment of consciousness only an asymmetric relation is taking place. When the asymmetric terms surrender and merge into unity, the symmetric, relation ceases and a new identity is born. However, to remedy the asymmetric nature of this relation, the roles have to be alternated constantly. When one kind of role is assigned to any one term, inequality is the inevitable result. For example, in traditional chauvinistic thinking only man plays the active, aggressive role whereas woman has the opposite role. We stereotype man and woman when we assign completely separate roles to them instead of alternating these roles. When society further reinforces these stereotypes through institutionalized discrimination, male chauvinism is the inescapable consequence.

It seems clear to me that inequality is not a necessary consequence of asymmetric roles. Difference or asymmetry cannot and should not be avoided, for it is the source of dynamism and action. What should be avoided is the stereotyping and solidifying of these roles. Many feminists seem to think that if we deny the difference in human relations, equality will prevail. However, sexuality is not the only difference or asymmetry in human relations. When a person relates to any other person, that relation, if it is a relation at all, contains an asymmetric dimension. Thus, even in homosexual or lesbian relations chauvinism can develop.

A note of caution should here be added. Even though the symmetric and the asymmetric relations in a duality are distinct from each other, they are not separate from each other. A separation of them would destroy the possibility of a real relation. Essence and existence are

distinct in the conceptual structure, but united in their
concrete reality. Man and woman are concrete universals.
In other words, our sexed bodies and asexual personhoods
are one and the same. Bonhoeffer has correctly observed
that "escape from the body is escape from being man (and
woman) and escape from the spirit as well. Body is the
existence-form of spirit, as spirit is the existence-form
of body."[5] The implication is this that if we opt for the
symmetric dimension alone, that is the transcendent, we
deny the reality of the asymmetric dimension, that is the
immanent. This is what has happened in western theological
thought and Ms. Daly seems to adopt the same posture.[6]

What implications has this analysis for theology?
Theology deals with our relation with God. This relation
also contains a symmetric and an asymmetric dimension. As
a person God establishes a commonality or symmetry with us.
This is both the justification and necessity of the anthropomorphism of God. God, of course, can and has been conceived as universal power or energy, as a philosophical
Being; but conceived as such, God is not to be worshipped
but to be explained in philosophical analysis and demonstration. Such a view of God does not give rise to existential relations with people. To personify God is not,
as Ms. Daly asserts, to reify God.[7] If we must pursue the
absolute transcendence of God then we have to go beyond
being as well. Buddha realized this. The absolute transcendence of God entails that God be above things, persons
and being--*Nirvana*--and that man and women be empty of
being--*śunya*. This is the ultimate transcendence: the
apophatic, silent and unknowable infinite void. With such
a God people cannot relate but can only vanish. This is
the basic orientation of original Buddhism. Yet in short
order Buddha's followers personified Buddhist deities in
profusion. The Buddhist pantheon outnumbers that of any
other religion. This confirms the fact that the personification of God is both a human and religious necessity.

Moreover in our relation to God, the asymmetric dimension manifests itself as well. Both eastern and western mystics express their union with God in terms of sexual polarities: God is the bride or groom of the human soul. We should not dismiss the Shakti and Tantric traditions of Inida and Tibet without further reflection because they sound too offensive to our pious ears. In Shakti, sexuality, especially female sexuality, is the embodiment of the immanence of God. Sex, and everything that comes from it, is divine.

Certainly, to make God totally immanent is not only idolatrous and sacrilegious but also debasing of our own nature. This has happened in the eastern religious experience from time to time. Tantric practices have been known to degenerate into unadulterated sexual orgies. Conversely, in the West the immanent realities of people and of this world have been debased in the pursuit of transcendence. When transcendence gets out of hand, when a person flies higher and higher and loses touch with the depths of his being, then religion becomes a vacuous or even a self-negating death-ethic for the human community. There is something tragic, for example, about a Jonathan Livingston Seagull, soaring so high above his fellows that they can no longer understand him and he them. Jonathan utterly transcends the seagull world. He takes no pleasure in eating fish or basking in the sun; he disdains the seagull mating game which tie him to earth. A cross-cultural theology can compliment and safeguard both eastern and western religious traditions.

In conclusion I propose that cross-cultural theologizing could serve as a critique of various theologies, as a methodology for future theology, and as a metatheology. In today's world it is not only preferable but imperative that liberation theology in particular should adopt a cross-cultural approach if it is to be liberating at all.

NOTES

[1] As reported in *National Catholic Reporter* (October 17, 1975).

[2] From Rāmaprasād in *Sources of Indian Tradition*, ed. deBarry (New York: Columbia University, 1958) 364-63.

[3] Mary Daly, *Beyond God the Father* (Boston: Beacon, 1973) 33.

[4] Cf. ibid., pp. 33, 68, 97; and Rosemary Ruether, *Liberation Theology* (New York: Paulist Press, 1972) 19.

[5] Dietrich Bonhoeffer, *Creation and Fall* (London: SCM, 1959) 45-46.

[6] Cf., Daly, *Beyond God the Father*.

[7] Ibid., p. 33.